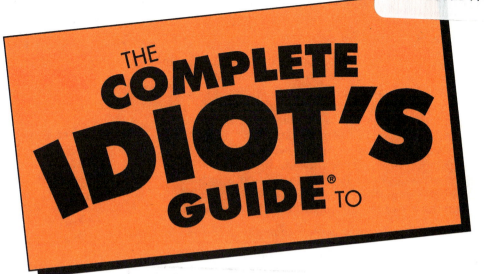

THE COMPLETE IDIOT'S GUIDE® TO

Online Search Secrets

by Michael Miller

201 W. 103rd Street, Indianapolis, IN 46290

The Complete Idiot's Guide to Online Search Secrets

Copyright© 1999 by Que

International Standard Book Number: 0-7897-2042-6

Library of Congress Catalog Card Number: 99-61481

Printed in the United States of America

First Printing: July 1999

01 00 99   4 3 2

Trademarks

Warning and Disclaimer

Publisher
Greg Wiegand

Development Editor
Gregory Harris

Managing Editor
Thomas F. Hayes

Project Editor
Tom Stevens

Copy Editor
Barbara Hacha

Indexer
William Meyers

Proofreader
Tricia Sterling

Technical Editor
Patrick Grote

Interior Designer
Nathan Clement

Cover Designer
Michael Freeland

Copy Writer
Eric Borgert

Layout Technicians
Cynthia Davis-Hubler
Brad Lenser
Steve Geiselman

Contents at a Glance

Introduction

Contents

Part 3: The *Unusual* Suspects: General Search Sites You Probably Didn't Know About, But Should Have   117

10 The Next Generation: Newer, Better Search Engines   119

11 Paying for Information: Subscription Search Sites   133

12 Madame Librarian: Online Libraries and Encyclopedias   139

About the Author

Michael Miller is a writer, speaker, consultant, and the President/Founder of The Molehill Group, a strategic consulting and authoring firm based in Carmel, Indiana. More information about the author and The Molehill Group can be found at www.molehillgroup.com, and you can email the author directly at author@molehill-group.com.

Michael Miller has been an important force in the book publishing business since 1987. In his most recent position of Vice President of Business Strategy for Macmillan Publishing, he helped guide the strategic direction for the world's largest reference publisher and influence the shape of today's computer book publishing market. There are few who know as much about the computer industry—how it works, and why—as does Mr. Miller.

As the author of 30 best-selling nonfiction books, Mr. Miller writes about a variety of topics. His most recent books include *The Complete Idiot's Guide to Online Auctions*, *Lycos Personal Internet Guide*, *Sams Teach Yourself MORE Windows 98 in 24 Hours*, and *Webster's New World Vocabulary of Success*. Upcoming titles include *The Complete Idiot's Guide to Surfing the Internet with WebTV* and a new edition of his all-time bestseller, *OOPS! What to Do When Things Go Wrong*.

From his first book (*Ventura Publisher Techniques and Applications*, published in 1988) to this, his latest title, Michael Miller has established a reputation for practical advice, technical accuracy, and an unerring empathy for the needs of his readers. Many regard Mr. Miller as the consummate reporter on new technology for an everyday audience.

Dedication

To my dear friend Beth Ogren, for service above and beyond the call of duty.

Acknowledgments

I'd like to thank the usual suspects at Que, including but not limited to Greg Wiegand, Gregory Harris, and Tom Stevens. I'd also like to thank the powers that be at Pearson Education who enabled my full-time writing career.

Tell Us What You Think!

As the reader of this book, *you* are our most important critic and commentator. We value your opinion and want to know what we're doing right, what we could do better, what areas you'd like to see us publish in, and any other words of wisdom you're willing to pass our way.

As a Publisher for Que, I welcome your comments. You can fax, email, or write me directly to let me know what you did or didn't like about this book—as well as what we can do to make our books stronger.

Please note that I cannot help you with technical problems related to the topic of this book, and that due to the high volume of mail I receive, I might not be able to reply to every message.

When you write, please be sure to include this book's title and author as well as your name and phone or fax number. I will carefully review your comments and share them with the author and editors who worked on the book.

Fax: 317-581-4666

Email: `office_que@mcp.com`

Mail: Greg Wiegand
          Publisher
          Que
          201 West 103rd Street
          Indianapolis, IN 46290 USA

Introduction

Don't you hate trying to find stuff on the Internet? First, you have to choose one of the hundreds of available search sites—should you use Yahoo! or Excite, AltaVista or Lycos?—then you have to figure out what words to search for, and then you get to dig through pages and pages and *pages* of results (most of which have no bearing on what you were searching for in the first place!), and then maybe, just *maybe*, you find a page that looks like it might have some of the information you were searching for. There *has* to be a better way to find things online!

Well, I have some bad news and some good news for you. The bad news is, there *isn't* a better way. The only way to find information online is to search for it, using some sort of search engine or directory. Sorry.

The good news is, while you still have to search for stuff, there are *better* ways to search, things you can do that will help you find exactly what you're looking for without the tons of irrelevant results you typically get with a standard Net search. And those search secrets are here, in this book, in your hands.

Who This Book Is For

The Complete Idiot's Guide to Online Search Secrets is written for anyone who's ever tried to find anything on the Internet. Whether you're using America Online or a local Internet service provider, whether you're a Netscape Navigator user or an Internet Explorer fan, whether you just started Web surfing yesterday or have been on the Internet since the days before the World Wide Web even existed, you still need to search for stuff, and you still need the search secrets that are revealed in this book.

If you're a newer Internet user, you'll want to read this entire book from front to back. I'll tell you all about how information is stored on the Internet, and show you how to get the best results from all the major search sites.

If you're a more experienced Internet user, you'll really appreciate all the inside information layered throughout this book. I'll show you the best places to look for specific types of information, and why you should use one site instead of another.

No matter what type of user you are, you'll get maximum use from all the secrets and strategies I present on how to always find what you're looking for—without getting overwhelmed by extraneous results. I'll train you how to *think* like a researcher, so that you're never more than a few clicks away from the information you need.

I do assume a few things about you. I figure that you already have a personal computer (and know how to use it!), that you have an Internet connection, that you have a Web browser (Internet Explorer, Netscape Navigator, or the America Online browser), and that you know your way around Internet basics—that you know how to click on hyperlinks and enter Web page addresses and that sort of thing. I *don't* assume that you know everything there is to know about online searching—because if you did, you wouldn't be reading this book!

What You'll Find In This Book

The Complete Idiot's Guide to Online Search Secrets is composed of 39 relatively short chapters, each of which concentrates on specific ways you can maximize your Internet search results. The chapters are organized into nine general parts, as follows:

> ➤ Part 1, "Getting Started: Where and How to Find Information on the Web," is a brief introduction to the concept of how information is stored on the Internet—and how you can find it. This is a great place to start *before* you start futzing around with individual search engines and directories.

> ➤ Part 2, "The Usual Suspects: How to Get the Best Results from the Major Search Sites," focuses on how to best use the "Big Seven" search sites—Yahoo!, AltaVista, HotBot, Lycos, Excite, Infoseek, and Northern Light.

> ➤ Part 3, "The *Unusual* Suspects: General Search Sites You Probably Didn't Know About, But Should Have," examines some of the best but least-known search sites on the Internet, including Ask Jeeves!, Metacrawler, and LEXIS-NEXIS.

> ➤ Part 4, "Getting Personal: How to Find People and Addresses," shows you how to find all sorts of personal information on the Internet, including street addresses, phone numbers, personal Web pages, and genealogical data. You'll even find out how to find the love of your life via online personal ads.

> ➤ Part 5, "Getting Down to Business: How to Find Business and Financial Information," shows you how to look up businesses via online yellow pages, how to find detailed company and financial information, and how to enhance your career with online job listings.

> ➤ Part 6, "Getting a Bargain: How to Find Things for Sale," shows you how to search for the best deals in online auctions and online classified ads.

> ➤ Part 7, "Getting Technical: How to Find Computer-Related Stuff," shows you how to find all manner of technical information and files on the Internet, from troubleshooting solutions to Usenet newsgroup postings to email mailing lists to MP3 audio files.

> ➤ Part 8, "Getting Particular: How to Find Specialized Information," shows you how to find information about specialized topics, such as medicine and education.

> ➤ Part 9, "Getting Smart: Sanity-Saving Search Secrets," is the part of the book *everybody* should read, because it reveals the secret strategies you need for successful searches, and the tips and advice that will make you both an effective and an efficient online searcher!

In addition, I've included The Complete Idiot's Search Site Directory (the book's appendix), which lists the URL for every search site mentioned in this book, in alphabetical order. You will also find invaluable the tear-out card at the front of this book, which includes report cards for the Big Seven search sites, as well as a special search site feature comparison—keep it next to your computer at all times to help you quickly identify the right site for your specific online search needs.

How to Do the Things You See in This Book

To get the most out of this book, you should know how it is designed. I've tried to put things together in such a way as to make reading the book both rewarding and fun. So, here's what to do when you see any of the following:

➤ Links and anything clicked or selected on a Web page are presented in **bold color**; click a link to go to the corresponding Web page.

➤ Anything you need to enter—into a search box, for example, or into a form—is presented in `mono text`; enter this text as written to proceed.

➤ New terms are presented in *italicized text*; pay close attention to these terms.

Extras

To pack as much information as possible into *The Complete Idiot's Guide to Online Search Secrets*, you are presented with additional tips and advice as you read the book. These elements enhance your knowledge, or point out important pitfalls to avoid. Along the way, you'll find the following elements:

Sniff This Out

These boxes contain warnings, notes, and other information you'll find useful for successful Web searching. Be sure to read each of these boxes—failure to do so might result in missing out on some important points.

Search Speak

These boxes contain high-tech info that provides more in-depth information about a topic related to the chapter. If you don't want to dig deeper into how Internet searching *really* works, you can skip over these boxes. If you want to impress your friends and loved ones with your mastery of arcane technical information, though, this is the place to look.

Get Ready to Search the Net

Still here? It's time to get started, so turn the page and prepare to learn how and where information is stored on the Internet—and the best ways to find it!

Part 1

Getting Started: Where and How to Find Information on the Web

Want to know more about how search engines and directories work? Want to know how to perform a rudimentary search that will work on just about any search site? If so, then this part of the book is for you. It's a good general overview to the topic of searching and search sites, and if you read nothing more than these chapters, you'll at least be a smarter searcher than you were before!

oooh...

All You Ever Wanted to Know About Search Sites and Directories

In This Chapter

➤ Discover just how big the Web is—and why it's so hard to find Web-based information

➤ Learn how directories differ from search engines

➤ Find out how spiders surf the Web to create search engine indexes

➤ Uncover the individual strengths and weaknesses of the Big Seven search sites

Like you, I enjoy the Internet. Really. I'm on it every day for several hours a day. Would I use something so much if I didn't like it?

Like most users, I probably spend the most time on the Net searching for stuff. I search for research data, company financials, background information, definitions of terms, phone numbers and addresses—you name it, I search for it.

But as much as I like the Internet in general, I really don't like searching in particular. In fact, some days I outright *hate* searching the Internet.

It's not because I'm not good at it. On the contrary, I'm a very good Internet searcher—one of the best, IMHO. I can find practically anything online, fast. As proof of my searching talents, all my friends come to me to find things for them online. (Of course, I could just have lazy friends....)

IMHO, It's a Timesaving Acronym

IMHO is an abbreviation common to the Internet. It stands for In My Humble Opinion.

No, the reason I hate Internet searching is because it's not easy—and it isn't even that logical. Searching the Web is more of an art than a science. The same query at different sites produces wildly different results, and you're better off relying on feel than you are on facts in determining where and how you search.

The very reasons why I hate searching the Web are the reasons why you purchased this book. (You did *purchase* this book, didn't you?) You want to perform better Internet searches, you don't want to waste as much time searching online, and you always—*always*—want to find what you're looking for.

You just made a good first step. Read on and I'll tell you all about how information is stored on the Internet—and why it's so hard to find.

The Needle in a Haystack Problem—How and Where to Find What You Need on the Internet

By one count, there are more than 300 million pages of information on the World Wide Web—and that number is doubling yearly. You would think that with all that information online, you'd be able to find what you need, wouldn't you?

Of course, you'd be wrong.

Information online is not stored or organized in any logical fashion. You have to realize that the Internet itself is not run or managed by any central organization; the Net is nothing more than a collection of millions of individual computers, all connected by a bunch of wires crisscrossing the globe. Nobody is in charge; therefore, everybody manages their own computers, called *servers*, any old way they want to.

There are no standards or guidelines for laying out Web pages so that certain types of information are always presented the same way, using the same words, positioned in the same place. There is no guarantee that the topic mentioned in a Web page's title is even mentioned in the text of the page. There is no assurance that a page that was on the Web yesterday will still be there tomorrow.

In short, the Web is a mess. And somewhere in that mess is the information you need. Somewhere, hidden on a single Web page deep within a particular Web site, stored on a overloaded Web server in some country connected somehow to the Internet, is that one piece of data you need. But where? And how do you find it?

If there are no rules governing how information is stored on the Internet, what procedures can you follow for retrieving information?

Fortunately, procedures do exist. Fortunately, you're not the first person to run into this little problem. Fortunately, entire industries have built up around the issue of searching for information on the Web. All you have to do is know where to look and how to ask.

The Old Ways to Find Stuff—Gopher, Veronica, Archie, and WAIS

But first, a little history—because, you see, this problem of retrieving data from the Internet is not a new problem.

Before there was the Web (like, pre-1994), there was the Internet. (The Internet itself has been around since the 1970s, in one form or another.) Even then, in the pre-Web days, lots of information was stored on Internet servers around the globe, and lots of users needed to find specific bits of that information. How did they do it?

Remember that the pre-Web Internet didn't have fancy graphics and clickable hyperlinks, so it should come as no surprise that all the data back then existed in text format only. That text was stored in various file formats on various computers, and four main tools were available for getting at those text files.

➤ **Gopher** is a tool for organizing files on dedicated servers, and it was extremely popular in universities across the U.S. Each Gopher server contained lists of files and other information, both at that specific site and at other Gopher sites around the world. Gopher worked similarly to a hierarchical file tree like that used in Windows Explorer—you clicked folder links to see their contents and navigated up and down through various folders and subfolders. Gopher was created at the University of Minnesota, and the UMN Gopher system still exists, to some degree, although functioning servers are becoming more rare. If you want to check it out, use your Web browser to go to gopher://gopher.micro.umn.edu.

➤ **Veronica** is a server-based tool used to search multiple Gopher sites for information. You used Veronica somewhat like you use one of today's Web search engines—you entered a query and clicked a **Search** button, which generated a list of matching documents. I would suggest you check out Veronica yourself, but it's hard to find a working Veronica server these days.

➤ **WAIS**, which stands for *wide area information server*, lets you use the old text-based Telnet protocol to perform full-text document searches of Internet servers. WAIS was more powerful than Veronica but was quickly superseded by the Web and Web-based search tools.

➤ **Archie** is a tool for searching FTP sites—Internet servers that store files for downloading. You used Archie to hunt for specific files to download.

Evidence that the world existed before the Web— a still-functioning Gopher server at the University of Minnesota.

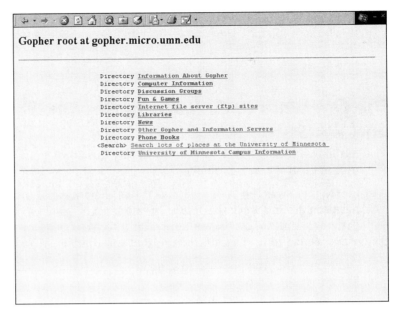

Of course, after the Web came along, these old tools went the way of the horse carriage and buggy whip. Although you still find a few old Gopher servers up and running on one college campus or another, very little new information has been added to these servers since 1994. For that reason, I mention them here purely for their curiosity value.

The New Ways to Find Stuff—Search Engines and Directories

With the advent of the World Wide Web in 1994 (or thereabouts), data started migrating from Gopher and FTP servers to Web servers. Boring old text documents got dusted off and spruced up with graphics and hyperlinks, and Microsoft and Netscape started battling back and forth about who had the better Web browser. In short, the Internet was stood on its head as the Web became the dominant infrastructure—and as millions of new users flooded the Internet monthly.

As the number of individual Web pages grew from tens of thousands to hundreds of thousands to millions to tens of millions to hundreds of millions, it became imperative for people to quickly and easily find their way around all those pages. With the explosion of the Web, then, came a new industry of cataloging and indexing the Web.

And the two main ways of organizing the Web were *search engines* and *directories*.

The Difference Between Search Engines and Directories—and Why You Should Care

You may look at sites such as Yahoo!, Excite, and AltaVista as serving similar functions, which they do. The reality, though, is that some very real differences exist in how they go about organizing the Web.

One approach to organizing the Web is to physically look at each Web page and stick each one into a hand-picked category. When you get enough Web pages collected, you have something called a *directory*.

A directory doesn't search the Web—in fact, a directory only catalogs a very small part of the Web. But a directory is very organized and very easy to use, and lots and lots of people use Web directories every day. In many ways, these Web directories look and work like traditional print Yellow Pages.

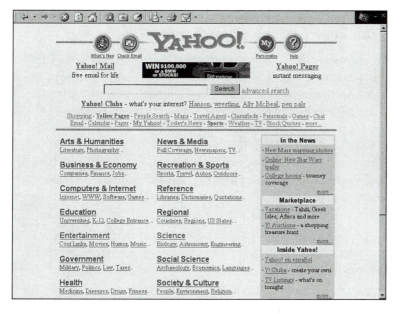

Yahoo!, a well-organized directory that contains one million hand-picked Web sites.

The single most popular Web site today is a directory. Yahoo! catalogs more than one million individual Web sites in its well-organized directory, and people seem to like it—even though Yahoo!'s directory content represents less than 1/100th of one percent of the total number of pages currently published on the Web.

It's important to note that a directory is *not* a search engine. A *search engine* is not powered by human hands; instead, a search engine uses a special type of software program (called a *spider* or a *crawler*) to roam the Web automatically, feeding what it finds back to a massive bank of computers. These computers hold *indexes* of the

11

Web—in some cases entire Web pages are indexed; in other cases only the titles and important words on a page are indexed. (Different search engines operate differently, you see.)

In any case, as the spiders and crawlers operate like little robot Web surfers, the computers back at home base create a huge index (or database) of what the robots found. Some search-engine indexes contain up to 150 million entries—which means, of course, that even the best search engine still leaves more than half the Web untouched and unavailable to searchers.

The Engines Behind the Engines

Although many search engines employ their own proprietary search technologies, others rely on technologies licensed from third parties. The two largest suppliers of behind-the-scenes search technology are Inktomi (www.inktomi.com) and Direct Hit (www.directhit.com). These two players service some of the largest search sites, including Yahoo!, HotBot, MSN Search, and Snap. Problems arise when multiple search sites use the same search technology, because this sometimes results in near-identical results from multiple search sites. (For example, for the longest time I kept getting very similar results from HotBot and MSN Search.) If you find yourself getting similar results from two or more search sites, it probably means that they're sharing technology—and that you can eliminate the duplicative sites from your Favorites list!

When you go to a search engine such as AltaVista or HotBot or Excite or Lycos, you enter a *query* into a little search box on the search engine's home page. This query represents, to the best of your descriptive ability, the specific information that you're looking for. When you click the **Search** button, your query is sent to the search engine's index—not out to the Internet itself. (You never actually search the Web itself, you only search the index that is created by the spiders crawling the Web.) The search engine then creates a list of pages *in its index* that match, to one degree or another, the query that you entered.

12

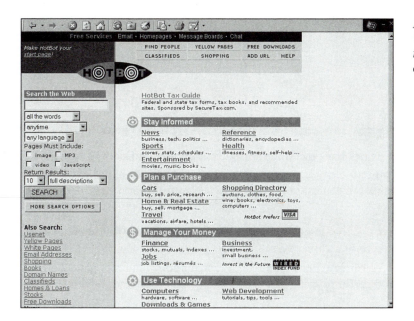

HotBot, one of the largest Web search engines, with more than 110 million entries in its index.

And that's how you get results from a search engine.

So, which is better, a directory or a search engine? It all depends on what you want.

➤ If you want the most results, use a search engine.

➤ If you want hand-picked results, use a directory.

➤ If you want the most current results, use a search engine.

➤ If you want the best-organized results, use a directory.

It's tempting to say that search engines deliver quantity and that directories deliver quality, but that isn't always the case. Some of the best and most powerful search engines—such as HotBot and Northern Light—can deliver quality results matching or besting those from the top directories. To complicate matters even further, many search engine sites have recently added smaller Web directories as part of their services.

The most popular search engine sites include AltaVista, AOL NetFind, Excite, HotBot, InfoSeek, Lycos, MSN Search, Northern Light, and WebCrawler. The most popular directory site is Yahoo!—but it's also the most popular search site, period. Yahoo! doesn't offer a Web search engine, although you can search the entries in its directory.

Which is more popular, then—search engines or directories? People seem to like them both—at least as long as they find what they're looking for.

13

Searching for Information About Search Engines

The topic of search engines has developed into a burgeoning bedroom industry on the Internet. If you're really into search engines—how they work and what the latest developments are—here are a handful of Web sites to add to your Favorites list.

➤ **Search Engine Watch** (www.searchenginewatch.com) The premiere site for search engine news and reviews.

➤ **Portal Hub.com** (www.portalhub.com) Not about search engines per se, but rather about the portals. into which many search engines have evolved.

➤ **Search Engines in Review** (www.blueangels.net) Reviews of search engines from the point of view of getting your Web site listed.

➤ **Spider's Apprentice** (www.monash.com/spidap.html) Tips on using the top Web search engines.

Where to Go Searching

By several counts, more than 200 separate search engines and directories exist on the Internet. That's a lot—certainly more than I've personally visited. With that many options available, you almost need a search engine to search for a search engine!

I tend to divide all these search sites into two major categories: The Big Seven and Everybody Else.

The Big Seven

Seven search sites—*The Big Seven*—receive the bulk of the search traffic on the Web. It's not (in all cases) that these are the better search engines; in fact, some of the search services offered by these sites are rather lame. That said, if everybody's using them, they can't be all bad—so in Chapters 3 through 9 of this book, I show you how to get the best results from the Big Seven sites.

> ### When a Search Site Becomes a Portal
>
> In a drive to become more of an end-destination for users, most of the Big Seven search sites—and several of the Everybody Else sites, too—have given up the purity of being *just* a search engine. By adding proprietary content, communities, and (in some cases) commerce, these sites claim to be *portals* to the entire Internet. In this way, sites such as Yahoo!, Lycos, and Excite compete to some degree with commercial online services, such as America Online. In this book I evaluate these sites only on their search capabilities, not on their additional content or worthiness as a portal. You may decide to use Excite as a portal (because it's a pretty good portal) but still do your searching at AltaVista or Northern Light—which is exactly what I do!

Just who are the Big Seven? In alphabetical order, they are

➤ **AltaVista** (www.altavista.com)   The largest and one of the most powerful search engines. See Chapter 4, "Scale the Heights of AltaVista," for more information on AltaVista.

➤ **Excite** (www.excite.com)   A run-of-the-mill search engine attached to a fairly decent portal. See Chapter 7, "Electrify Your Searches with Excite," for more information on Excite.

➤ **HotBot** (www.hotbot.com)   Another large and powerful search engine, slightly easier to use than AltaVista. See Chapter 5, "Serve Up Hot Searches at HotBot," for more information on HotBot.

➤ **Infoseek** (infoseek.go.com)   Another undistinguished search engine, now part of Disney's GO Network and portal. See Chapter 8, "Seek Important Information at Infoseek," for more information on Infoseek.

➤ **Lycos** (www.lycos.com)   Yet another average search engine attached to a Web portal—but with a unique user-edited Web directory. See Chapter 6, "Go Get It at Lycos," for more information on Lycos.

➤ **Northern Light** (www.northernlight.com)   The least known but perhaps most powerful of the Big Seven, comprising a very large search engine with an additional Special Collection database culled from 5,400 publications. See Chapter 9, "See the Search Lights with Northern Light," for more information on Northern Light.

➤ **Yahoo!** (www.yahoo.com)   The only pure Web directory in the Big Seven and, by most reckonings, the singlemost popular search site on the Internet—not a lot of content, but organized very well with an easy-to-use interface. See Chapter 3, "Surf Yahoo!," for more information on Yahoo!.

Actually, it's hard to go completely wrong with any of these Big Seven sites. Although some are better than others, none are really teeth-gnashingly bad. That said, there are some major differences between these sites; see Table 1.1 for a more detailed comparison of features.

Table 1.1   Comparison of the Big Seven Search Sites

	AltaVista	Excite	HotBot	Infoseek	Lycos	Northern Light	Yahoo!
URL	www. altavista. com	www. excite. com	www. hotbot. com	infoseek. go.com	www. lycos. com	www. northern light.com	www. yahoo. com
Pros	Big and fast; powerful search options; multiple language searches and translations	Intelligent Concept Extraction finds related ideas in addition to keywords; very fresh content; good summaries	Big and fast; wide variety of powerful and easy-to-use search options; very easy to narrow searches	Portal links to other Disney sites (ESPN.com, ABCNEWS. com, Disney.com, Mr. Showbiz)	MP3 search for music files; FTP search for shareware/ freeware downloads	Big and fast; on-the-fly organization of results into Custom Search Folders; proprietary Special Collection provides results when other search engines don't	Very easy to use; well-organized categories; can either browse or search the directory
Cons	Relevancy of rankings is sometimes poor; the number of matches can be over-whelming; can be difficult to narrow searches	Limited selection of search commands; Power Search is hard to find; can be difficult to narrow searches	Could be confusing to inexperienced users	Relatively small size; limited search commands	Very limited search commands in basic search; relatively small size	Fees charged for searching Special Collection ($1-$4 per article); requires registration	Very small size; doesn't use Boolean operators
Search engine?	Yes	Yes	Yes	Yes	Yes	Yes	No
Directory?	Yes	Yes	Yes	Yes	Yes	No	Yes

16

	AltaVista	Excite	HotBot	Infoseek	Lycos	Northern Light	Yahoo!
Other Sources	Usenet, LookSmart Web directory, AV Photo & Media Finder	Usenet, Web Site Guide directory	Usenet, Open Directory	Usenet, GO Network, Directory	Usenet, MP3, audio, sounds, Open Directory	Special Collection of 5,400 unique publications	Usenet, Yahooligans! directory for children, Yahoo! Image Surfer for pictures
Content size	150 million	55 million	110 million	70 million	50 million	125 million Web pages and 4 million full-text articles in the Special Collection	1 million
Pages crawled per day	10 million	3 million	10 million	NA	6-10 million	3 million	NA
Freshness	1 day to 4 weeks	1 day to 3 weeks	1 day to 4 weeks	1 day to 2 months	2 to 5 weeks	1 day to 4 weeks	4 weeks to 1 year
Implied connector	OR	AND	Menu selectable (default to AND)	AND/OR	AND	AND	OR
Boolean operators (in standard search)	AND, NEAR, NOT, OR (advanced search only)	AND, AND NOT, OR (use of Boolean operators overrides concept-based search)	AND, NOT, OR	AND, NOT	AND, NOT, BEFORE, ADJ, FAR, NEAR (advanced search only)	AND, NOT, OR	Unavailable
Wildcards/ Truncation	*	Automatic truncation	*	None	Automatic truncation (period after keyword forces exact match)	* and %	*
Cost	Free	Free	Free	Free	Free	Web search free; Special Collection search fee-based	Free

To help simplify things, I tend to cluster the Big Seven sites into three main groups

➤ **The big and the powerful**   AltaVista, HotBot, and Northern Light. With big indexes (over 100 million entries) and powerful search tools, these are the best places to find just about anything—even though it may take a bit of effort.

➤ **The easy-to-use**   Yahoo!. The smallest index, but the best organized. This is the best site for beginning and casual searchers, with highly qualified results and an easy-to-use interface.

➤ **The middle of the pack**   Excite, Infoseek, and Lycos. It's hard to recommend these guys because they really don't bring much special to the table. They're not the biggest or the most powerful, and they're not the easiest to use. They're just kind of average. Serious searchers skip these sites.

In other words, if you want the most results and the most control over your searches, go either to AltaVista, HotBot, or Northern Light. If you want the most-qualified results and the easiest-to-use interface, go to Yahoo!.

Everybody Else: The Other 200 (or so...) Search Sites

The category that I call Everybody Else includes every single search site or directory not in the Big Seven. I tend to group these sites into a handful of major categories, as follows:

➤ **The runners-up**   These are sites that almost made the Big Seven—typically sites associated with major browsers or online services. Chief among the runners-up are AOL NetFind (www.aol.com/netfind/), LookSmart (www.looksmart.com), MSN Search (home.microsoft.com), Snap (www.snap.com), and WebCrawler (www.webcrawler.com).

➤ **The next generation**   These are smaller and/or newer search engines and directories that offer new technology or approaches to searching the Web. In other words, these are the guys to keep your eyes on. Chief among the next generation are Ask Jeeves! (www.askjeeves.com), GOD: Global Online Directory (www.god.co.uk), Google! (www.google.com), About.com (www.about.com), and whatUseek (www.whatuseek.com). See Chapter 10, "The Next Generation: Newer, Better Search Engines," for more information on these up-and-comers.

➤ **The metasearchers**   These are search engines that let you search multiple search engines and directories from a single page. The top metasearchers include Dogpile (www.dogpile.com), InferenceFind (www.infind.com), Internet Sleuth (www.isleuth.com), Mamma (www.mamma.com), MetaCrawler (www.go2net.com), SavvySearch (www.savvysearch.com), Search Spaniel (www.searchspaniel.com), SuperSeek (www.super-seek.com), and WebTaxi(www.webtaxi.com). See Chapter 13, "Kill Two Birds with One Stone at Meta-Search Sites," for more details.

➤ **The pay-per-viewers**   These are professional search sites that charge for access, such as Dialog (www.dialogweb.com), Lexis-Nexis (www.lexis-nexis.com), and ProQuest Direct (www.umi.com/proquest/). See Chapter 11, "Paying for Information: Subscription Search Sites," for more information.

➤ **The libraries**   These sites include both the online arms of traditional libraries, and the new generation of completely digital Web-based libraries, such as Argus Clearinghouse (`www.clearinghouse.net`), Berkeley Digital Library SunSITE (`sunsite.berkeley.edu`), Electric Library (`www.elibrary.com`), Internet Public Library (`www.ipl.org`), Library of Congress (`lcweb.loc.gov`), My Virtual Reference Desk (`www.refdesk.com`), and the New York Public Library Digital Library Collections (`digital.nypl.org`). See Chapter 12, "Madame Librarian: Online Libraries and Encyclopedias," for more information.

➤ **The encyclopedias**   These are online versions of traditional encyclopedias as well as completely new Web-based encyclopedias, such as Encarta Online (`www.encarta.msn.com`), Encyclopedia Britannica Online (`www.eb.com`), Encyclopedia.com (`www.encyclopedia.com`), Funk & Wagnalls Knowledge Center (`www.fwkc.com`), and Letsfindout Kids' Encyclopedia (`www.letsfindout.com`). These sites are also covered in Chapter 12.

➤ **The specialists**   These are search engines and directories that specialize in a particular type of search or a specific type of content. They include Usenet newsgroup searchers, mailing-list directories, email and phone number directories, online auction searchers, MP3 search engines, shareware and freeware directories, and business and financial information databases. You'll find specialist search sites covered in Chapters 14 through 37 of this book.

Who's Related to Whom?

It's a little-known fact that many of the major search sites and portals are related to one another, generally through several convoluted series of acquisitions over the past few years. For example, Excite owns WebCrawler and AOL NetFind—except in Europe, where NetFind is powered by Lycos. Lycos owns Wired Digital, which owns HotBot, and licenses the Open Directory from Netscape (which used to use Excite for its own search—remember?). AltaVista gets its directory services from LookSmart and some intelligent searching technology from Ask Jeeves!. InfoSeek provides search services for WebTV and Search.com, and is itself part and parcel of Disney's GO Network. I'm not sure anyone can truly keep track of all the acquisitions and alliances, but it makes for some pretty interesting behind-the-scenes stories, I'm sure.

So, Which Search Site Should You Use?

The easy answer is that you should use the site most appropriate to your needs and your individual searching style.

But that's a cop-out, and I know it.

So I'll answer that difficult question by telling you which search sites I use. (And that's right, I said sites—plural!)

Believe it or not, for an everyday type of query, I actually start with Yahoo! more often than not. Yes, I know it has the least amount of content. Yes, I know its search tools are the most primitive. But, gosh darn it, it's just so well organized, and I know that what few results it comes up with are probably worth checking out!

Then I take advantage of Yahoo!'s links to other search engines and automatically pop my query into AltaVista. If I don't like what I get there, I head either to HotBot or Northern Light.

Now, that search process was for a run-of-the-mill type of query. If I'm doing some heavy-duty searching for something I know will be hard to track down, I head straight to Northern Light. I get the best results there, and I love the way the results are organized into their Custom Search Folders.

Finally, if I'm doing a topic-specific search, I'll try to find a site or two that specializes in that topic area. If I can search a topic-specific database or topic-specific archives, that's normally more efficient and more reliable than relying on the general search engines to find specialized information.

Are the search engines I use the right ones for you? That's for you to determine!

The Only Constant Is Change

The information presented in this book is current as of when I wrote it. (Spring 1999, for those of you keeping track.) Given the dynamic nature of the Internet, however, I guarantee you that some things will have changed by the time you read this book—somebody will have acquired somebody else, switched search technologies, added features, or *something*. I apologize; it's just the way it is, and I can't do anything about it. (You gotta love this Internet thing, don't you?)

The Least You Need to Know

➤ The World Wide Web contains more than 300 million pages of information, which is doubling each year; the best search engine has 150 million pages indexed, and the best directory catalogs have only one million pages.

➤ No standards or guidelines exist for organizing information on the Web.

➤ A directory hand-picks Web sites and organizes them into logical categories.

➤ A search engine uses special "spider" software to automatically surf the Web and create an index to the sites it finds; users then query that index to find matching sites.

➤ The Big Seven search sites are AltaVista, Excite, HotBot, Infoseek, Lycos, Northern Light, and Yahoo!.

Chapter 2

Word Up: How to Search with Keywords and Wildcards

Searching is easy. It's getting good results that's hard. To get good results—results that zero in precisely on the information you want without throwing in pages and pages of irrelevant data—you need to know the right way to search. And the right way to search is all about asking the right questions.

Imagine you're a detective questioning a suspect, and you only have a limited number of questions you can ask. Do you waste a question by asking, "Where were you on the night of the crime?" The suspect can answer that question many ways, most of them vague: "California." "Home." "Out." "Someplace better than here."

A better question is one that is more precise and that allows less latitude in how it is answered. "Were you at 1234 Berrywood Lane on the night of the crime?" For this question, only two answers are acceptable: "Yes" or "No." Either of these answers gives you the information you're looking for, with no chance for evasion or misinterpretation.

Searching the Web is like playing detective. Ask the right questions and you get useful answers. Ask vague questions and you get useless answers.

It's that simple.

Why You Can Never Seem to Find What You're Looking for on the Internet

You search and you search and you search, yet you never seem to find exactly what you're looking for. Why is that?

It could be because you don't know how to construct effective search queries (and we'll get to that soon), but even properly constructed queries won't always find the information that best answers your questions. That's because the Internet isn't nearly as orderly as we'd all like to believe.

You see, the Internet is like a bunch of file cabinets in a great big office. You can walk from file cabinet to file cabinet (surf from Web site to Web site), riffle through the file folders in any particular file drawer (browse through the pages on any site), and scan the papers within any individual folder (read the contents of any individual Web page). After all that work, you still might not be able to find what you were looking for.

Think about it: How many times have you tried to find a specific piece of information in your office—and failed? Did you always go to the right file cabinet? Did you always find the right folder? Were the folders always organized the way you thought they'd be organized? Did the folders you looked in always contain the papers you thought would be there? And did the papers you read always contain the information you wanted—worded in precisely the manner you expected?

Of course not. Papers and folders and files are all created and organized by human beings, and human beings (1) are not perfect, (2) seldom think perfectly logically, and (3) rarely think alike.

Guess what? It's the same way on the Web.

Human beings create Web pages. Human beings assemble multiple pages into Web sites. Human beings (or software programs created by human beings) attempt to index and organize all that information on all those Web sites in a useful manner.

Which explains why you can never find what you were looking for on the Internet.

The Internet—Bigger and Badder Than Any Office

Another reason why it's so hard to find anything online is that the Internet is big—really, *really* big! The Internet contains more than 300 million individual "documents"—and that number is doubling yearly! Just think of it—300 million poorly conceived and poorly organized documents, all filed and indexed by human beings. Ouch! (It makes your office look manageable, doesn't it?)

To look for information created and managed by a human being, you have to think like that human being. Did the person writing about Internet Explorer call it "Internet Explorer," "Microsoft Internet Explorer," just "Explorer," "IE," "IE5" (including the version number), or was it called a "browser," a "Web browser," or even (somewhat incorrectly) a "navigator?" You see, any or all of those words and phrases could refer to the single thing you thought you were looking for. If all you do is look for one of these words or phrases, you could skip right over important information that happens to use a slightly different word or phrase.

The best search engines in the world can't anticipate human beings who use alternate words, or (heaven forbid!) use the wrong words by mistake. But you, as a master Internet searcher, must somehow learn to overcome these human shortcomings if you're to find all the information you wish to find.

So here's your challenge: You have to learn how to think like the people who created and organized the information you're looking for. If you're looking for old plastic model kits, you have to realize that some people call them "kits" and some call them "model kits"; some call them "plastic model kits" and some call them "models"; some call them by name ("Aurora model kits") and some call them "ready-to-assemble kits"; some even have poor spelling skills and call them "modle kits."

When you construct your queries, think through all the different ways people refer to the topic you're looking for. Think like the people who put the information together, like the people who create the Web pages. Visualize the results you'd like to find and what they might look like on a Web page. Then, and only then, should you construct your query, using the keywords and operators and modifiers you need to return the results you visualized. Master this skill, and you'll almost always find what you want.

Searching 101: The Basic Parts of Every Search Site

Every search site includes two basic components you need to perform a search: a *search box*, into which you enter your query, and a ***Search*** *button*, which you click to initiate your search (sometimes pressing **Enter** also does the trick). These components may be at the top of some pages, on the left or right side of others, or even at the bottom of a select few. They may even have funny names, such as Lycos's **Go Get It!** button. But these items are always there, and they always work the same way.

Some sites have *additional components* that let you exert more control over your searches. For example, HotBot includes a number of pull-down lists and check boxes you can use to narrow your search parameters. If a site has more components, and if they're truly useful to you, great. If not, you can probably exert similar control by fine-tuning the keywords and operators in your search query.

Many of the major sites offer *advanced search modes* or pages. In some cases, the advanced search simply uses a series of forms to perform the same functions as modifiers and operators in complex queries. In other cases, the advanced search is the only place where you can perform Boolean operations. In still other cases, the advanced search actually offers a host of extra functions that are not found anywhere else on the site. In any case, if an advanced mode exists, you should probably check it out— even though you may not end up using it.

Finally, every search site generates many, many pages of *search results.* Although some results pages include additional types of information, all list the Web pages that best match your search, sorted in descending order of relevancy to your query. Some listings include brief descriptions of the matching sites, some let you view additional pages similar to the selected match, but all let you click a link to go directly to the matching page.

A typical search box and ***Search*** *button from AltaVista—enter your query into the search box, and then click the* ***Search*** *button to start your search.*

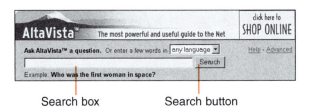

Search box   Search button

The bottom line is that only three components are totally necessary on a search site, and all search sites include all three.

➤ **The search box**   This is where you enter your query.

➤ **The Search button**   This is what you click to initiate your search.

➤ **The search results page**   This is where you find Web pages that match your query; click the links to go to the matching pages.

The Correct Way to Search

Is there one correct way to perform an online search? No, of course not; every searcher has a preferred style and approach.

However, there are a handful of general search guidelines that I recommend you follow.

1. Start by thinking about what you want to find. What words best describe the information or concept you're looking for? What alternate words might be used instead? Are there any words that can be excluded from your search to better define your query?

2. Determine where you should perform your search. Do you need the power of AltaVista, HotBot, Northern Light, or the better-qualified results of Yahoo!? Are there any topic-specific sites available you should use instead of these general sites?

3. Construct your query. If at all possible, try to use Boolean expressions (they're more flexible). Use as many keywords as you need—the more the better. If appropriate (and available), use the site's advanced search page or mode.

4. Click the **Search** button to perform the search.

5. Evaluate the matches on the search results page. If the initial results are not to your liking, refine your query and search again—or switch to a more appropriate search site.

6. Select the matching pages that you wish to view and begin clicking through to those pages.

7. Save the information that best meets your needs.

Sounds pretty logical, doesn't it? I'm going to bet, however, that you regularly skip over at least half of the steps in this list. Pay particular attention to the first two steps (thinking about how and where to search), and step 5 (evaluating your results and refining your search). The key to better searching is better planning—and learning from your mistakes.

The bottom line? Think before you search, and spend more time learning from your results afterward.

How to Perform a Basic Search—On *Any* Search Site

As you learned in the last chapter, there are many different kinds of search sites—including general search engines, general Web directories, specialized search engines, and specialized directories. And every site you go to works in a slightly different way, using a slightly different logic (and technological infrastructure) to perform its search operations. To master the intricacies of every single search site would appear to be an insurmountable task.

Fortunately, some common logic is used in almost all the major search sites. This logic is represented by a series of commands, modifiers, and operators that work in similar fashion across most search engines and directories. If you can master these basic skills, you'll be 80 percent of the way toward mastering each individual site.

The following sections show you the common skills you can use on just about any search site you come across.

Use the Right Words

When you construct your query, you do so by using one or more *keywords*. Keywords are what search engines look for when they process your query. Your keywords are compared to the index or directory of Web pages accessible to the search engine; the more keywords found on a Web page, the better the match.

Use the Right Words to Talk About the Right Words

The individual words that you enter into a search box are called *keywords*. Collectively, all your keywords (and the operators and modifiers between the words) combine to form a *query*. Just remember that a query is composed of keywords, not the other way around, and you'll have it straight.

You should choose keywords that best describe the information you're looking for—using as many keywords as you need. Don't be afraid of using too many keywords; in fact, using too few keywords is a common fault of many novice searchers. The more words you use, the better idea the search engine has of what you're looking for. Think of it as describing something to a friend—the more descriptive you are (that is, the more words you use), the better the picture your friend has of what you're talking about.

It's the same way when you "talk" to a search engine.

If you're looking for a thing or a place, choose keywords that describe that thing or place in as much detail as possible. For example, if you're looking for a car, one of your first keywords would, of course, be car. But you probably know what general type of car you're looking for—let's say its a sports car—so you might enhance your query to read sports car. You may even know that you want to find a foreign sports car, so you change your query to read foreign sports car. And if you're looking for a classic model, your query could be expanded to classic foreign sports car. As you can see, the better your description (using more keywords), the better the search engine can "understand" what you're searching for.

If you're looking for a concept or an idea, you should choose keywords that best help people understand that concept or idea. This often means using additional keywords that help to impart the meaning of the concept. Suppose you want to search for information about senior citizens; your initial query would be senior citizens. What other words could you use to describe the concept of senior citizens? How about words such as elderly, old, or retired? If these words help to describe your concept, add them to your search—like this: senior citizens elderly old retired. Trust me—adding keywords like these results in more targeted searches and higher-quality results.

One other thing to keep in mind is to think about alternative ways to say what it is that you're looking for. (In other words, think about synonyms.) If you're looking for a car, you could also be looking for a vehicle, an automobile, an auto, or for transportation. It doesn't take a search guru to realize that searching for car vehicle automobile auto transportation will generate better results than simply searching for car.

When You Don't Know the Right Words, Use Wildcards

What if you're not quite sure of which word form to use? For example, would the best results come from looking for auto, automobile, or automotive? Many search sites let you use *wildcards* to stand in for parts of a word that you're not quite sure about. In most instances, the asterisk character (*) is used as a wildcard to match any character, or group of characters, from its particular position in the word to the end of that word. So, in our example above, entering auto* would return all three words—auto, automobile, and automotive.

Wildcards are very powerful tools to use in your Internet searches. I like to use them when I'm searching for people and I'm not totally sure of their names. For example, if I'm searching for someone whose name might be Sherry or Sheryl or Sherylyn, I just enter sher* and I'll get all three names back in my results. To take it even further, if all I knew is that the person's name started with an "s," I'd enter s*—and get back Sherry and Susan and Samantha as matches.

Wildcards can also return unpredictable results. Suppose I'm looking for Monty Python, but I'm not sure whether Monty is spelled "Monty" or "Montey," so I search for mon*. Unfortunately, this wildcard matches a whole bunch of "mon" words, including Monty—and money, monsters, and Mongolia. In other words, if you go too broad on your wildcards, you'll find a lot more than what you were initially looking for.

Everything's Wild, Automatically

Some search sites don't use wildcards, but instead use what is called *automatic truncation*. On these sites, a wildcard is assumed at the end of every word—so just entering mon will return Monty, money, monsters, and all the rest. Automatic truncation is supposed to work best with plurals (enter monster and get both "monster" and "monsters" automatically), but it can also work to your detriment, in the form of too many irrelevant returns.

Modify Your Words with +, –, and " "

A *modifier* is a symbol that causes a search engine to do something special with the word directly following the symbol. Three modifiers are used almost universally in the search engine community.

➤ + (always include the following keyword)   Use the + modifier when a keyword must be included for a match. For example, searching for +monty +python will return Monty Python pages or pages about pythons owned by guys named Monty—because any matching page must include both the words, but not necessarily in any order.

➤ – (always exclude the following keyword)   Use the – modifier when a keyword must never be part of a match. For example, searching for +monty –python will return pages about guys named Monty but will not return pages about Monty Python—because you're excluding "python" pages from your results.

➤ " " (always search for the exact phrase within the quotation marks)   Use the " " modifier to search for the precise keywords in the prescribed order. For example, searching for "monty python" will return only pages about the British comedy troupe Monty Python—you're searching for both the words, in order, right next to each other.

Use AND, NOT, and OR in a Boolean Search

Modifiers are nice, but they're not always the most flexible way to modify your query. The preferred parameters for serious online searching are called *Boolean operators*.

Boolean Logic

Boolean logic is a form of algebra in which all values are reduced to either TRUE or FALSE. So a *Boolean expression* results in a value of either TRUE or FALSE (for example, if a page matches all conditions of a query, the result is TRUE) and contains *Boolean operators*, such as AND, OR, or NOT. For that matter, the less-than (<) and greater-than (>) signs are also Boolean operators, although you won't find them used on any search engine I'm aware of. By the way, Boolean logic was named after nineteenth-century mathematician George Boole and is widely used in both mathematics and computer programming.

The most common Boolean operators you'll be able to use at most search sites are the following:

➤ **AND** (a match must contain *both* words to be TRUE)   Searching for monty AND python will return Monty Python pages or pages about pythons owned by guys named Monty, but not pages that include only one of the two words. The more words connected by AND operators, the more precise your search and the fewer matches you'll receive. Remember, however, that in an AND search, you're searching for both the words, but *not necessarily in order*—if you want to search for both words in order, next to each other, you want to search for the exact phrase, which you do by putting the phrase in quotation marks, like this: "monty python".

➤ **OR** (a match must contain either of the words to be TRUE)   Searching for monty OR python will return pages about guys named Monty or pythons or Monty Python. With an OR search, you're searching for *either* monty *or* python, so both words don't have to appear on the same page to make a match. The more words connected by OR operators, the less precise your search—but the more matches you'll receive.

➤ **NOT** (a match must exclude the next word to be TRUE)   Searching for monty NOT python will return pages about guys named Monty but will not return pages about Monty Python—because you're *excluding* "python" pages from your results. (NOTE: At some search engines, this must be used in the form AND NOT.)

In addition, Boolean searching lets you use parentheses, much as you would in a mathematical equation, to group portions of queries together to create more complicated searches. For example, suppose you wanted to search for all pages about balls that were red or blue but not large. The search would look like this:

```
balls AND (red OR blue) NOT large
```

A handful of other Boolean operators are also available, such as ADJ or NEAR or FAR, that have to do with *adjacency*—how close words are to each other. However, very few search engines use these adjacency operators, so you probably won't have much of an opportunity to use them.

Define **Where You Want to Search with Meta Words**

Some search engines include what are called *meta words,* which are operators that enable you to restrict searches to specified parameters. A meta word is actually a pair of words—a keyword followed by a value, separated by a colon, such as this: keyword:value.

Most meta words let you restrict searches to parts of a document. For example, the meta word title: restricts searching to the title of the Web page; the meta word text: restricts searching to the text of the page.

Suppose you wanted to search for Web pages that had the word "molehill" in their title; you would enter the command `title:molehill`.

No Spaces in Meta Words

Be careful to include only *one* value word after a meta word because that's all most search engines recognize. For example, a search engine will see `title:monty python` and only view `title:monty` as the meta word; the `python` will be viewed as a separate keyword. You can get around this, in some instances, by grouping multiple words in quotation marks, as an exact phrase—in other words, you can legally search for `title:"monty python"`.

Keep in mind, however, that not all search engines let you use meta words, and the meta words you can use—and how they work—differ somewhat from site to site. It's probably best to check out a site's Help file before attempting to use meta words.

But How Does It Work in the Real World?

Okay, all that theory about modifiers and operators was nice, but how do you make practical use of it in the real world of Internet search engines? Read on and you'll get some hands-on experience with constructing useful search queries.

Everything You Can Do All in One Place: A Quick Reference to Common Search Operations

First, because all these modifiers and operators are easy to forget, Table 2.1 presents a quick list of which commands to use to perform specific search operations.

Table 2.1   Common Search Operations and Commands

To Do This:	Use This Command:	Example:
Non-Boolean Modifiers		
Search for part of a word	*	`mon*`
Must include a word	+	`monty +python`

To Do This:	Use This Command:	Example:
Must exclude a word	–	monty –python
Search for an exact phrase	" "	"monty python"
Boolean Operators		
Include both words	AND	monty AND python
Include at least one word	OR	monty OR python
Exclude pages that contain a word	NOT or AND NOT	monty NOT python *or* monty AND NOT python
Group words or phrases together	()	(monty python)

Practice Makes Perfect—Examples of Some Common and Some Complex Queries

Now we'll try a few real-world examples of both common and complex search queries.

Suppose you're preparing a report on reptiles. Your query would be simple:

```
reptile
```

Although you could put a wildcard (*) after the word "reptile" (so that you could also catch the plural, "reptiles"), that isn't necessary on most search sites. Most sites automatically search for plurals, so I decided to just use the singular and let the search engine do the rest. (By the way, if I wanted to be safe, I could have entered reptil*, which would catch "reptile," "reptiles," and "reptilian.")

The problem with this query, of course, is that you'll get about a zillion hits, most of them fairly vague and irrelevant. So we'll make some more assumptions.

Suppose that your report is focusing on reptile mating behavior. You could enter the following query:

```
reptile mating behavior
```

And you'd probably get some okay results. But it may pay to insert some synonyms for mating and make the word "behavior" optional. This would be a better query:

```
reptile AND (mating OR reproduc* OR sex OR courtship) behavior
```

Take a closer look at that last query. I started out by thinking of several synonyms for mating—reproduce, sex, and courtship—and included them all in a big OR expression, joined by parentheses. Then, instead of using the word "reproduce," I put a wildcard after the "c" to give us reproduc*. I put the wildcard there so that I could pick up any or all of "reproduce" or "reproducing" or "reproduction"—that is, I inserted the wildcard after the last common letter, which was the "c." Finally, I wanted the word "behavior" to be in the query, but not necessarily a required keyword, so I stuck it on the end by itself, without any modifier or operator that would dictate its appearance. The result is a query that should give us precisely what we want.

But what if the search engine you're using doesn't let you use Boolean operators? Then it gets a little trickier, but you can still get similar results. Just use modifiers to create the following query:

```
+reptile mating reproduc* sex courtship behavior
```

Most search engines that don't use Boolean operators use the assumed OR between all the words—so just listing the words without operators is the same as putting an OR between the words. For those words that must be included (the AND words), use the + modifier. In this example, the only *required* word is "reptile"—the other words are optional. Note that non-Boolean searches don't let you use parentheses for grouping, so we lose some of the desired functionality of the initial query. (That's why most serious searchers prefer to use Boolean expressions whenever possible.)

Now we'll look at one more example, one that forces you to *exclude* some phrases. Suppose you want to look for comedy clubs in New York but can't stand Jerry Seinfeld. Here's what a Boolean-type query might look like:

```
(comed* AND club) AND "New York" NOT Seinfeld
```

We'll look at this one phrase by phrase. First, I wanted to look for pages that had the words "comedy" and "club" in them, but not necessarily used together. (I can envision a page saying something like "this is a classy club with today's hottest comedy acts.") I also didn't want to limit the results to matching the word "comedy"— "comedians" would also be a good match—hence the wildcard after the "d." Now, I made "New York" into an exact phrase (complete with capital letters) because, well, New York is always New York. Because I want only comedy clubs in New York, I connected the two phrases with an AND. Finally, the NOT in front of Seinfeld weeds out any page on which Mr. Seinfeld's name appears.

Sometimes NOT is AND NOT

Some search engines don't let you use NOT by itself, requiring instead that it be preceded by an AND. So the query in the running example would become (comed* AND club) AND "New York" AND NOT Seinfeld. Remember to check the instructions for each individual search site for specific details.

Here's the same query in a non-Boolean fashion:

```
+comed* +club +"New York" -Seinfeld
```

In this instance, the non-Boolean search works just as well as the Boolean version. The +'s serve the same functions as the ANDs, and the – works as well as the NOT. We do lose the parenthetical grouping of "comed* club," but that ends up not being such a big thing.

Seem simple enough? Usually you can come up with the right query just by talking through what you really want to look for. When in doubt, say it out loud—if you can't understand what you just said, chances are the search engine can't, either!

The Bottom Line—Ten Tips You Can Use at Just About Every Search Site

Follow these 10 tips to improve your search results across most search sites:

➤ **Tip #1: Use nouns as keywords**   Verbs and conjunctions are either ignored by the search engines or are too common to be useful. Remember—search for specific things.

➤ **Tip #2: Use descriptive or specific words to narrow your search**
Using multiple words helps the search engine get a handle on the concept you're looking for—the more words the better. Instead of searching for a ford, search for a 1964 ford mustang.

➤ **Tip #3: Search for synonyms**   Is it big or is it large? Use big OR large OR huge to catch all possible variations.

➤ **Tip #4: Put the important stuff first**   You get different results with sport car than you do with car sport; the first word gets greater weighting.

➤ **Tip #5: Search for specific phrases**   Use quotes to search for exact phrases. If you want to search for the movie *Heavy Metal*, search for "heavy metal"— searching for heavy metal (without the quotation marks) will return a lot of sites about heavy filing cabinets made of metal!

➤ **Tip #6: Group like items**   Think of your query as an algebraic expression. Group related items in parentheses, and think left-to-right. If you want to search for heavy metal or music sites that don't include Def Leppard, write it like this: ("heavy metal" OR music) NOT "def leppard". If, on the other hand, you want to search for all heavy metal sites but only those music sites that exclude Def Leppard, then your query would look like this: "heavy metal" OR (music NOT "def leppard").

➤ **Tip #7: Truncate words or use wildcards**   If you want to pick up both singular and plural versions of your keywords, don't search for the plural! Many search engines use automatic truncation, so searching for truck will return both truck and trucks (and trucking, for that matter). For those engines that don't automatically truncate, stick a "*" wildcard after the keyword (truck*, using the current example).

➤ **Tip #8: Use appropriate capitalization** Searching for Whitewater will give you sites that mention the political scandal; looking for whitewater will return sites about rafting and canoeing.

➤ **Tip #9: Refine your searches—then refine them again** You seldom get perfect results on the first try. Look at the results from your initial query and try to figure out why you're getting too many or too few matches. Based on what you deduce, either add or subtract keywords from your query, and then search again. Keep repeating this process of refinement until you finally find what you're looking for.

➤ **Tip #10: Look for help** All search sites have online help files, tip pages, or files of frequently asked questions (FAQs). Look for this online help to find the precise way to word your queries on that specific site.

One More Tip: Save Your Searches!

If you actually manage to execute a search that results in a perfect set of matches, you probably want to save your results so you can access them again in the future. Learn how to save specific results pages as Bookmarks or Favorites within your Web browser—this way, you can click the bookmark or favorite and return to that ideal page of results, without need to replicate the query from scratch.

The Least You Need to Know

➤ The key to successful searching is to plan through your search in advance and then refine your search results afterward.

➤ Learn to think like the people who create and organize the information—remember to think of alternate ways to say what you're looking for.

➤ Most search engines use the same general commands.

➤ You can modify keywords with + (include), –(exclude), and " " (exact phrase).

➤ Boolean operators let you connect words with AND (must include both words), OR (must include either word, not necessarily both), and NOT (must exclude the following word).

Part 2

The Usual Suspects: How to Get the Best Results from the Major Search Sites

Chances are, you're already a heavy user of one of the "Big Seven" search sites—Yahoo!, AltaVista, HotBot, Lycos, Excite, Infoseek, or Northern Light. Chances also are that you're dissatisfied with the results you're getting from these sites. This part of the book goes into detail on how to use each of these popular sites—how to perform advanced searches, and how to get the best results. Use these chapters as a handy reference to the sites you use most often!

Chapter 3

Surf Yahoo!

In This Chapter

➤ Understand why Yahoo! is the most popular site on the Web—despite its many limitations

➤ Learn how to browse through Yahoo!'s hierarchy of categories

➤ Master Yahoo!'s limited searching capabilities

➤ Use Yahoo!'s other directories to find kid-friendly sites and image files

Yahoo! (www.yahoo.com) is the most popular site on the entire World Wide Web. More people visit Yahoo! than any other site on the Web—over 30 million per month— which automatically makes it the most popular of all the numerous search sites. Chances are that you use Yahoo! on a regular basis.

Despite its popularity, however, Yahoo! is not the best search site available—not by a wide margin. In fact, if you want to generate a lot of results or are hunting for a somewhat obscure topic, Yahoo! is a site to avoid.

Just take a look at Yahoo!'s report card. Of the Big Seven search sites, Yahoo! has

➤ **The least content**   Yahoo! only indexes about one million pages—compared to 50 to 100 million pages indexed on other sites.

➤ **The oldest content**   It can take months—or even years—for Yahoo!'s human editors to add a page to the Yahoo! directory.

➤ **The fewest power tools**   You can't use your Boolean AND, OR, or NOT operators here.

In other words, not much is there, and most of what is there is somewhat out of date. So, if the site's so bad, why is it so popular?

Report Card

Address:	www.yahoo.com
Search Engine:	No
Directory:	Yes
Size:	D
Freshness:	C
Ease of Use:	A
Power:	D
Extras:	Yahooligans! directory for kids and Yahoo! Image Surfer for pictures; provides same-query access to other search engines

Why Everybody Wants to Yahoo!

Yahoo's saving grace is that it is the easiest search site for average surfers to use, bar none. For the average Web user, ease of use beats completeness any day.

What makes Yahoo! so easy to use? First, even though it looks like a search engine, it isn't; it's just a very large Web *directory*. Second, the sites listed in the Yahoo! directory aren't automatically grabbed off the Web by spider software, they're added by hand. Third, the same human beings that add the sites to the directory also arrange them in a very logical series of topics and subtopics.

Remember, Yahoo! is a directory, not a search engine. That means that a finite number of listings are in the Yahoo! database—a little more than one million pages as of this writing. This compares to more than 50 million pages on normal search engines, such as Excite and Lycos, and more than 100 million pages on the very best search engines, such as AltaVista, HotBot, and Northern Light. The trade-off for a lower page count is higher quality—fewer "bad" and duplicative pages are present on Yahoo! than on any other search site.

The bottom line is that Yahoo!'s human dimension makes it easy to use and guarantees a certain quality (but not quantity) of results. So if you're searching for a popular topic (not too obscure) and you want a few good results, Yahoo! is a good place to start. Then, if you can't find what you're looking for on Yahoo!, lots of other sites are available to search next!

More Than You Ever Wanted to Know About Yahoo!

Yahoo! has an interesting history—it came into being almost in spite of itself. David Filo and Jerry Yang were students at Stanford University in 1994, in the early days of the World Wide Web. As a convenience to themselves, they started keeping track of their favorite sites on the Web, collecting and classifying hundreds and then thousands of different Web pages. As their little hobby grew more time-consuming, Filo and Yang created a custom database to house their Web links, and they made the database available for free on the Web. They named the database Yahoo! (supposedly an acronym for Yet Another Hierarchical Officious Oracle) and, after about a year, moved their site from the overloaded Stanford servers to the larger-capacity servers of Netscape Corporation.

In the spring of 1995, Yang and Filo began to realize the commercial appeal of their increasingly popular site; they accepted some venture capital and turned Yahoo! into a full-time business. Since going public in 1996, Yahoo! has become one of the highest-flying Internet stocks on the market—and one of the first Internet-related companies to actually turn a profit. (If you had invested $100 in Yahoo! stock when it first went public, that stock would have been worth more than $1,500 less than three years later!)

The Chief Yahoos

Today, Yahoo! is run by a team of professional managers, including Chairman/CEO Timothy Koogle (ex-Motorola) and President/COO Jeff Mallett (ex-Novell). Filo and Yang remain on board as "Chief Yahoos," providing important strategic and technical direction for the rapidly expanding company.

Of course, the Yahoo! of today is a far cry from the database that resided on Filo and Yang's personal workstations at Stanford. Yahoo! has expanded well beyond a simple Web directory (even though most Yahoo! visitors still use the site primarily for searching). Today, Yahoo! is a full-fledged Web *portal*, a site that not only directs you to content across the Internet, but also contains its own proprietary content and services—everything from stock quotes to online auctions, interactive chat, and free email.

In addition, international versions of Yahoo! are available for more than 20 countries, from Australia to the United Kingdom. As you can see, Yahoo! is more like America Online than it is a simple search site—although searching is what we're interested in right now.

Yahoo!—you can search its Web directory or take advantage of its many services, including free email, news, and stock quotes.

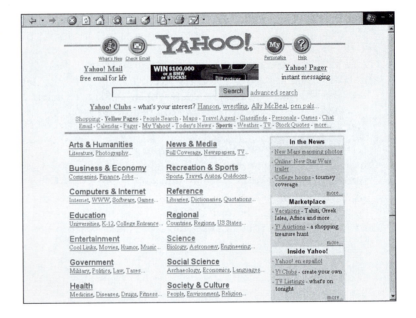

How Yahoo! Ranks Your Results

Did you ever wonder how a particular page ended up at the top of the search results list? Yahoo! uses three criteria to rank its results:

➤ **Keywords** If you've entered multiple keywords, those Web pages that match more of your keywords rank higher than those pages that match fewer keywords.

➤ **Inclusion in title** If your keywords are included in the Web page's title, then that page is ranked higher than one in which your keywords are found only in the body or URL of the page.

➤ **Category** Remember that Yahoo! is a directory composed of multiple categories and subcategories arranged in hierarchies. Those categories that are higher up in the Yahoo! tree hierarchy are ranked higher than those lower in the hierarchy.

I find that Yahoo! actually does a pretty good job of listing the best sites first. In fact, if you're fed up with getting hundreds or thousands of irrelevant results from other search engines, Yahoo!'s shorter but better qualified lists of matches can be a breath of fresh air!

Less Content—and Fewer Descriptions!

The great things about Yahoo! are its well-thought-out categories and its hand-picked selection of sites. Unlike other (smaller) directories, however, the sites in Yahoo!'s directory are not accompanied by helpful descriptions. All you get are the names of the sites and the URLs—nothing more. Most other directories, such as the user-edited Open Directory and Lycos Top 5 percent, include brief descriptions of the sites they list. To me, site descriptions are one of the most appealing features of directories—and Yahoo! doesn't have them.

Finding Web Pages with Yahoo!—The Easy Ways

There are two ways to find things on Yahoo!: *browsing* and *searching*. Let's look a little at each.

Browsing Yahoo! Categories

The first way to find things on Yahoo! is to navigate through the topic classifications on the Yahoo! home page. You do this by clicking a category on the Yahoo! home page, which displays a listing of subcategories within the main category. Then you click a subcategory to display subcategories of that subcategory, and so on, until you get to actual Web page links. (In other words, you browse from the general to the specific.)

As an example, suppose you're looking for information on crocodiles. You start by clicking the **Science** link on Yahoo!'s home page. When the Science listings appear, you look at all the subtopics available (from Acoustics to Web Directories) and decide to click **Animals, Insects, and Pets**. After deciding that crocs are neither insects nor pets, you need to choose yet another subtopic from the next page displayed (which, in this case, runs the gamut from Animal Behavior to

@Yahoo!

You'll notice that some categories end with the "@" sign, such as Dinosaurs@. This means that the particular category is listed in more than one location within the Yahoo! directory.

Xenotransplantation—the use of live animal cells in human patients). If you know your species, you know that crocodiles are reptiles, so you click **Reptiles and Amphibians**. When the next page appears, you click **Reptiles**, and when the next page appears, you click **Crocodiles and Alligators**. Finally, you see the Crocodiles and Alligators page, which has about a dozen links to sites that have something to do with crocs, with the most relevant sites listed at the top of the page.

Keep Your Place

As you navigate through the various subtopics in the Yahoo! directory, it's easy to forget just where you are. To help you remember where you are and where you've been, a simple navigation line is shown at the top of every Yahoo! category page. For example, the Crocodiles and Alligators page is at the end of the following category tree: Home>Science>Biology>Zoology>Animals, Insects, and Pets>Reptiles and Amphibians>Reptiles>Crocodiles and Alligators. Note that this category tree includes two branches that you didn't visit: Biology and Zoology. Clicking links in a Yahoo! listing sometimes jumps you to subcategories not in a direct path from where you currently are. However, the nice thing about Yahoo!'s navigation tree is that you can click any subtopic within the tree and jump there directly. In our current example, clicking **Reptiles and Amphibians** takes you directly to the Reptiles and Amphibians page you visited earlier, and clicking **Home** takes you back to the Yahoo! home page.

This searching by browsing is certainly a no-brainer way to navigate the Yahoo! directory, but it's very time-consuming, and, if you're like me, you often don't know what things go in which categories. I much prefer the second way of finding things on Yahoo!—by searching.

Simple Searches

Even though Yahoo! is a directory—not a search engine—Yahoo! still employs a search engine that enables you to locate subjects in its directory. Try to keep that clear—you can't search the Web from Yahoo!, but you can search Yahoo! itself.

I find searching Yahoo! preferable to browsing Yahoo!; even though the Yahoo! directory only holds a million pages, that's still too many pages to browse through expediently. So if you use Yahoo! a lot, you should learn how to search the directory.

The Yahoo! search box is at the top of Yahoo's main page. Searching Yahoo! is as simple as entering your keyword or words and then clicking the **Search** button.

Search Within a Browse

You can actually search while you're browsing—which is a great way to find specific information within some of the larger, less manageable categories. After you've browsed through a category, type a query into the search box at the top of the page, pull down the list next to the search box, select **just this category**, and then click the **Search** button. Yahoo! searches within the current category for the keywords you entered.

Yahoo! returns three types of results in the following order:

➤ **Yahoo! category matches**   This first cut of the data lists those Yahoo! categories that match your search parameters (such as the Home>Science>Biology>Zoology>Animals, Insects, and Pets>Reptiles and Amphibians>Reptiles>Crocodiles and Alligators category mentioned earlier). Click any category match to display Yahoo!'s complete site listings for that category. This is typically a short list of categories; if your search doesn't directly match any Yahoo! categories, nothing is listed here.

➤ **Yahoo! site matches**   The second type of results lists sites in the Yahoo! directory that match your search parameters. The results do not list individual pages within a site—only the main page of the site itself. Yahoo! displays these results grouped within large Yahoo! categories. Typically this list is larger than the category matches.

➤ **Web pages**   This final type of results goes outside of the Yahoo! directory (using the Inktomi search engine, which is also used by HotBot and several other search sites) to list individual Web pages that meet your search criteria. Note that these Web page listings are not available when you're browsing through Yahoo!'s category lists.

You can scroll to the bottom of any Yahoo! results page and click the **Categories**, **Web Sites**, or **Web Pages** links to go directly to those types of listings. You can also click the **Related News** links to find news headlines about your search topic or click the **Net Events** link to find any online chat events concerning the topic at hand.

Yahoo! search results, with the closest matches listed first. Just click a link to go to the matching page.

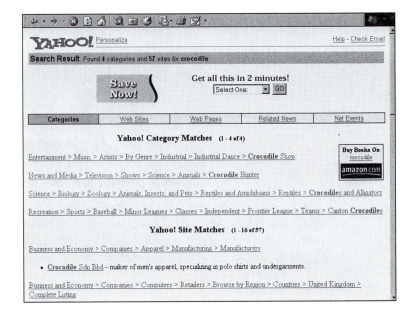

In my searching, I normally don't find the Yahoo! Category Matches too useful (although they do let you quickly see how related items are categorized), so I'll typically go directly to the Yahoo! Site Matches. If I can't find what I need there, I move outside of the Yahoo! directory proper to Inktomi's Web Pages listings.

Search Other Search Sites from Yahoo!

At the very bottom of every Yahoo! search results page are links to other Web search sites, such as AltaVista, HotBot, Infoseek, and Lycos. If you click any of these links, you're taken directly to that search page, with your current search criteria automatically plugged into the new search engine and the results already displayed. I like to start my searches at Yahoo!, and then—if I don't find what I'm looking for—I use the bottom-of-page links to automatically launch the same search in a different search engine. (By the way, if you click the **More** link at the bottom of the page, you display Yahoo!'s Searching the Web category, which lists a variety of other search sites and resources.)

Fine-tuning Your Yahoo! Search

Yahoo! lets you use a limited number of wildcards and operators to fine-tune your search—much fewer than with other search sites. Table 3.1 lists the commands you can use to fine-tune your Yahoo! search results.

Table 3.1   Yahoo! Search Parameters

To Do This:	Use This Command:	Example:
Search for part of a word	*	mon*
Must include a word	+	monty +python
Must exclude a word	–	monty –python
Search for a complete phrase	" "	"monty python"
Only search in the title of the page	t:	t:monty python
Only search in the URL of the page	u:	u:monty python

Note that Yahoo! search does not use Boolean operators—a major drawback for serious searchers.

The Automatic OR

If you enter more than one word in a query with no operator between them, Yahoo! will assume you want to look for either word and automatically insert an OR between the words. In other words, Yahoo! automatically searches for pages that contain any of your keywords. As a result, if you're looking for a title or phrase, consider enclosing it in quotes or using plus signs to indicate required keywords.

Find More Stuff with Yahoo!'s Advanced Search Options

Not satisfied with the quality of results from a standard Yahoo! search? Then click the Advanced Search link on Yahoo!'s home page to access Yahoo!'s Advanced Search Options.

Yahoo!'s Advanced Search Options—Tell Yahoo! whether you want an exact phrase match, whether to imply AND or OR operations, and whether to limit results to newer listings.

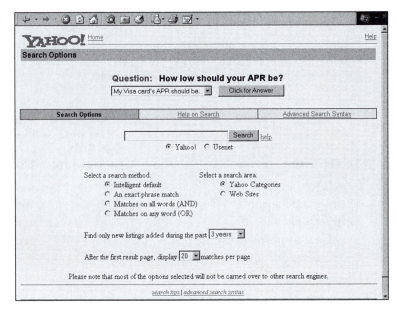

Most of what you can do on the Advanced Search Options page you can do with normal commands and operators from the standard Yahoo! search. However, a few additional parameters are available from this page, including

➤ **Search the Web or Usenet**   Instead of searching the Web, you can search Usenet newsgroups by clicking the `Usenet` option. This is the only way to search Usenet on the Yahoo! site.

➤ **Intelligent default**   This is the standard Yahoo! search mode.

➤ **An exact phrase match**   This has the effect of putting quotation marks around your keywords to search for an exact phrase.

➤ **Matches on all words (AND)**   This changes the default OR operator to AND, enabling you to search for pages that include all the words in your query.

➤ **Matches on any word (OR)**   This returns you to the default OR mode to search for any of the words in your query.

➤ **Search Yahoo! categories**   This limits your search to Yahoo! categories only—it doesn't search for individual Web pages.

➤ **Search Web sites**   This limits your search to sites in the Yahoo! directory only—it doesn't search for matching Yahoo! categories.

➤ **Find only new listings**   You can elect to search for sites listed in the Yahoo! directory only within the past day, three days, one week, one month, three months, six months, or three years. This helps you to narrow your search to relatively newer sites.

➤ **Display XX matches per page**   This customizes the number of results listed per page—after the initial page, that is.

Should you use Yahoo!'s Advanced Search Options? I don't, unless I want to limit the age of the pages I'm looking for. (And even then, Yahoo!'s human editors take way too much time to add new pages to their directory—which means that Yahoo! isn't likely to have the newest pages, anyway.) All in all, this is a pretty lame advanced options page when compared to similar pages on other search sites.

Find Even More Stuff with Yahoo!'s Other Directories

Yahoo! offers two additional directories for more specialized searching—the Yahooligans! directory for kids and the Yahoo! Image Surfer directory for pictures and graphics files.

Finally, a Kid-Safe Directory for Your Family

Yahooligans! (www.yahooligans.com) is a kids-oriented directory that is part of the Yahoo! family of services. It works just like its parent directory, which means you can find sites by either browsing through categories or directly searching. The difference is that this directory includes categories and sites of particular interest to children and teenagers.

A few other differences exist in how Yahooligans! works, including

➤ Yahooligans! lists a maximum of only 100 matches per query.

➤ Yahooligans! search does not head back out to the Web for Web page matches (as the Yahoo! search does, using Inktomi).

➤ The Yahooligans! directory does not include sites with any content inappropriate for younger Web surfers.

➤ Yahooligans! includes some additional services especially for children, including a link to Cool Web sites, a What's New page, and Club Yahooligans!, complete with a newsletter, hats, t-shirts, and other goodies.

All in all, this makes Yahooligans! a pretty good kid's site, although Lycos's Search Guard (discussed in Chapter 6, "Go Get It at Lycos") does a better job of searching the Web while still filtering out inappropriate material.

A Picture Is Worth a Thousand (Key)Words

You can try to search for pictures and graphics through a normal search engine, but your results will be hit-and-miss. (Just try entering your topic plus the keywords picture or graphic.) A somewhat better—and infinitely more enjoyable—way to search for picture files is by using the Yahoo! Image Surfer.

Image Surfer is located at `ipix.yahoo.com`. It works pretty much the same as the regular Yahoo! directory—you can either browse through categories of pictures or search for specific types of pictures. The results pages display up to six different "thumbnails"; click a thumbnail to go to the page where that picture is displayed.

This is what you get when you search for "yasmine bleeth" with the Yahoo! Image Surfer—just click the image to go to the host site.

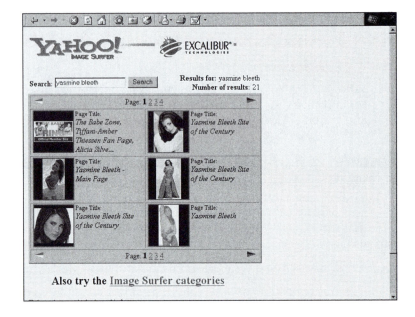

If you choose to browse through the categories, you find a few interesting features that you don't find while using the search function. These include

➤ **Visual search**   Click this link to display more pictures like the one you selected.

➤ **Image info**   Displays detailed information about the selected image, including the URL of the page containing the image.

➤ **Random**   Click this link to display a random selection of images in this particular category.

Yahoo! Image Surfer isn't the largest directory of images on the Web—AltaVista Photo Finder (`image.altavista.com`) and Lycos Image Gallery (`www.lycos.com/picturethis/`) are top competitors—but it does work pretty well. In particular, I find the search feature to be particularly spot-on. If you're looking for pictures, I'd give it a try.

Now You Found It; How Do You Keep It?

If you want to download a picture you found on the Web onto your hard disk, right-click anywhere on the picture and select the Save Picture option from the pop-up menu in your Web browser. Remember to go to the host page first and save that picture—the thumbnail displayed by Image Surfer is generally too small and low-resolution to be of much good to you.

You can also turn any image your Web browser displays—even a page's background—into Windows desktop wallpaper by right-clicking and choosing the Set As Wallpaper command.

The Least You Need to Know

➤ Yahoo!, located at www.yahoo.com, is the most popular Web search site—even though it has the least amount of content.

➤ Yahoo! is a directory, not a search engine, and has only about a million pages indexed.

➤ You can find Web pages at Yahoo! either by browsing through categories or by using Yahoo!'s search capabilities.

➤ You can't use Boolean operators at Yahoo!, although you can use *, +, −, and " ".

➤ If you want a search site that your kids can use, try the Yahooligans! directory at www.yahooligans.com.

➤ If you want to find pictures and graphics on the Web, try Yahoo! Image Surfer at ipix.yahoo.com.

Chapter 4

Scale the Heights of AltaVista

In This Chapter

➤ Understand how AltaVista indexes and ranks more than 150 million individual pages—more than any other free search engine

➤ Learn how to use powerful operators and options to fine-tune your AltaVista searches

➤ Discover how to search for foreign-language pages—and translate any foreign-language pages you may find

➤ Use AltaVista's other search services to filter out offensive content or find photos and art work on the Web

If Yahoo! has the best organization but the least amount of content, as I described in the previous chapter, AltaVista is Yahoo!'s mirror image—it has the most listings of any search site (over 150 million pages), but it's the most disorganized mess you'll ever find. For those of you who value quantity over quality, AltaVista is the site for you!

AltaVista (www.altavista.com) has many things going for it, including

➤ The most robust search spider, which results in...

➤ The most content of any free search site

➤ A versatile set of search tools

➤ The capability to search in multiple languages

In short, AltaVista is the biggest and most powerful free search engine on the Web. (Northern Light, described in Chapter 9, gives AltaVista a run for its money, but you have to pay to access some of its content.) If you don't mind spending a little time to find what you want, it's a sure bet you can find it (somehow) using AltaVista.

Report Card

Address:	www.altavista.com
Search Engine:	Yes
Directory:	Yes
Size:	A
Freshness:	A
Ease of Use:	B
Power:	A
Extras:	Incorporates the LookSmart Web Directory; includes AV Family Filter and AV Photo & Media Finder services

More Than You Ever Wanted to Know About AltaVista

AltaVista is a product of Digital Equipment Corporation, the big computer hardware company (since acquired by Compaq Computer). It's not surprising, then, that AltaVista gets most of its power from state-of-the-art computer hardware, not necessarily from sophisticated indexing (spider or crawler) software.

In the spring of 1995, key personnel at Digital embarked upon a project to catalog the World Wide Web. Initially, this project was conceived as a way to demonstrate Digital's newest product, the Alpha 8400 (TurboLaser), a computer that could run database software a hundred times faster than the competition. Digital thought it would be good for the company's image to build a database of the Web and provide free access to it for every Web user.

At the time, Digital estimated that all the text on the entire Web probably amounted to less than one terabyte (a thousand gigabytes) of data—which, although large, isn't so large that it's uncapturable. Digital believed that every single word on the Web could be indexed, which would make AltaVista far more powerful than any other existing search engine.

The goal, then, was to capture essentially the entire Internet on the computers at Digital's Palo Alto labs. To accomplish this task, Digital created a special indexing program, named Scooter, and paired it with the massive computer power at Digital's fin-

54

gertips. This combination of raw computing power and specialized indexing software created the first full-text index of the entire Internet.

Today, that full-text index that we now call AltaVista is huge, comprehensive, fast, and powerful—capable of searching for complete phrases via complex queries at no loss of speed. In other words, AltaVista is the mother of all Web search engines, the end product of a brute-force approach to indexing the Web.

The Index Becomes a Portal

Of course, in today's Internet space, being a mere search engine—even if you're the biggest and the most powerful search engine—just isn't enough. Following the current trends, Digital is attempting to position AltaVista as a full-featured Web *portal*, just like Yahoo!, Excite, Lycos, and all the rest, complete with news, stock quotes, free email, and all the other geegaws and gadgets that users supposedly want. In my humble opinion, AltaVista is a lousy portal—but a great search engine!

How AltaVista Ranks Your Results

AltaVista uses a proprietary algorithm to rank the Web page matches on your results page. In doing so, it takes the following factors into account:

➤ How many keywords are contained on a page

➤ Where the keywords appear on a page

➤ How close together the keywords are on a page

Some special combination of these factors determines a page's ranking, although AltaVista's ranking capability leaves a little to be desired. More often than not, I find the information I'm looking for on the second or third page of results, not on the first. AltaVista's brute-force approach does appear to deliver a massive quantity of matches; however, it falls a little short in the quality-of-ranking department!

Finding Web Pages with AltaVista—The Easy Way

Standard searching with AltaVista is relatively simple. Just enter a query (one or more keywords) into the search box at the top of the page, and then click the Search button. The results are displayed 10 to a page, with some of the keywords on each page listed under the page's title and URL.

AltaVista's home page— Enter a query in the search box at the top of the page or browse through the LookSmart categories along the left side.

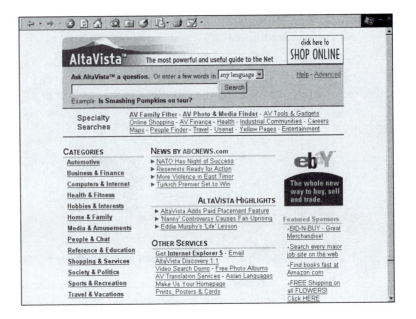

Powered by Jeeves

AltaVista now features technology licensed from the Ask Jeeves! site. The "Ask AltaVista" options lets you type a question in plain English (complete with question mark) into AltaVista's search box. When you do this, the Ask Jeeves! technology will return—in addition to traditional AltaVista Web site matches—a series of questions similar to the one you ask. Just select a question to access a site that provides the precise answer. You can learn more about how Ask Jeeves! works in Chapter 10, "The Next Generation: Newer, Better Search Engines."

AltaVista offers the useful option of refining your standard search results. When you click the **Refine your search** link at the top of the search results page, you're taken to a page where certain related keywords are listed; use the pull-down lists next to each term to exclude it or include it in a new search of the initial results. Click the **Search** button to search the current results with the current refinements, or click the **Refine Again** button to display more keywords to exclude or include. You can also click the **Graph** link to display these sub-keywords in graphic form, somewhat like an organization chart or a flow chart.

Browsing on a Search Engine?

Now that AltaVista is purportedly a portal, it attempts to offer Yahoo!-like browsing capabilities directly from its home page. But because the AltaVista search engine doesn't organize the Web (it only searches it), Digital has had to partner with LookSmart to offer a browsable Web directory. When you click one of the categories listed along the left side of the AltaVista home page (and then click down through the subsequent subcategories, in hierarchical fashion), you're really browsing through the LookSmart Web directory. LookSmart is a smaller directory than Yahoo! (only 250,000 entries compared to Yahoo!'s one million plus), but it does offer brief overviews of every site in its index, which Yahoo! doesn't.

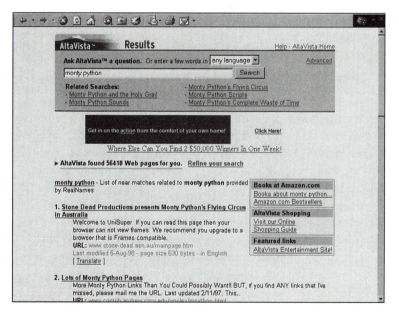

AltaVista's search results—Click a link to go to the matching page or click **Refine your search** *to perform a new search within these results.*

AltaVista offers a handful of additional search options off the standard search results page, including

➤ Related searches For some queries, AltaVista recognizes related searches you might want to try, and it lists them at the top of the search results page, directly under the search box. As an example, I entered the query monty python, and AltaVista recommended the following related searches: Monty

57

Python and the Holy Grail, Monty Python Sounds, Monty Python's Flying Circus, Monty Python Scripts, and Monty Python's Complete Waste of Time.

➤ **RealNames matches**   Near the top of the results page is a link to Web sites whose names are "near matches" to your query. This is one way to search for branded names, and it works really well if you're looking for the Web site of a major corporation, such as Coca Cola.

➤ **AltaVista recommends**   This link, at the bottom of the search results page, takes you to a related category in the LookSmart Web directory.

➤ **AltaVista knows the answers to these questions**   Using technology from Ask Jeeves! (see Chapter 10, "The Next Generation: Newer, Better Search Engines"), AltaVista attempts to generate a question related to your query. As an example, I entered the query crocodile hunter, and this feature generated the question "How can I get assistance in planning a hunt?" Click the **Answer** button to get the answer to the question, or the **More Answers** link to generate a page that enables you to create additional questions to ask.

Search in a Foreign Language

AltaVista lets you initiate a search of Web pages in a particular foreign language. Above the search box on the home page are the words "Or enter a few words in," and a pull-down list. Select a language from the pull-down list, enter your keywords (in that language), and click the **Search** button. AltaVista returns pages in that language that match your query. For any search, if you get a matching page that isn't in English (or whatever language you happen to speak), you can have AltaVista translate that page into one of several major languages. Just click the **Translate** link at the end of the listing, select the type of translation you want (English to French, Spanish to English, and so on), and click the **Translate** button. AltaVista does the best it can to translate the selected page into the selected language; the translation is seldom perfect, but it's often better than not being able to read the page at all!

Fine-tuning Your AltaVista Search

The basic AltaVista search enables you to use a surprising number of wildcards and operators to fine-tune your search. Table 4.1 lists the commands you can use to fine-tune your search results.

Table 4.1   AltaVista Standard Search Parameters

To Do This:	Use This Command:	Example:
Search for part of a word	*	mon*
Must include a word	+	monty +python
Must exclude a word	–	monty –python
Search for a complete phrase	" "	"monty python"
Only search in the title of the page	title:	title:monty python
Only search in the URL of the page	url:	url:monty
Only search in the text of a page (not in an image, link, or URL)	text:	text:monty python
Only search in hyperlinks within a page	anchor:	anchor:monty python
Only search for pages with a link to a specific URL	link:	link:www.molehillgroup.com
Only search for pages on a specific computer	host:	host:www.molehillgroup.com
Only search for pages within a domain	domain:	domain:com
Only search for pages containing specific image files	image:	image:monty.jpg
Only search for specified Java applet	applet:	applet:clock

Note that the standard AltaVista search does not use Boolean operators—you have to select the Advanced option to go Boolean!

The Automatic OR

If you enter more than one word in a query with no operator between them, AltaVista assumes you want to look for either word and automatically inserts an OR between the words. In other words, AltaVista automatically searches for pages that contain *any* of your keywords. Therefore, you may want to get into the habit of using plus signs or quotation marks for multi-keyword searches.

A few things are worth noting about AltaVista's search options. First, unlike other search engines, AltaVista lets you specify where you want to search. Suppose, for example, that you want to look for reviews of computer hardware, and you know that CNET (at www.cnet.com) has some pretty good reviews. You can enter the following query to restrict your search to the CNET site:

```
host:www.cnet.com +computer +review
```

You can also limit your search to a particular domain type. For example, if you wanted to search for scholarship information but wanted to avoid commercial sites and search only on true education sites, you could use this query:

```
domain:edu scholarship
```

Or maybe you want to search for any sites that link to your site. Using my personal site (www.molehillgroup.com) as an example, the query would look like this:

```
anchor:www.molehillgroup.com
```

In any case, AltaVista's powerful operators enable you to fine-tune your search in ways that other search engines can't.

Find More Stuff with AltaVista's Advanced Options

More savvy searchers can access AltaVista's Advanced mode by clicking the (surprise!) **Advanced** link on AltaVista's home page. (This link also appears on all subsequent results pages.)

Just In Case

AltaVista keywords are semi-case-sensitive. If your keyword is lowercase, AltaVista returns lowercase, uppercase, and mixed results. If your keyword is uppercase, it returns only uppercase results. If your keyword mixes upper- and lowercase, it returns only exact matches. So searching for bbc will return "BBC," but searching for BOB will *not* return "Bob" or "bob."

The key additions in the advanced mode are

➤ The capability to use Boolean operators

➤ The capability to limit matches to a range of dates

If you want to use Boolean operators, you have to enter your query in the Enter Boolean Expression box. Table 4.2 lists the Boolean operators you can use.

Table 4.2   AltaVista Advanced Mode Boolean Operators

To Do This:	Use This Command:	Example:
Search for both keywords	AND	monty AND python
Search for either keyword	OR	monty OR python
Exclude a word	AND NOT (must be used with another operator)	monty AND NOT python
Search for pages that contain both specified words within 10 words of each other	NEAR	monty NEAR python

If you enter only a Boolean expression, AltaVista returns your results in an *unranked* list. (Yuck!) What you need to do, then, is enter your Boolean expression and then enter some other keywords in the normal search box—because AltaVista will rank your results based on the keywords in the search box.

Suppose, for example, you want to look for pages about either Monty Python or John Cleese, but not including Eric Idle, and you're particularly interested in the Dead Parrot sketch. You would enter the keywords `dead parrot` in the search box and the phrase `"monty python" OR "john cleese" AND NOT "eric idle"` in the Boolean box.

Boolean Yes, Exclude/Include No

If you use Boolean expressions in AltaVista's advanced mode, you can't use + and – to include and exclude words.

Find Even More Stuff with AltaVista's Specialty Searches

Although the real attraction of AltaVista is its powerful Web search engine, the site also offers a handful of other, more specialized, searches. These include a special filtered search for children, a search fine-tuned for finding photos, and a search engine for Usenet newsgroup articles.

Filter the Filth with AV Family Filter

If you want your kids to surf the Net but you don't want them to be exposed to dirty pictures and language, you want to check out the AV Family Filter. This is a content filter that sits on top of the standard AltaVista search to filter out potentially offensive content.

AV Family Filter works by automatically categorizing pages so that offensive pages are separated from the rest of your search results. It reviews the content of pages using proprietary technology supplied by SurfWatch, and it also removes inappropriate pages reviewed by AltaVista editors and users.

The kind of content that AV Family Filter guards against includes the following:

➤ Drugs, alcohol, and tobacco
➤ Gambling
➤ Hate speech
➤ Sexually explicit language and photos
➤ Violence

AV Family Filter also incorporates ChatBlock technology, which blocks access to Internet chat rooms and channels while you're searching.

Using AV Family Filter is easy. Just click the AV Family Filter link on AltaVista's home page. When the AV Family Filter page appears, click the Start AV Family Filter button. On the next page, you'll need to supply a password (and don't give it to your kids!); then click the Continue button. After you confirm your password, you're notified that AV Family Filter is now turned on. Click the Return to Search button to go back to the AltaVista home page and resume searching.

When AV Family Filter is activated, a red + sign appears on all your pages, just to remind you that your results are being filtered. In my experience, AV Family Filter works pretty well at filtering out the bad stuff, although it's your call as to how much good stuff gets thrown out with the bad. You can turn off AV Family Filter at any time by clicking the AV Family Filter link, entering your password, and then clicking the Cancel AV Family Filter button.

Look for Pretty Pictures with AV Photo & Media Finder

When you click the AV Photo & Media Finder link on AltaVista's home page, you're taken to one of the better search engines available for pictures, graphics, video, and audio files. This isn't just a simple directory (like Yahoo! Image Surfer), but a specialized search engine that indexes millions of individual pictures and sounds on the Web.

AV Family Filter Limitations

If you use AV Family Filter, you do limit your AltaVista search options to a small degree. You won't be able to search Usenet newsgroups, and you'll only be able to search English-language pages.

You use AV Photo & Media Finder the same as you would the standard AltaVista search (which means no Boolean operators). First, you select whether you want to search for Images, Videos, or Audios. Then you pull down the from list and choose to search either The Web and Collections (which searches the entire Web) or Premiere Collections Only (which limits your search to a smaller number of higher-quality collections). Then you enter your query in the Search box and click the Search button, and AV does its thing.

To access some more advanced search features, just click the Options link. On the page that follows, you can choose to limit your search to Photos, Art Works (also known as "line art"), Color, or Black & White images. You can also choose to exclude buttons and simple graphics from your search, as well as select different options for displaying your results.

Your results are displayed in thumbnails, up to 12 on a page. For each thumbnail, the picture size and resolution are displayed, and you can click the About the picture link to view a variety of details about the graphic—format (jpeg, gif, and so on), transparency, and which Web pages contain the picture. To go to the page containing the picture, click the picture itself.

Where Are the Dirty Pictures?

When you first access AV Photo & Media Finder, you are (by default) in *filtered mode*, which uses the AV Photo & Media Filter technology to automatically filter out offensive content, such as sexually explicit pictures. If offensive content is what you're really looking for, click the **Click here to choose unfiltered option** link and follow the onscreen instructions.

What AV Photo & Media Finder displays for a query on the keywords `batman +robin`—*Click any thumbnail to go to the host page.*

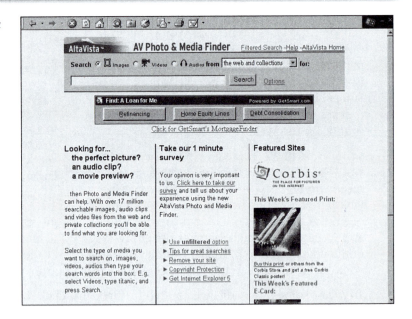

If you find a picture you like and want to see others that have the same look and feel, click the **Visually Similar** link. This displays more thumbnails that are supposedly similar to the original photo, generally in color or tone—but not necessarily in content. (Beware—this sometimes returns some very bizarre results!)

Of all the photo and image finders on the Web, I like AV Photo Finder best. It does a pretty good job of finding what I want, and it always returns a large number of results.

Now You Found It; How Do You Keep It?

If you want to download a picture you found on the Web onto your hard disk, right-click anywhere on the picture and select the **Save Picture** option from the pop-up menu in your Web browser. Remember to go to the host page first and save that picture—the thumbnail displayed by AV Photo Finder is generally too small and low-resolution to be of much good to you.

You can also turn any image your Web browser displays—even a page's background—into Windows desktop wallpaper by right-clicking and choosing the **Set As Wallpaper** command.

Search Usenet Newsgroup Articles

AltaVista, like the DejaNews site (see Chapter 25), enables you to search Usenet newsgroup articles posted in the past two weeks. To access AltaVista's Usenet search function, click the Usenet link on AltaVista's home page.

You use the same wildcards and operators to search Usenet as you do to search the Web with a standard AltaVista search. A handful of new operators are available, however, as described in Table 4.3.

Table 4.3   AltaVista Usenet Search Parameters

To Do This:	Use This Command:	Example:
Find articles posted by a specific person or email address	from:	from:bruce@gotham.com
Find articles containing a specific text in the subject field	subject: "xxx"	subject:"wealthy socialite"
Find articles posted to a specific newsgroup	newsgroups:	newsgroups:alt. comics.batman
Find articles with specific text in the summary	summary:	summary:batman

Search Your Hard Disk with AltaVista Discovery

One last thing about AltaVista—you can actually use the AltaVista technology to search your hard disk! To do this, you have to download and install the free AltaVista Discovery software.

To do this, click the AltaVista Discovery link toward the bottom of AltaVista's home page, and then click the Download Now link on the following page. You'll need to be running either Windows 95, Windows 98, or Windows NT and have at least 16MB memory and 32MB free hard-disk space. Further instructions are on the download page.

Basically, AltaVista Discovery installs a search bar on your Windows desktop. From this bar you can choose to search your downloaded email, documents on your hard disk, the Web, or any Web pages you've recently browsed. If you have trouble finding things on your computer, you might want to check it out.

The Least You Need to Know

➤ AltaVista, located at www.altavista.com, is the biggest and most powerful search engine on the Internet, with more than 150 million pages indexed.

➤ You can use a variety of operators in AltaVista's standard search, including *, +, −, " ", title:, url:, and text:.

➤ You can use Boolean operators AND, OR, AND NOT, and NEAR in AltaVista's Advanced mode.

➤ AltaVista enables you to search for pages in specific languages.

➤ AltaVista now incorporates the LookSmart directory, which lets you browse 250,000 preclassified Web pages.

➤ The AV Family Filter enables you to filter out offensive content from your AltaVista searches.

➤ The AV Photo Finder is arguably the best search engine for photos and artwork on the Internet.

➤ You can download free software to use AltaVista technology to search your own computer.

Chapter 5

Serve Up Hot Searches at HotBot

In This Chapter

➤ Find out why HotBot may be the best free search engine on the Web

➤ Discover how HotBot's easy-to-use options can help you fine-tune your searches

➤ Learn how to create complex search queries with HotBot's numerous and powerful search commands

Although AltaVista is the current king of the Web search engines, HotBot—which is owned by Lycos as part of the *Wired Digital* network of sites—is increasingly a close runner-up and the search engine of choice for many serious researchers.

Why is HotBot (www.hotbot.com) such an up-and-coming search site? First, HotBot's index is almost as big as AltaVista's (110 million pages compared to 150 million pages for AltaVista). Second, HotBot includes some very powerful search tools that are as easy to use as selecting an item from a pull-down list. Third, HotBot's ranking of results appears to be slightly more intelligent than those of its competitors.

In other words, HotBot is

➤ Big

➤ Powerful

➤ Easy to use

➤ Relatively smart

Report Card

Address:	www.hotbot.com
Search Engine:	Yes
Directory:	Yes
Size:	A
Freshness:	A
Ease of Use:	A
Power:	A
Extras:	Incorporates the user-edited Open Directory

How HotBot Ranks Your Results

HotBot seems to be "smarter" than other search engines in ranking the results of your queries. How does it do it? HotBot uses a combination of the following factors to rank your results:

➤ Keywords in the title of the page

➤ Keywords in the page's META tags

➤ Frequency of keywords throughout the document

➤ Document length

These criteria don't seem all that complicated, so some hidden intelligence must be going on behind the scenes. It really doesn't matter, though; however they do it, I find that the quality of HotBot's rankings are superior to those of most other search engines, especially those of AltaVista. Something in HotBot's ranking scheme must be working!

Finding Web Pages with HotBot—The Easy Way

Standard searching with HotBot is relatively simple. Enter a query (one or more keywords) into the search box in the Search the Web section of HotBot's home page, then click the **Search** button.

Search box   Look For list   Date list   Language list

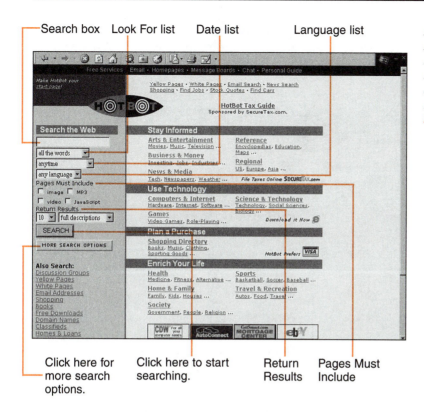

HotBot's home page—Enter a query in the search box, make your selections from the pull-down lists and check boxes, then click the **Search** *button.*

Click here for more search options.

Click here to start searching.

Return Results

Pages Must Include

The Automatic AND

If you enter more than one word in a query with no operator between them, HotBot assumes you want to look for pages that contain *both* words and automatically inserts an AND between the words. (This assumes that you have **All the Words** selected from the Look For list, which is the default selection.) In other words, HotBot automatically searches for pages that contain all your keywords, unless you instruct it otherwise—by pulling down the **Look For** list and selecting **Any of the Words**.

69

HotBot's results are displayed 10 to a page, and list each page's title, description, and URL. The final line of each listing reads "See results from this site only." When you click the **this site only** link, HotBot displays similar pages from the parent Web site.

*HotBot's search results—Click a link to go to the matching page or click **this site only** to look at related pages on the same site.*

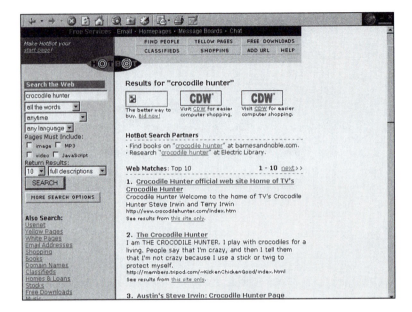

At the bottom of each results page are links to Lycos, About.com, and other search engines. Click on one of these links to redirect your search to these other sites, automatically—it's a nice way to get a second opinion on your query!

Fine-tuning Your HotBot Search

To help you narrow your search parameters, HotBot offers some of the most powerful—and easiest-to-use—tools available on any major search engine. I find it amazing that HotBot puts these powerful tools on their basic search page; many search sites reserve these tools for their advanced searches, if they offer them at all! (And HotBot adds even more tools to its advanced search, discussed later in this chapter.)

70

Just In Case

HotBot keywords are semi-case-sensitive. If your keyword is lowercase, it returns lowercase, uppercase, and mixed results. If your keyword is uppercase, it returns only uppercase results. If your keyword mixes upper- and lowercase, it returns only exact matches. Therefore, searching for bbc will return "BBC," but searching for BOB will not return "Bob" or "bob."

Narrowing Your Search with the Pull-Down Lists

The easiest way to fine-tune your search results is by using the pull-down lists and check boxes in the section directly below HotBot's search box. Using these simple tools, some of what you can do is described in the following list:

➤ **Define what you're looking for**   The Look For list lets you tell HotBot how to interpret the keywords you entered into the search box. You can select from the following options:

  ➤ **All the words**   Inserts an automatic AND between all your keywords so that HotBot retrieves Web pages that include all words in your query (this is the default).

  ➤ **Any of the words**   Inserts an automatic OR between all your keywords so that HotBot retrieves Web pages that include any (but not necessarily all) words in your query.

  ➤ **Exact phrase**   Inserts automatic quotation marks around your entire query so that HotBot retrieves Web pages that include all your keywords in their exact order.

  ➤ **The page title**   Restricts your search to Web page titles only; it ignores the actual text of the Web pages.

  ➤ **The person**   Use if you're searching for a person; enter the first and last name as your query.

  ➤ **Links to this URL**   Use if you're looking for pages that link to a specific page; enter a specific URL as your query.

  ➤ **Boolean phrase**   Use if you want to use Boolean operators in your search query. Probably the most useful option on the entire page!

➤ **Add age parameters to your search**   Pull down the **Date** list and select an age parameter to narrow your searches to Web pages created during a specific time frame.

➤ **Search foreign-language pages**   Pull down the **Language** list and select a language to restrict your searches to pages created in a specific language.

➤ **Look for pages that contain specific elements**   Go to the check boxes in the Pages Must Include section to restrict your searches to pages that include images, video, MP3 audio clips, or JavaScript.

➤ **Refine an existing search**   After you've completed an initial search, click the **Search these results** box to search the existing results with additional parameters.

➤ **Modify how HotBot displays your results**   Go to the Return Results section to change how many matches are displayed on a page and whether HotBot displays full descriptions (the default), brief descriptions, or URLs only.

Make a special note of that Boolean Phrase option—you'll need it to use some of the commands discussed in the next section.

Narrowing Your Search Within the Search Box

In addition to the options available from the pull-down lists and check boxes, HotBot also lets you use a large number of wildcards and operators to fine-tune your search. You can use these commands within the search box itself, without having to make any selections from the pull-down lists. (One exception: To use the Boolean operators AND, OR, or NOT, you have to select the Boolean Phrase option from the first pull-down list.)

Table 5.1 lists all the commands you can use.

Table 5.1   HotBot Search Parameters

To Do This:	Use This Command:	Example:
Search for part of a word	*	`mon*`
Must include a word	+	`monty +python`
Must exclude a word	–	`monty -python`
Search for a complete phrase	" "	`"monty python"`
Search for both keywords	AND	`monty AND python`
Search for either keyword	OR	`monty OR python`
Exclude a word	NOT	`monty NOT python`
Search for pages only within a domain	domain:	`domain:com`
Search only in the title of the page	title:	`title:monty`

To Do This:	Use This Command:	Example:
Restrict the number of pages retrieved	depth:	`depth:5`
Restrict search to pages created after a specified date	after:*day /month /year*	`after:15/1/99`
Restrict search to pages created before a specified date	before:*day /month /year*	`before:15/1/99`
Restrict search to pages created within the last specified time period	within:*x/ period*	`within:6/months`
Restrict search to pages that include embedded files with the specified extension	outgoing urlext:*ra*	`outgoingurlext:jpg`
Restrict search to pages that include Acrobat files	feature: Acrobat	`feature:Acrobat`
Restrict search to pages that include embedded Java applets	feature: applet	`feature:applet`
Restrict search to pages that include ActiveX controls	feature: activex	`feature:activex`
Restrict search to pages that include audio files (WAV, MIDI, and so on)	feature: audio	`feature:audio`
Restrict search to pages that include plugins	feature: embed	`feature:embed`
Restrict search to pages that include the Flash plugin	feature: flash	`feature:flash`
Restrict search to pages that include HTML forms	feature: form	`feature:form`
Restrict search to pages that include HTML frames	feature: frame	`feature:frame`
Restrict search to pages that include image files (GIF, JPEG, and so on)	feature: image	`feature:image`
Restrict search to pages that include embedded scripts	feature: script	`feature:script`
Restrict search to pages that include Shockwave files	feature: shockwave	`feature:shockwave`
Restrict search to pages that include HTML tables	feature: table	`feature:table`
Restrict search to pages that include video files	feature: video	`feature:video`

continues

Table 5.1 **CONTINUED**

To Do This:	Use This Command:	Example:
Restrict search to pages that include VRML files	feature: vrml	`feature:vrml`
Restrict search to pages that include JavaScript	script language: javascript	`scriptlanguage: javascript`
Restrict search to pages that include VBScript	script language: vbscript	`scriptlanguage: vbscript`

More Powerful Than the Average Word: Meta Words

Operators that enable you to restrict searches to specified parameters are called **Meta words**. A Meta word is actually a pair of words—a keyword followed by a value, separated by a colon, like this: **keyword**: *value*. Be careful to include only one value word after a keyword because that's all the search engine recognizes. For example, the search engine sees **title:monty python** and views only **title:monty** as the Meta word; **python** is viewed as a separate keyword.

That is a pretty powerful list of search commands! However, you should know a few things about these commands.

First, you can use the Boolean operators AND, OR, and NOT only if you first pull down the **Look For** list and select **Boolean Search**. Selecting any other options from the Look For list causes HotBot to ignore any Boolean expressions you enter in your query.

Second, unlike some other search engines, HotBot lets you mix and match query modifiers (+, –, *, and " ") with Boolean operators, but it won't let you use query modifiers with Meta words. So a query such as `crocodile +within:6/months` won't work; use `within:6/months crocodile` instead.

Finally, if you use the `feature:` Meta word, make sure you put your keywords first in the query, and the Meta word last. For example, to look for a Monty Python video, you would enter this query: `"monty python" feature:video`.

Constructing Some Complex Queries

Now let's look at some of the more complex queries you can construct with HotBot's search options.

One very useful thing you can do is to restrict your searches by date. That is, you can search for pages created either before or after a specified date or within a specified age range. For example, suppose you're looking for some old data on automobile sales, pre-1997. You would instruct HotBot to look for pages created before January 1, 1997 as follows:

```
before:1/1/97 automobile sales
```

You can also limit your search to a particular domain type. For example, if you wanted to search for scholarship information but wanted to avoid commercial sites and search only on true education sites, you could use this query:

```
domain:edu scholarship
```

It's also possible to limit your search to pages that include specific elements, such as images, sounds, and even specific file types. Suppose you wanted to look for Monty Python pages that contain pictures or graphics; you would enter this query:

```
feature:image "monty python"
```

The bottom line is that you can string together some pretty complex queries from HotBot's standard search box. Let's see how complicated an example we can create. How would you construct a query to search for recent pages that list episodes of the *Crocodile Hunter* TV show and that contain either sound or picture files but don't mention Steve Irwin's dog Sui? Try this:

```
within:6/months "Crocodile Hunter" AND episode AND (feature:image OR
feature:sound) NOT Sui
```

Now, the problem with creating too complex a query is that it sometimes narrows your search just a tad too far. In the case of our *Crocodile Hunter* example, the search is so narrow it doesn't return *any* results! When this happens, remove a few parameters from the query and try it again! (In other words—don't get *too* carried away with HotBot's powerful search parameters!)

Find More Stuff with More Options

If all these options aren't enough for you, HotBot offers even more search options when you click the **More Search Options** button. In this more advanced search area, you'll find the following:

➤ **Look For**   Same as the Look For list on the main page; you can determine how your query is interpreted by HotBot. (Note, however, that the default selection on this page is Boolean Phrase; I guess HotBot assumes that if you got this far, you're using Boolean operators!)

➤ **Language**   Same as the Language list on the main page; you can restrict your search to pages in a specific language.

➤ **Word Filter**   This works pretty much the same as the + and – modifiers in the search box. You can choose from **must contain**, **must not contain**, and **should contain**, which is kind of an in-between option not available otherwise.

➤ **Date**   This works pretty much like the Date list on the main page, but with additional parameters that mimic functionality of the `after:` and `before:` Meta words.

➤ **Pages Must Include**   Same as the Pages Must Include options on the main page, with additional options for Shockwave, Java, ActiveX, VRML, Acrobat, and VBScript.

➤ **Location/Domain**   Selects **Domain** functions the same as the `domain:` Meta word, enabling you to restrict your searches to a particular type of Web site. The **Continent** option is exclusive to this page, letting you restrict your search to sites in specific regions.

➤ **Page Depth**   Pretty much exclusive to this page, this lets you instruct HotBot how deep within a site you wish to search: Any Page on the site, the Top Page of a site only, a Personal Page within a site, or a user-selected Page Depth (similar to the `depth:` Meta word).

➤ **Word Stemming**   Exclusive to this page, turning on Word Stemming lets you search for grammatical variations on your keywords. For example, if you search for `thought`, the word-stemming feature also finds pages that include the words "think" and "thinking."

➤ **Return Results**   Same as the Return Results section on the main page, which lets you customize your search-results page.

You can obtain most of the functionality from the More Options page by using HotBot's numerous search commands in the standard search box. However, you might want to check out the word-stemming function, which applies a kind of limited artificial intelligence to your searches and can eliminate some of the guesswork that goes into selecting the right keywords for a query.

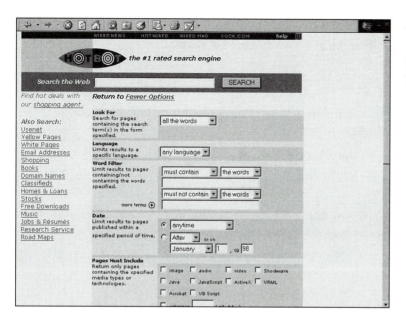

HotBot's More Options search page—helping you fine-tune your search even further than you can with normal search operators.

HotBot Now Has an Open Directory

One of the latest changes to HotBot is the addition of the Open Directory, licensed from Netscape. When you click one of the categories listed along the right side of the HotBot home page (and then click down through the subsequent subcategories, in hierarchical fashion), you're really browsing through the user-edited Open Directory. The Open Directory is an interesting project, in that the management of the directory is done by volunteer editors—essentially, it's the Web's first "open source" directory. Or, as Netscape puts it, the "largest human-edited directory of the Web." Read more about the Open Directory in Chapter 10, "The Next Generation: Newer, Better Search Engines."

The Least You Need to Know

➤ HotBot is a big, fast, powerful, and easy-to-use search engine that returns an intelligent ranking of results.

➤ You can narrow your search results by using the pull-down lists and check boxes on HotBot's main page.

➤ HotBot also lets you use a large variety of powerful search commands to fine-tune your search, including +, −, *, " ", AND, OR, NOT, domain:, and depth:.

➤ Selecting **More Options** lets you access more advanced search options from an expanded series of pull-down lists and search menus.

Chapter 6

Go Get It at Lycos

In This Chapter

➤ Learn how to perform both basic and advanced Lycos searches

➤ Find and download all types of files from the Internet with Lycos's FTP Search

➤ Search for songs in MP3 format with Lycos's unique MP3 Search

➤ Discover Lycos' unique version of the user-edited Open Directory

Lycos is an average, somewhat undistinguished, search engine. It falls below AltaVista and HotBot in terms of speed, power, and size (50 million entries, compared to 100 million plus for the two leaders), but it's still larger and more powerful than directory-based services such as Yahoo! Its basic search functions are fairly unremarkable, but it does offer a glimpse of power searching with its Advanced Search page.

In short, Lycos isn't a bad little search engine, but it's not the best you can find—it's average.

So if better search engines exist, why would you use Lycos? In addition to its ubiquitous portal capabilities (lots of content categories, free email, home-page building, and the like), Lycos does offer a handful of unique features, including

➤ Search Guard filtering for kid-safe searching

➤ A search engine for FTP files

➤ A Pictures and Sounds search engine

➤ A unique, new search engine for MP3 music files

➤ Unique implementation of the user-edited Open Directory

Although the MP3 and FTP search engines are relatively unique (as of this writing, anyway), it's hard for me to strongly recommend Lycos as your sole search engine—just as it's hard for me to say anything really bad about it. Lycos is a nice, average search site that is good enough for most users—but not a great choice for power searchers.

If you want a directory alternative to Yahoo!, however, you should check out Lycos' implementation of the Open Directory, the largest user-edited directory on the Web.

Report Card

Address:	www.lycos.com
Search Engine:	Yes
Directory:	Yes
Size:	B
Freshness:	C
Ease of Use:	B
Power:	C
Extras:	Includes user-edited Open Directory, MP3 Search, Pictures & Sounds Search, FTP Search, and Search Guard for kid-safe searching

Like the Site? Then Read the Book!

If you want to learn more about the entire Lycos site, including all its portal capabilities, check out *Lycos Personal Internet Guide* from Que (ISBN 0-7897-1831-6), written by yours truly.

An Itsy-Bitsy Spider...

Like all search engines, Lycos's search engine is built on a special software program called a *spider*. Spider software automatically roams the Web and catalogs new pages and sites as they're created. What's interesting is that a lycos is a certain type of spider—so the Lycos search engine got its name from a lycos spider!

Basic Searching at Lycos—The Easy Way

As with most search engines, it's easy to do a basic Web search with Lycos. Enter your keyword(s) in the Search For box, and then click the **Go Get It!** button.

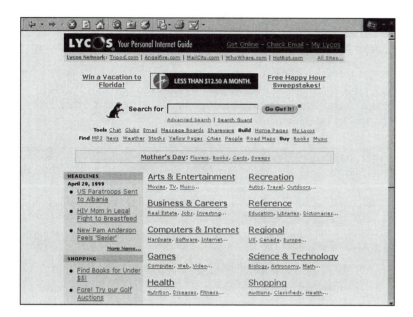

The Lycos home page looks confusing, but all you need to worry about is the Search For box (where you enter your query) and the **Go Get It!** *button (which initiates your search).*

Check This Out

The Automatic OR

If you enter more than one word in a query with no operator between them, Lycos assumes you want to look for pages that contain either of the words; it automatically inserts an OR between the words. In other words, Lycos automatically searches for pages that contain *any* of your keywords. Therefore, you may want to get into the habit of using plus signs or quotation marks for multi-keyword searches.

Depending on your search, Lycos returns different kinds of results. You may see *categories* from Lycos' Open Directory (their edited Web directory), *Web Sites* from the Open directory, *News & Media* articles about the topic, or (the one you really want) matching *Web Pages*. To go to a matching page, click its title.

At the bottom of each results page is a link to HotBot, which is owned by Lycos. Click this link to redirect your search to HotBot automatically—it's a nice way to get a second opinion on your query!

There are two other types of information you *may* see on your search results page, depending on the topic. *First and Fast* presents handpicked sites (or Lycos-specific content) especially relevant to the search topic. *Featured On Lycos* presents other areas of the Lycos network that might be relevant to your search.

A typical page of Lycos search results—Click the title to go to a page.

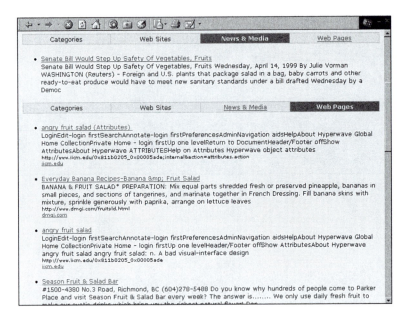

Fine-tuning Your Lycos Search

Lycos doesn't have quite the same basic searching power as do some other search engines. In fact, Lycos's basic searching is fairly lame. Table 6.1 lists the few commands you can enter into Lycos's Search For box to narrow your search parameters.

Table 6.1   Lycos Search Parameters

To Do This:	Use This Command:	Example:
Match a word *exactly*	.	monty.
Search for part of a word	$	mon$

To Do This:	Use This Command:	Example:
Search for a complete phrase	" "	`"monty python"`
Exclude pages that contain a word	–	`monty -python`
Require a word on a page	+	`monty +python`

Nothing Wild

Note that Lycos doesn't use wildcards, as most search engines do. Instead, it uses something called *assumed truncation*. With assumed truncation, the search engine assumes a wildcard at the end of every keyword you enter. For example, if you enter `mel`, Lycos returns the words "mel," "melanie," "melon," "melodious," and so on. If you don't want to assume truncation—that is, if you want to search for an exact word—put a period at the end of a word (like this: `mel.`).

Find Better Stuff with Lycos Advanced Search

Given the weakness of Lycos's basic search engine, to fine-tune your results at all you need to use the Lycos Advanced Search. Use Lycos Advanced Search when your standard searches prove either fruitless or too fruitful.

To use Lycos Advanced Search, click the **Advanced Search** link. You now have access to the following options:

➤ **Search for**   Pull down this list to select how you want to search. You can choose from the following options:

 ➤ **Any of the words (OR query)**   Searches for any of the listed words, in any order. This is the equivalent of the standard Lycos search.

 ➤ **Natural language query**   This option lets you pose a question—in natural language—to Lycos. For example, you could enter `what comedy team included john cleese?` and hope to get the correct answer. (However, Lycos's natural language query doesn't always work all that well.)

 ➤ **All the words (any order)**   Searches for pages that include all the words you listed, in any order. For example, searching for `monty python` would return sites that included the words monty and python—including where the words were used in different sentences.

➤ **All the words (in order)**   Searches for pages that include all the words you listed, as long as they appear in the order listed. For example, searching for monty python would return a page with the phrase "My name is Monty, and this is my Python," but it would not return a page with the phrase "This is my Python, and his name is Monty."

➤ **All the words (within 25 words, any order)**   Searches for pages that include all the words, as long as the words are within 25 words of each other, in any order.

➤ **All the words (within 25 words, in order)**   Searches for pages that include all the words, as long as the words are within 25 words of each other *and* are used in the order specified.

➤ **All the words (adjacent, any order)**   Searches for pages where all the words listed are in a row, but not necessarily in the order listed. For example, you could search for python monty and still return Monty Python.

➤ **The exact phrase**   Searches for a phrase exactly as entered. For example, searching for monty python would return pages only about Monty Python.

➤ **Look for**   Check the boxes for what kind of content you want to search for—in effect, telling Lycos where you want to search. You can choose from Any Content (that is, a standard Web search), Books, Cities, Downloads, Dictionary, FTP Search, Message Boards (Lycos's proprietary discussion groups), Music (by artist), News, Newsgroups (Usenet, that is), Pictures, Personal Home Pages, Recipes (!), Sounds, Stock (by symbol), Top 5% Sites (Lycos' old, pre-Open Directory Web directory), and Weather (by city).

➤ **Search the...**   Determine whether you want to search the entire document (the Web page, that is), the page title only, the page URL, or all the pages on a selected Web site. (If you select to search an entire Web site, enter the main URL for that site in the box.)

➤ **Select a language**   Choose which language (English, Spanish, and so on) you wish to search in—good for searching for foreign-language pages.

➤ **Sort results by ranking importance**   Give a ranking (low, medium, high) to the importance of each of the following search criteria: Match all words, Frequency of words, (words listed) Near beginning of text, (words) Close together, (words as they) Appear in title, and (words) In exact order.

➤ **Display**   Select how many matches to display on the search results page.

In addition, when you use the Advanced Search page, you can now use Boolean expressions in your query. Lycos recognizes the Boolean operators described in Table 6.2.

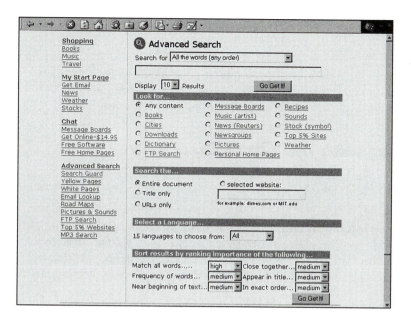

Use Lycos Advanced Search to add a little power to your queries— You can select where and how you search for items and use Boolean operators.

Table 6.2   Lycos Advanced Search Boolean Operators

To Do This:	Use This Command:	Example:
Search for both words	AND	`monty AND python`
Search for either word	OR	`monty OR python`
Exclude a word	NOT	`monty NOT python`
Search for words right next to each other, in any order	ADJ	`monty ADJ python`
Search for words within 25 words of each other, in any order	NEAR	`monty NEAR python`
Search for words appearing 25 or more words apart, in any order	FAR	`monty FAR python`
Search for words in this exact order, any distance apart	BEFORE	`monty BEFORE python`

It's a shame that more of these advanced options aren't available from Lycos's basic search page. It's not a bad collection of search tools for those few who bother to click through and use them.

A Few Unique Things About Lycos—The Other Stuff

If the Lycos search engine is undistinguished, a few other features on the Lycos site make Lycos stand out from the other search sites. These include a unique new Web directory, a kid-safe search filter, and a new search engine for MP3 music files.

Selected Searching with the Open Directory

Like most other search sites, Lycos also includes a search directory. In Lycos' case, they license the increasingly popular Open Directory from Netscape—and call it the Lycos Open Directory.

The Open Directory is an interesting project, in that the management of the directory is done by volunteer editors—essentially, it's the Web's first "open source" directory. Or, as Netscape puts it, the "largest human-edited directory of the Web." (Read more about the Open Directory in Chapter 10, "The Next Generation: Newer, Better Search Engines.")

Note that the Lycos Open Directory isn't just the Netscape Open Directory (found at directory.netscape.com) with Lycos' name on it. Lycos has employed over 10,000 volunteer editors to edit the directory, an implementation that goes well beyond what Netscape itself has done with the original Open Directory. Lycos has also excluded some non-Web material (such as news archives and encyclopedia data) and is applying its own relevancy mechanisms to rank the Open Directory listings.

When you click one of the categories listed along the right side of the Lycos home page (and then click down through the subsequent subcategories, in hierarchical fashion), you're really browsing through the Open Directory. You can access a Search box for the Open Directory (and find out more about the Directory itself) by going directly to www.lycos.com/directory/information.html.

Even though the Open Directory only has 500,000 listings (versus Yahoo!'s 1 million plus listings), it's still a pretty good edited directory to use when you value quality over quantity of results.

Kid-Safe Searching with Search Guard

Lycos has created a special gateway to the Web called Search Guard, which is designed to give users the capability to screen out adult content from their Web surfing; it blocks users from searching for pornographic or offensive words and from accessing Lycos's Chat, email, and message board functions. If you're worried about your children seeing inappropriate responses when they search for information on the Web, Search Guard isn't a bad way to go.

To use Search Guard, start by clicking the **Search Guard** link on the Lycos home page, or go directly to the registration page at personal.lycos.com/safetynet/

86

`safetynet.asp.` Read through the introductory material and click through until you reach the Search Guard Control Panel page. Fill in all the information as appropriate, and then select which level of filtering you wish to enable. When you click **Submit**, Search Guard is activated, and you can return to the Lycos home page and surf the Web as usual. To turn off Search Guard, click the **Search Guard** link on the Lycos home page and select the appropriate option on the Search Guard Control Panel page.

Find Files to Download with FTP Search

If you like to download files off the Internet—utilities, shareware programs, picture files, or whatever—then Lycos's FTP Search may be of interest to you. With FTP Search, you can search more than 100 million files and then automatically link to their FTP sites for downloading.

You access FTP Search by clicking the **FTP Search** link on the Lycos home page or by going directly to `ftpsearch.lycos.com`. Enter one or more keywords to describe the file you're looking for, and then pull down the **File Type** list and select the type of file you want. When you click the **Go Get It!** button, FTP Search generates a list of matching files.

It Can Only Guard So Much...

Note that Search Guard only filters information accessed through the Lycos Web site and search engine; it does not filter information accessed at any other site or through any other programs.

When you click the link to the file you wish to download, your browser automatically initiates the download process. After the file download is completed, you'll need to manually install the file as directed; in most cases, installation involves running a file named setup.exe or install.exe. Some files are downloaded in compressed ZIP format; before you install these files, you'll need to unzip the file using a zip/unzip utility, such as WinZip.

See Chapter 27, "Search for Files to Download," for more information on finding files on the Internet.

Searching for Stuff You See and Hear with Pictures & Sounds

Lycos includes a somewhat serviceable search engine for picture and sound files, which you can access by clicking the **Pictures & Sounds** link on the Lycos home page (or by going directly to `www.lycos.com/picturethis/`). Although Lycos does include a rudimentary directory of images (and these categories are listed first on the Pictures & Sounds page), you want to scroll to the bottom of the page to the search box. Select whether you want to search for pictures, sounds, or MP3 files (more about them in the next section), enter your keyword(s), and then click **Go Get It!**.

Whether you searched for pictures or sounds, you'll only see a list of matches—no picture thumbnails here, unfortunately. For that reason, I prefer the AV Photo Search feature on AltaVista—not only does it do a better job searching for pictures, it also displays the results in thumbnail fashion!

The Latest Thing in Audio—Search for MP3 Music Files

Know this: MP3 is revolutionizing the music industry.

MP3 is a new format for compressing music to fit within reasonably sized computer files while maintaining near-CD-quality sound. A typical three-minute song in MP3 format only takes up 2MB of disk space.

Although large record companies despise MP3 (they fear the threat of unauthorized copying), Internet users—particularly college students—love it, and have wholeheartedly embraced the format. MP3 has quickly become the standard for music on the Web.

Lycos was the first major search site to activate an MP3-specific search engine. Lycos's MP3 Search indexes more than a half-million MP3 files on the Net, with hundreds of new songs added daily.

You access MP3 Search by clicking the **MP3 Search** link on the Lycos home page, or by going directly to mp3.lycos.com. You can enter either an artist or a song name; click **Go Get It!** to initiate the search. When the search results appear, click any link to download the MP3 file.

Getting ready to search for MP3 files with Lycos's MP3 Search— which also contains links to a variety of other MP3 resources, including MP3 players and encoders.

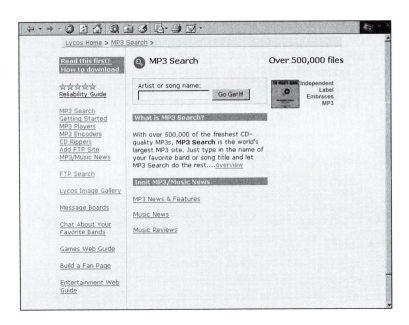

See Chapter 29, "Search for Music and Sounds," for more information on finding MP3 files on the Internet.

The Least You Need to Know

➤ Lycos is a fairly average search engine with a handful of unique features—including FTP Search and MP3 Search services.

➤ You can use only a limited number of operators in a basic Lycos search, chief among them are +, −, and " ".

➤ You can't use Boolean expressions in a standard Lycos search, but you can in the Lycos Advanced Search.

➤ If you want any control at all over your searching, you probably should go directly to Lycos Advanced Search.

➤ Lycos's Search Guard is a good way to filter out inappropriate content from your searches.

➤ Lycos FTP Search enables you to search through more than 100 million files for immediate downloading.

➤ Lycos MP3 Search enables you to search for and download music in the new MP3 format.

➤ The Lycos Open Directory is the world's largest user-edited directory of Web sites, and a plus if you value quality over quantity in your search results.

Chapter 7

Electrify Your Searches with Excite

In This Chapter

➤ Discover how Excite's Intelligent Concept Extraction differs from standard keyword searching

➤ Learn how to put together an effective search using keywords, modifiers, and Boolean operators

➤ Browse through Excite's Web Page Guide to find recommended sites that match your interest

On the surface, Excite (www.excite.com) is a fairly average search engine and portal, comparable to Lycos and other similar sites. Despite its moderate size (55 million pages indexed) and run-of-the-mill search tools, however, some interesting power resides just beneath the surface of Excite.

In addition to the standard keyword searching that all other sites offer (and Excite does let you use Boolean operators on its basic search page), Excite also offers what it calls *Intelligent Concept Extraction* (*ICE*), which searches for concepts and ideas in addition to searching for keywords.

ICE is a limited form of artificial intelligence—it actually tries to understand what you're searching for, conceptually, rather than just trying to match keywords. For example, if you search for `historical musical instruments`, Excite will (of course) return sites that include all those keywords, but will also find sites relating to early instruments, instrument collections, and other early music topics.

You'll find that because of ICE, Excite's search results are somewhat different from those of other search engines—and, in many cases, superior. It's the one thing that makes Excite unique as a search engine.

Report Card

Address:	www.excite.com
Search Engine:	Yes
Directory:	Yes
Size:	B
Freshness:	A
Ease of Use:	B
Power:	B
Extras:	Intelligent Concept Extraction (ICE) for conceptual searches

Conceptual Searching

Essentially, the ICE technology understands relationships between words. ICE looks for words that frequently appear close together in Web pages, because that often implies a broader concept that may be different from the literal meaning of the individual words. By recognizing the concept behind the words, ICE can then suggest additional words and phrases that are related to the key concept.

One other nice thing about ICE technology is that it learns about related concepts from the Web pages that it finds, and it learns more from each new page that it indexes. So the more you fine-tune your search, the more "intelligent" your results will be.

Take the example of the query `elderly people`. ICE recognizes the relationship between the words and the concept behind them; it adds terms such as "retired people" and "senior citizens" to its search. In other words, ICE figures out that the term "elderly people" is related to the term "senior citizens." This is different from a traditional keyword search, in which pages including "senior citizens" wouldn't match the query `elderly people`, even though they're ways of expressing the same concept.

So if you're descriptive enough in your conceptual query, you don't have to worry about including a lot of synonyms in your search phrase, as you might have in a more traditional search. And you might even be surprised by Excite's results—sometimes ICE identifies conceptual relationships that even you hadn't thought of!

Basic Searching with Excite

Basic searching with Excite is no different from searching with other search engines. Go to the Excite home page, enter your query in the search box, and click the **Search** button.

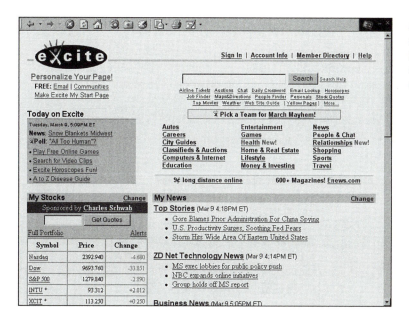

Excite's home page—You can search for keywords (using Boolean operators) or enter a more conceptual query.

Remember, however, that Excite lets you search for ideas and concepts in addition to keywords. Excite's Intelligent Concept Extraction technology finds relationships that exist between words and ideas, resulting in matches that contain words related to the concepts for which you're searching. So try something different with Excite—try selecting your keywords to best describe the general concept you're looking for, rather than to elicit the most "hits" on a page.

Reading the Results

Excite's Search Results page is a little different from those at other search sites. You get a lot of different types of results on Excite's page—some useful, some not. You'll see the following:

Order Boolean with No ICE

If you want to try a conceptual search, you have to give up your Boolean operators. The minute you include AND, AND NOT, or OR in your query, Excite automatically turns off the ICE technology.

➤ **Search Wizard**   This is what Excite calls the words listed below the search box on the Search Results page. Excite's Search Wizard suggests words that it believes are closely related to the subject of your query; check any words you want to add to your query, and then click the **Search Again** button to refine your search.

➤ **Web Site Guide**   These are links to specific categories in Excite's Web Site Guide directory. Click a link to see all the Web sites listed in that category.

➤ **Web Results**   These are your traditional search results, listed 10 pages at a time, most relevant pages first. Each listing includes the site's title, percentage match, URL, and a brief description. Click the **Search for more documents like this one** link to search for similar pages.

➤ **News Articles**   This section lists recent news articles related to your query.

➤ **Discussions**   This choice lists Usenet newsgroups and Excite communities related to your query.

*Excite's search results—Click **Web Results** to go directly to the standard Web page matches.*

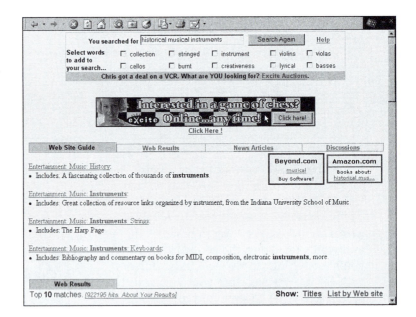

Don't dismiss the News Articles and Discussions links as irrelevant to your search. You'd be surprised how much additional information you can find in Usenet newsgroups and in the occasional news report. It's also sometimes worth your while to browse through the preselected sites in the Web Site Guide, in addition to the matches returned by the Excite search engine.

In other words, don't ignore any potential source of information related to your query!

Consolidate Your Results

If you want to see all the matching pages within larger Web sites, click **List by Web Site**. This compresses your results to show only the names of the URLs and the relevant links within them, and it ranks the sites themselves by percentage match. It's a good way to see which sites have the most information related to your query—and then you can go directly to those sites. (It also helps reduce the clutter when you have multiple matches from the same site.)

Fine-tuning Your Excite Search

Excite lets you use a handful of Boolean operators and other search commands directly in its basic search box. Table 7.1 lists all the commands you can use with Excite; just remember that using Boolean operators turns off the conceptual search technology.

Table 7.1   Excite Search Parameters

To Do This:	Use This Command:	Example:
Search for part of a word	*	`mon*`
Exclude pages that contain a word	–	`monty -python`
Require a word on a page	+	`monty +python`
Include both words	AND	`monty AND python`
Include at least one of the words	OR	`monty OR python`
Exclude pages that contain a word	AND NOT	`monty AND NOT python`
Search for a complete phrase	" "	`"monty python"`

Advanced Searching with Excite Power Search

Although it's a little difficult to find, Excite offers a collection of advanced search tools it calls Power Search. With Power Search you can fine-tune your searches to a finer degree than you can with the standard Excite search.

The Automatic AND

If you enter more than one word in a query with no operator between them, Excite assumes you want to look for both words and automatically inserts an AND between the words.

To access Power Search, you have to scroll to the bottom of the Excite home page and look for the little link called **Power Search**. Don't worry, most people don't see it at first—I certainly didn't. I don't know why Excite hides this, but it's worth looking for!

From the Power Search page, you have access to the following search options:

➤ **I want to search**   This pull-down list lets you direct your query to the Web, Excite's Web Site Guide (listed as "selected sites"), to a current news feed, and to country-specific versions of Excite (great for searching for non-English pages).

➤ **My search results CAN contain**   Select whether you want to search for individual words or exact phrases that can—but don't necessarily have to—appear in matching pages.

➤ **My search results MUST contain**   Select whether you want to search for individual words or exact phrases that have to appear in matching pages.

➤ **My search results MUST NOT contain**   Select whether you want to search for individual words or exact phrases that should not appear in matching pages.

➤ **Display my results by document with**   Enables you to select how you wish to display your results.

➤ **Display the top 40 results grouped by Web site**   Check this to display URLs only (no summaries), grouped by site.

Excite's Power Search— Select options from the pull-down lists and enter the keywords that CAN, MUST, and MUST NOT appear on matching pages.

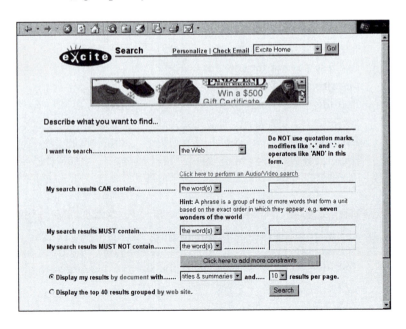

Power Search essentially lets you construct complex queries without the need to learn and use modifiers (+, –, " ") and Boolean operators. Therefore, you can't use modifiers and Boolean operators within the search fields in Power Search—which would be redundant, in any case.

Search for Audio and Video

Excite has hidden a real gem of a search engine deep within the bowels of its site. After you've found the Power Search page, look for the **Click Here to Perform an Audio/Video Search** link. When you click this link, you'll see a page that enables you to search for audio and video files on the Web. Basically, this little search engine searches for Real Audio and Real Video format files; you use it the same as you would the normal Excite search engine.

One Other Thing to Browse Through: Excite's Web Site Guide

Like most of the other search sites, Excite includes a Web site directory with listings chosen and organized by real human beings. Excite's directory is called the Web Site Guide, and you access it by clicking the **Web Site Guide** link at the top of the Excite home page.

You browse through the Web Site Guide the same as any directory, such as Yahoo! Just click a category, then click a subcategory, then click another subcategory, and so on until you find the listing of sites you're interested in.

When you finally get to a listing of sites, you'll find the page divided into Recommended Web Sites and Other Web Sites. The recommended sites generally come with short overviews; more often than not, these are some really good sites. They're not always the *best* sites, of course, because Excite's editors don't get to look at every site available. But the recommended site section isn't a bad place to start looking for what you want to find.

The Least You Need to Know

➤ Excite differs from other search engines in that it offers Intelligent Concept Extraction, the capability to search for concepts and ideas in addition to keywords.

➤ You can use the standard modifiers (+, –, " ") and Boolean operators (AND, AND NOT, OR) in Excite's standard search box—although using the Boolean operators turns off the conceptual searching technology.

➤ Excite's Power Search lets you construct complex searches through a series of pull-down lists.

➤ The Web Site Guide presents a directory of recommended sites, hand-picked by Excite's editors.

Seek Important Information at Infoseek

Like Lycos and Excite, Infoseek (infoseek.go.com) is a nondescript little search engine with a moderate amount of content (45 million entries), a moderate selection of search tools, and nothing really unique to make it stand out from the crowd. That said, it does an acceptable—but not outstanding—job of searching, is relatively easy to use, and—because it's part of Disney's GO Network—is used by millions of searchers daily.

Like many other search engines, Infoseek also includes an Advanced Search option (which lets you modify your search with form-based tools), a smallish Web directory (imaginatively called the GO Network Directory), and a kid-safe search filter (dubbed GOguardian). By the way, if you go to the GO Network portal (www.go.com), you'll see that it's the same page as the Infoseek home page—Infoseek and GO are now one and the same.

By the way, GO isn't a bad portal in and of itself. Disney's family of Web sites—all integrated into the GO Network—include not only Infoseek, but also the ABC.com, ABCNEWS.com, ESPN.com, Family.com, and Mr. Showbiz sites.

If you happen to use the Infoseek or GO Network portals, you can use Infoseek for your basic searching. For more comprehensive searching, however, you're better off trying one of the bigger and more powerful search engines, such as AltaVista, HotBot, or Northern Light.

Report Card

Address:	infoseek.go.com
Search Engine:	Yes
Directory:	Yes
Size:	B
Freshness:	B
Ease of Use:	B
Power:	B
Extras:	Includes the GO Web Directory, part of Disney's GO Network

Basic Searching at Infoseek—The Easy Way

Basic searching at Infoseek is pretty easy. Just enter your query into the search box, then from the pull-down list select where you want to search, and click the **Search** button. You can choose to search Web Sites (the default search), News articles, Companies, the GO Network Directory, or Usenet Newsgroups.

Searching at Infoseek—
Enter your query, choose
your collection, and GO.

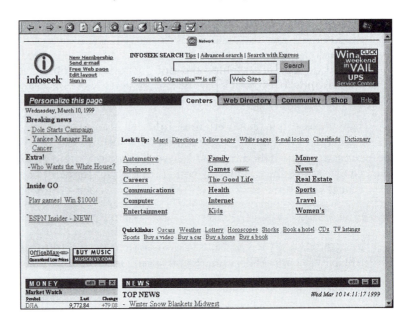

The Automatic AND/OR

If you enter more than one word in a query with no operator between them, Infoseek assumes you probably want to look for pages that contain both words, and it gives preferential treatment to pages that contain both words. However, it still returns pages that include either word—thus, the query first second would read something like "first and/or second." If you want to guarantee an AND-type result, put the + modifier in front of both keywords; if you want to guarantee an OR-type result, put a comma between the words.

The search results page lists three types of results:

➤ **Recommended**   Infoseek directs you first to the "communities" appropriate to your query on the GO Network. These results are, more often than not, proprietary content on one of Disney/GO's Web sites and are only occasionally related to what you are really looking for.

➤ **Directory topics**   These results are categories within the GO Network Directory that match your query. Generally they are worth checking out because they are hand-picked sites.

No Boolean

Sorry, folks, Infoseek doesn't offer Boolean searching anywhere on its site. That means no AND, OR, or NOTs in any of your searches.

➤ **Infoseek Web search results**   These listings are the matches you really wanted to see, displayed 10 to a page. To go to a matching page, just click its title. To view pages with comparable content, click the **Find similar matches** link; to see all results from a given site, click the **Grouped results from** link.

A typical page of Infoseek search results—Ignore the Recommended section, browse through the Directory topics, or go directly to the individual matches in the Infoseek Web search results.

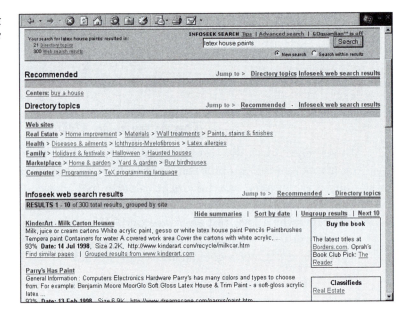

Fine-tuning Your Infoseek Search

In addition to the usual modifiers and operators you find at most search engines, Infoseek also offers a few unique search commands. Most interesting is the pipe (|), which enables you to combine a narrow search within a broader search. The proper syntax is *narrow|broad*, where the second term is the broad category, and the first term is a narrower category within the broad category.

Suppose, for example, you want to search for drums within the broad category of instruments. Your query would look like this: drums¦instruments. Kind of neat.

Table 8.1 lists all the commands you can enter into Infoseek's search box.

Table 8.1   Infoseek Search Parameters

To Do This:	Use This Command:	Example:
Search for a complete phrase	" "	"monty python"
Search for either word	,	monty, python
Exclude pages that contain a word	–	monty –python
Require a word on a page	+	monty +python
Search within a larger search	*narrow\broad*	monty¦comedy
Search all pages within a site	site:	site: molehillgroup.com

To Do This:	Use This Command:	Example:
Search only pages that contain the keyword in the URL	url:	`url:monty`
Search only in hyperlinks within a page	link:	`link:monty`
Search only in the title of a page	title:	`title:monty`
Search for pages that contain the keyword in a picture label	alt:	`alt:monty`

Nothing Wild—or Truncated

Note that Infoseek doesn't use wildcards, as most search engines do. It doesn't even use so-called automatic truncation. To Infoseek, a word is only a word; nothing else is assumed. (One exception—Infoseek does use something called "intelligent pluralization," which means that Infoseek seeks plural or singular forms of keywords.)

Find Better Stuff with Infoseek Advanced Search

Infoseek does offer a form-based Advanced Search, which enables you to do Boolean-like searches without using Boolean operators.

When you click the **Advanced Search** link from Infoseek's home page, you're presented with a form containing a series of pull-down lists and text boxes. The first pull-down list tells Infoseek where on a page to look for your keywords—in the whole Document (page), in the Title, in the URL, or in any Hyperlink within the page. The second pull-down list tells Infoseek whether the page must, should, or should not contain the keyword. The third pull-down list tells Infoseek whether it's looking for a phrase, a proper name, or an individual word or words.

Finally, you can change the way you want your results displayed and select which collection you wish to search, as well as which individual countries you wish to search. Leave as much blank as you want, and click the **Search** button to get things going.

103

Infoseek's Advanced Search enables you to do Boolean-like searches just by filling out the individual parts of this form.

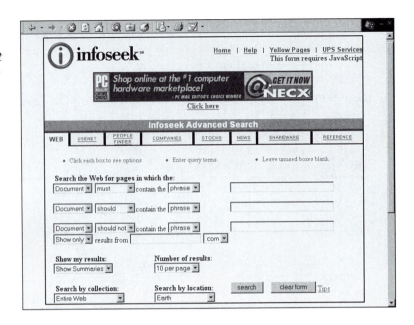

Kid-Safe Searching with GOguardian

Like several other search sites, Infoseek (and the entire GO Network) provides a service to filter out inappropriate adult content from search results. GOguardian is Infoseek's content filter, and you can turn it on and off by clicking the **Search with GOguardian** link on Infoseek's home page; when the Search with GOguardian page appears, select **GOguardian On** and click **OK**.

Go Browsing Through the GO Network Directory

Like most other search sites, Infoseek includes a human-assembled Web directory, which Infoseek calls the GO Network Directory. You get to it by clicking the **Web Directory** tab on Infoseek's home page.

The GO Network Directory works like most other directories; just click through the categories and subcategories until you come to the subcategory you want to investigate. Sites in the directory come with a very brief description, along with a three-star

104

ranking system. One star means the site is good, two stars means very good, and three stars are reserved for what GO's editors claim are the best sites. You may even occasionally come across a site that has been given the GO Network Award for Web Site Excellence; this reward is reserved for the very best of the best sites, as chosen by the GO staff.

Express Searching from Your Desktop

If you really like the way Infoseek searches, you can download and install a version of Infoseek that runs from your computer's desktop. Infoseek Express is a software program that integrates with your Web browser to offer additional search-related features, including the capability to search several search engines simultaneously. I can't say I'm a fan of this software, but if you want to check it out, click the **Search With Express** link on Infoseek's home page and follow the onscreen instructions.

The Least You Need to Know

➤ Infoseek is part of Disney's GO Network and offers a medium-sized content index with moderate searching power.

➤ You can use only a limited number of operators in an Infoseek search, chief among them are +, −, and " ".

➤ You can't use Boolean expressions in either the standard or Advanced Search modes.

➤ The GO Network Directory is Infoseek's obligatory Web directory.

➤ GOguardian is Infoseek's kid-safe search filter.

Chapter 9

See the Search Lights with Northern Light

In This Chapter

➤ Discover why Northern Light is the preferred search engine for many professional searchers

➤ Find out how the 5,400 publications in Northern Light's Special Collection add four million possible matches to your information searches

➤ Master complex queries using modifiers and Boolean operators or using Northern Light's Power Search function

➤ Learn how to browse through your search results in Custom Search Folders

Of all the Big Seven search sites, Northern Light is the one you're least likely to know about. Chances are, in fact, that you've never even heard of it.

That's a mistake you should correct—if you haven't used Northern Light yet, you're missing out on one of the best search sites on the entire Internet!

Northern Light (www.northernlight.com) is a large and powerful search engine, very much a direct competitor to AltaVista and HotBot. It has more than 125 million entries in its index, and it claims (by taking duplicate entries into account) to have indexed more individual sites than AltaVista (which has a 150 million-entry index).

To fine-tune your searches, Northern Light includes a good collection of search tools (including full Boolean operation from the standard search box), as well as an easy-to-use Power Search form. Northern Light's results are listed both by percentage match (relevancy ranking) and by subtopic, grouped into what Northern Light calls *Custom Search Folders*. No other search engine sorts its results in such a logical and easy-to-use manner.

Beyond simple Web searches, Northern Light also offers an additional proprietary database, which you can access for a fee. (You pay the fee only when you read individual articles, not when you perform the actual search.) This database, called the *Special Collection*, includes more than four million full-text articles from more than 5,400 journals, newspapers, and magazines. The Special Collection includes information that you simply can't find collected anyplace else—search engine, directory, or otherwise.

In case you can't tell, I really like Northern Light; it's my search engine of choice. The superb organization of results into Custom Search Folders, the full complement of search tools (including Boolean expressions), and the extra reach of the Special Collection database, push Northern Light well ahead of its power-search competitors AltaVista and HotBot. If you don't mind paying a little for some of the results you want, I heartily recommend Northern Light for your special searching needs.

Creating a Northern Light Account

To access any of the fee-based parts of Northern Light (such as the Special Collection), you'll need to create a Northern Light account. Just click the **Accounts** button on the Northern Light home page, and then click either **Set Up an Enterprise Account** (if you're registering for an entire business or organization) or **Set Up a New Account** (if you're registering for yourself). You'll need to create a username and password, of course, and have a credit card handy (for billing purposes). Otherwise, follow the onscreen instructions and you'll be signed up in no time. Once a month Northern Light bills your credit card for the fees you've incurred in the past 30 days.

Don't let this registration process scare you away from Northern Light. Just remember that you don't need an account to access Northern Light's powerful basic search engine, only to read articles from the Special Collection. And you only get billed for those Special Collection articles you actually read, not for any hits listed on the results page.

Report Card

Address:	www.northernlight.com
Search Engine:	Yes
Directory:	No
Size:	A
Freshness:	A
Ease of Use:	A
Power:	A
Extras:	Includes the Special Collection, a proprietary, fee-based, full-text database of four million articles from 5,400 journals, magazines, and newspapers

What's So Special About the Special Collection?

Northern Light differs from the other major search engines in that it manages its own proprietary database of information, called the Special Collection. When you do a search on Northern Light, you're searching both the Web and the Special Collection; matches from the Special Collection are so noted on your search results page.

The Special Collection is high-quality information. Northern Light compiles abstracts and full-text articles from more than 5,400 journals, reviews, books, magazines, and newswires—the majority of which are not freely available on the Web. All total, the Special Collection represents four million additional pieces of information that you don't get with traditional search engines.

Unfortunately, the Special Collection doesn't come cheap. Although some of the sources in the Special Collection provide their information free of charge (book reviews and abstracts, for example), you must pay a fee for most of the Special Collection articles if you want to read them. (It doesn't cost anything to search for them, of course.) These full-text articles cost from $1 to $4 to access.

You Pay Only for What You Use

It doesn't cost anything to perform a search of the Special Collection, and it doesn't cost anything to browse through Special Collection listings on the search results page. It doesn't even cost anything to read a summary of a Special Collection article. After you read the summary, however, if you decide to read the entire article, you have to get out your credit card.

(By the way, you actually have access to any article you've purchased for two full days. To access the article after your initial visit, click the **Accounts** button on the Northern Light home page, enter your username and password, click the **Transactions** tab, and then click the title of the article you wish to reread.)

Finding Information with Northern Light—The Easy Way

A simple Northern Light search works the same as a search on any other search engine—enter your query into the search box and click the **Search** button.

Simple searching from Northern Light's home page—Make sure the **Search** *tab is selected, enter your query, and click the* **Search** *button.*

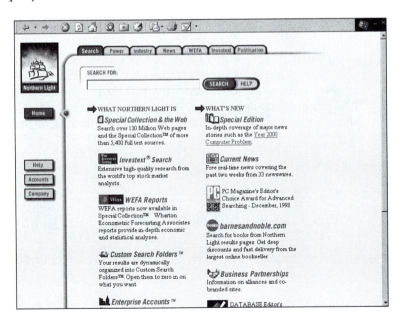

A normal Northern Light query searches all available sources, the Special Collection included. Note, however, that if you want to limit your query to only the Web or only the Special Collection, you'll need to do a Power Search, discussed later in this chapter.

The Automatic AND

If you enter more than one word in a query with no operator between them, Northern Light assumes you want to look for both words and automatically inserts an AND between the words. In other words, Northern Light automatically searches for pages that contain all your keywords.

Read the Results

Northern Light results are listed two ways—in the standard site match list (25 to a page) and in Custom Search Folders.

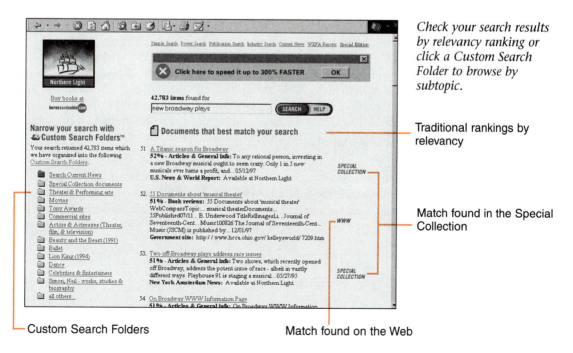

Check your search results by relevancy ranking or click a Custom Search Folder to browse by subtopic.

Traditional rankings by relevancy

Match found in the Special Collection

Custom Search Folders

Match found on the Web

Understanding a Match

Here's what you find for each Northern Light search result:

- ➤ **Title** Click the title of the Web page or Special Collection document to access the page or article.

- ➤ **Relevancy ranking** This shows how well (in percentage format) the page or document matches your query.

- ➤ **Type of document or Web site** Northern Light is unique in telling you what kind of site each match comes from (article, company information, commercial site, directory, encyclopedia, review, and so on), which makes it easier for you to decide if you really want to read it.

- ➤ **Summary** A brief overview of the matching page or document, including the date the page or document was last updated.

- ➤ **Source** This is either the Web page's URL or the document's source journal.

- ➤ **WWW or Special Collection** This icon tells you where Northern Light found the match—on the Web or in its Special Collection.

Filing Your Results in Folders

In addition to the traditional relevancy rankings, Northern Light also sorts your results into Custom Search Folders, located on the left side of your search results page. These Custom Search Folders help you better sort through your search results because they're organized by subtopic—with each subtopic generated dynamically according to the topic of your query.

As an example, if you search for new broadway plays, Northern Light generates Custom Search Folders for the following subtopics: Theater and Performing Arts, Movies, Tony Awards, Commercial sites, Actors and Actresses, Beauty and the Beast, Ballet, Lion King, Dance, Celebrities and Entertainers, and Simon, Neil. In addition, a "miscellaneous" folder (labeled "all others...") contains any matches that didn't fit within the other categories. (Northern Light also automatically generates Search Current News and Special Collection Documents folders for all queries.)

When you click a specific folder, a new search results page appears, listing only the matches that are contained in that folder—as well as a newly generated list of Custom Search Folders for that particular subtopic. Every time you drill down to a new level, new Custom Search Folders are created, helping you fine-tune your results until you find exactly what you're looking for.

Custom Search Folders Are *Not* Directory Categories

It's important to note that Northern Light's Custom Search Folders are not organized into preset categories like those you find in a traditional Web directory. Instead, the search engine creates new categories on-the-fly, every time you perform a Northern Light search, based on the content of your search query.

After you've clicked through a few levels of results, you may want to work your way back up the hierarchy of folders. To return to the previous level, click the topmost (blue) folder in the list.

Fine-tuning Your Northern Light Search

The basic Northern Light search lets you use a large number of wildcards and operators to fine-tune your search. Table 9.1 lists the commands you can use to narrow your search results—in both the standard search and the Power Search mode.

Table 9.1   Northern Light Search Parameters

To Do This:	Use This Command:	Example:
Search for part of a word	*	mon*
Search for a word with a single unknown character	%	mon%y
Must include a word	+	monty +python
Must exclude a word	–	monty –python
Search for a complete phrase	" "	"monty python"
Search for both keywords	AND	monty AND python
Search for either keyword	OR	monty OR python
Exclude a word	AND NOT	monty AND NOT python
Search for information about a specific company by company name	COMPANY:	COMPANY:microsoft

continues

Table 9.1   CONTINUED

To Do This:	Use This Command:	Example:
Search for information about a specific company by stock ticker	TICKER:	`TICKER:MSFT`
Search only in the URL of the page	URL:	`URL:monty`
Search only in the title of the page	TITLE:	`TITLE:monty`
Search only in the text of a page (*not* in the title or URL)	TEXT:	`TEXT:"monty python"`
Search only within a specific journal in the Special Collection	PUB:	`PUB:"bank automation news"`

Northern Light is unique in using two different wildcards to fill in missing parts of keywords. You can use the standard * wildcard to search for the missing last part of a word or the % wildcard to look for a single missing character.

For example, mon* will find "monty," "money," "monkey," or "Montgomery." Using mon%y will find only "monty" or "money." (Count the letters.) The % wildcard is great to use when you're not really sure how a word is spelled.

Add More Power to Northern Light

When you click the **Power** tab on Northern Light's home page, you're taken to Northern Lights Power Search. Here you can select specific sources, subjects, and types of documents that you wish to search.

The options on the Power Search page include the following:

➤ **Search For**   You can enter keywords you want to find anywhere in the document, only in the title, only in the publication name, or only in the Web page's URL. (Make sure you put a publication name in quotes; click the **list of publications** link to see all the publications available in the Special Collection.)

➤ **Select**   This option is where you tell Northern Light whether you want to search the Special Collection, the World Wide Web, or both (All Sources).

➤ **Select Date Range**   At your discretion, you can limit your search to pages or documents created within a specific range of dates; check the **Sort results by date** box to display your results in chronological order.

➤ **Select Sources**   Check one or more of the following sources you want to search: Journals and Magazines, News archives, Personal pages, Commercial Web sites, Non-profit Web sites, Educational Web sites, Military Web sites, or Government Web sites. You can also fine-tune your search by selecting only documents written in a specific language or Web sites originating in specific countries.

114

➤ **Select Subjects**   Narrow your search by selecting specific topics you want to search within. You can choose from Arts, Business and Investing, Computing and Internet, Contemporary Life, Education, Entertainment, Gov't Law and Politics, Health and Medicine, Humanities, Products and Services, Reference, Science and Mathematics, Social Sciences, Sports and Recreation, Technology, or Travel.

➤ **Limit Documents To**   This option provides another opportunity to narrow your search, this time by searching only the specific types of documents: Company Information, Directories and Lists, Event Listings, For Sale, Job Listings, Learning Materials, Press Releases, Questions and Answers, and Reviews.

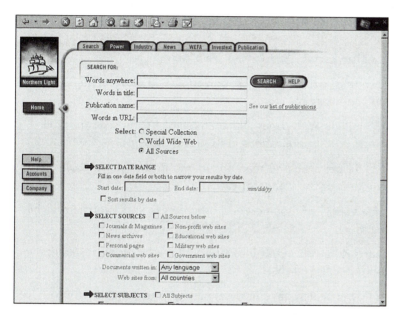

Use the check boxes and pull-down lists on the Power Search page to fine-tune your Northern Light search results.

Even More Types of Searches at Northern Light

In addition to Northern Light's standard search and Power Search, the site also offers a handful of specialized searches, all accessible by clicking the appropriate tab on the Northern Light home page. These specialty searches include the following:

➤ **Publication Search**   This option searches the Special Collection only, by specific publication or keyword.

➤ **Industry Search**   This choice searches both the Web and the Special Collection by specific industry category document types.

➤ **Current News**   This selection searches the previous two weeks of news stories from more than 70 sources, including AP Online, UPI, and PR Newswire. This page also includes continually updated headlines, weather, and sports information. (Note that news stories older than two weeks are available through your normal searches of the Special Collection, for a fee.)

➤ **WEFA Reports**   This newest option lets you search the Wharton Econometric Forecasting Associates (WEFA) Reports, which provide in-depth economic and statistical analysis of industries, countries, states, metropolitan areas, and commodities. This is the priciest part of Northern Light; these reports cost anywhere from $12 to $350. Also note that these reports are not in HTML format; instead, they're PDF files that require the Adobe Acrobat Reader for viewing.

The Least You Need to Know

➤ Northern Light is one of the largest, most powerful, and most intelligent search engines on the Internet.

➤ In addition to 125 million Web pages, Northern Light also indexes four million documents from 5,400 publications in its proprietary Special Collection.

➤ It costs from $1 to $4 per article to read documents in the Special Collection (but not to read results of the standard search).

➤ You can use a wide variety of modifiers and operators in your Northern Light queries, including +, −, " ", *, %, AND, OR, AND NOT, and PUB:.

➤ Northern Light sorts its search results into Custom Search Folders, dynamically generated for each specific search.

➤ Northern Light's Power Search page lets you narrow your search by source and type of document—as well as limit your searching to either the Web or the Special Collection.

Part 3

The *Unusual* Suspects: General Search Sites You Probably Didn't Know About, But Should Have

Did you know that there are over 200 different search sites on the Internet? So, if you've only been using one or two search sites, you've been missing out on some of the newer and more interesting search engines and directories currently available—including several sites that I guarantee will give you better results than Yahoo! or Excite or any of the other more popular search sites. Use this part of the book to explore new and better search engines and directories—sites that may very well become your favorite search sites!

The Next Generation: Newer, Better Search Engines

In This Chapter

➤ Learn how Ask Jeeves! makes keyword searching obsolete

➤ Discover how Google always puts the best result first

➤ Find out why About.com, Netscape Open Directory, and G.O.D. are good directory alternatives to Yahoo!

As powerful and advanced as they appear to be, the major search engines aren't always on the cutting edge of search engine technology. In fact, some of the major sites (Lycos and Infoseek come to mind), are downright primitive, search-technology–wise.

Some of the most interesting developments in search engine technology and usability are coming from outside the big boys' club. If you really want to see the next genera-tion of search sites, you have to look at a handful of little guys and what they're doing to make searching more accurate and more enjoyable.

Ask Jeeves! for What You Want

One of the more interesting next-generation search engines is Ask Jeeves! (www.askjeeves.com). What makes Ask Jeeves! unique is that it moves beyond simple keyword searching into natural-language query processing.

Just what is natural-language query processing? It's a fancy term for asking plain-English questions.

Just How Do You Ask Jeeves?

Suppose you want to find the current population of China. In a normal search engine, you have to structure a keyword-based request that looks something like this: `(population OR people) AND China`. With Ask Jeeves!, you formulate your request as a question: `How many people live in China?`

Ask Jeeves! then returns a page of related questions for which it knows the answer. Some of these questions might have variables in them that let you choose more appropriate phrases. For our example above, one of the questions listed by Ask Jeeves! was "Where can I find *demographic information for* the country *China*?" If demographic information isn't quite what you were looking for, you can pull down the list and select another item, such as "economic information for," or "geographical information for." Same thing with "China"; you can pull down that list and select another country.

Your original question

*Ask Jeeves! and generate a list of related questions—Click the **Ask!** button next to any question to go to the precise answer.*

Ask Jeeves!'s list of related questions for which it knows the answers

Possible matches to your query from traditional search engines

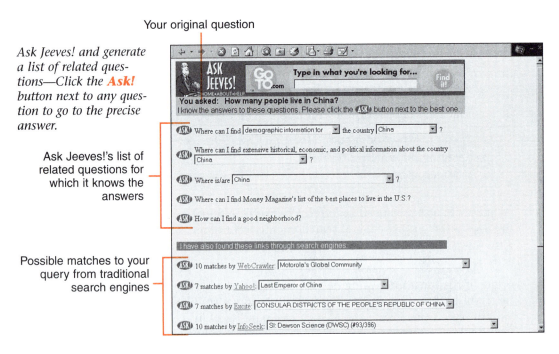

After you find a question that fits your query, click the **Ask!** button next to that question. Ask Jeeves! then returns one item—that's all, just *one*—that precisely answers the question. In the case of the China example, clicking **Ask!** next to the demographic information question returned a document that provided the exact number I was looking for (which, by the way is 1,236,914,658—estimated in July, 1998).

In addition to the new questions posed at the top of the Ask Jeeves! results screen, Ask Jeeves! also takes the initiative to feed your query into several of the major traditional search engines (Excite, Infoseek, Lycos, WebCrawler, and Yahoo!), and it presents their top findings in the bottom half of the page. Just select the appropriate item from one of the pull-down lists and click the related **Ask!** button; Ask Jeeves! takes you directly to that matching page.

As you can see, Ask Jeeves! doesn't give you pages and pages of results—it gives you the answer to your question. After all, do you really care how many matches you get to your query, or do you just want to get to the answer?

When Ask Jeeves! Has to Ask...

In response to some questions, Ask Jeeves! asks you a follow-up question before it returns its list of results. Think of this as a clarification needed by the search engine to give you the best possible answer.

Ask, But Spell It Correctly!

Ask Jeeves! can be thrown for a loop if you misspell one of the words in your question. For that reason, it has a built-in spell checker, which generates the message "I think you may have misspelled something" above the search results. If you see this message, click the message link to rephrase your question.

How Does Ask Jeeves! Work?

If you Ask Jeeves! how Ask Jeeves! works, you get a dabbling of technobabble with phrases such as "question-processing engine," "answer-processing engine," "natural-language processing," "templated questions," "context-sensitive knowledge base," and "meta-search engine."

If you ask *me* how Ask Jeeves! works, I give you two words: human beings. The Ask Jeeves! site employs a large staff who work full-time creating a huge knowledge base of questions. (At this writing, Ask Jeeves! has more than seven million questions in its knowledge base!) Thus, when you ask a question, chances are that question or one similar to it has already been asked—and answered. Ask Jeeves! doesn't try to reinvent the wheel with each new question or visitor.

The human beings are helped out just a little bit by technology, of course. Special software associates questions with concepts—and concepts with other concepts. Asking about Monica Lewinsky brings up questions associated both with presidential impeachment and Linda Tripp. Even though you didn't ask about those topics in particular, other users did, so Ask Jeeves! knows that they're related.

The result is a relatively "intelligent" search site, where the more precise your question, the more likely you'll get it answered.

Processing Questions and Answers

Although you don't need to understand how Ask Jeeves! works, technology-wise, it's interesting just how high-tech this search engine really is. When you Ask Jeeves! a question, the site's Natural Language Engine processes the meaning and grammar of your questions in plain English. The engine then matches your question to a "question template" in its knowledge base, using both semantic (word-oriented) and syntactic (grammar-oriented) parsing. In other words, Ask Jeeves! actually learns from each question you and other users ask.

Tips on Using Ask Jeeves!

To get the best use out of Ask Jeeves!, follow these tips:

➤ **Phrase your query as a question**   Forget about keywords, forget about modifiers and Boolean operators, just ask a simple question—in a complete sentence.

➤ **Ask a simple question, not a complex one**   In other words, search for one thing at a time.

➤ **Ask a narrow question, not a broad one**   Instead of just looking for information about travel, ask where you can find an online travel agent or which beaches allow nude sunbathing. Try to ask about *exactly* what you want to know—you'll be surprised at how often Ask Jeeves! knows the precise answer.

➤ **If a specific question doesn't work, ask a more general one**   If you can't find out how many left-handed albino dentists work in Des Moines, then step back a bit and just ask about Des Moinesian dentists in general.

The bottom line: Ask simple, direct questions—and keep revising your questions until you get the answers you're looking for.

Where Else Can You Find Jeeves?

You can find Ask Jeeves! technology in at least two other places on the Internet:

➤ **Ask Jeeves for Kids!** (www.ajkids.com)   This related site lets your kids ask typical, Ask Jeeves!, plain-English questions—with the added benefit of safety. On this site, every answer has been prescreened for kid-safe content.

➤ **AltaVista** (www.altavista.com)   The AltaVista site now features "Powered by Jeeves" technology. To use what AltaVista calls "Ask AltaVista," just type a question (complete with question mark) into AltaVista's search box. This generates Ask Jeeves! question-style results, as well as traditional AltaVista Web site matches.

Mind Boogling Results at Google

Google's home page is shocking in its simplicity.

It has no category listings, no news headlines, no stock tickers, no weather reports, and no blatant advertisements.

Just a logo is shown, along with a search box, two search buttons, and a link to some Help files and additional information (**More Google!**).

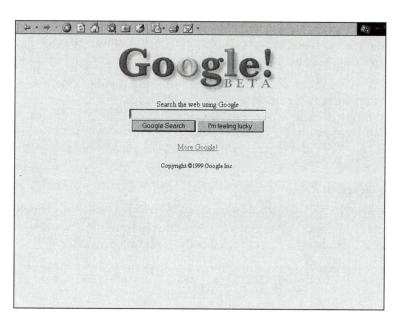

How much simpler can you get? Just enter your query and click the **Google Search** *button—no fuss, no muss.*

Google itself is a lot like its home page.

Google's claim to fame is that it does a very good job of returning the best results first—at the top of its search results list. Google is so sure of its capability to generate high-quality results that it puts an **I'm feeling lucky** button on its home page; click this button and you skip the standard results list and go directly (and blindly!) to the page that is the number one match to your query.

Just What *Is* a Google?

Technically, a *googol* (note the correct spelling) is 10 to the 100th power, which is a really big number—a one followed by 100 zeros. The Google guys say they picked the name because they want to "make huge quantities of information available to everyone...also, it sounds cool and has only six letters." They don't explain why they changed the spelling.

How Do You Use Google?

You use Google the same as you would any other search engine. Enter your query into the search box and click the **Google Search** button. (Or, if you want to go directly to the site of your number one match, click the **I'm feeling lucky** button.)

You can skip all the Boolean operators because Google doesn't use them. (Google uses an assumed AND between words, therefore it searches for *all* words in your query.) You can use + and – modifiers to include and exclude words, as well as " " to indicate exact phrases. Other than that, you don't have a whole lot of control over your Google searches.

How Does Google Work?

Google uses a special mathematical algorithm that rates a site or page based on which and how many other sites link to it. The ranking incorporates not only the number of sites that link to a page, but also the linking sites' own importance rating.

The result is as much a popularity contest as anything, but it seems to work most of the time.

For example, do a search for star wars. Thousands of home-grown Star Wars sites exist, but Google comes back with the official Star Wars site as its number one match.

When Should You Use Google?

Google works best for "official" queries for companies, proper names, and other discrete organizations and things. The search engine almost always ranks the official site at the top of its list.

However, the official site is not always the best source of information about any given topic. Sometimes the best match is actually a small, obscure site hiding away in some corner of the Web. The way Google works, if nobody links to that site, it won't come up as a match. So in Google's case, familiarity doesn't breed contempt, it breeds high-percentage matches.

The bottom line: Use Google if you want "official" information. Skip Google if you're looking for something more obscure.

whatUseek Is whatUget

Whatever else whatUseek (www.whatuseek.com) offers, it is, in my opinion, the next generation in *annoying* search engines! The main whatUseek site is jam-packed with multimedia geegaws and doodads, from a driving techno background beat to videogame-like blurps that issue forth whenever you move your cursor over an object. In fact, whatUseek is more like a videogame in appearance than a standard search site.

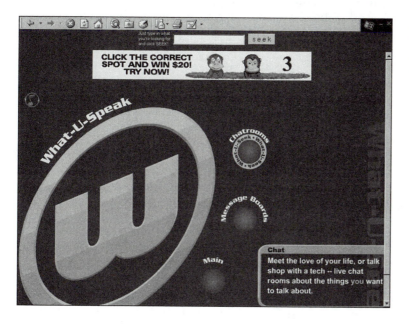

Zap! Pow! Blam! Using whatUseek is like playing a videogame—only more annoying.

Which some people may like. But I don't.

However, if you can push past the annoying interface, you'll find a pretty good next-generation search site.

whatUseek Without All the Flash

When you first access whatUseek, you have the option of entering the "animated" site I discuss, or using a more conventional non-animated site. To use the animated site, you have to have the Macromedia Flash plug-in installed in your Web browser. As to the non-animated version of whatUseek—well, without the flash, whatUseek starts to look like just another search engine or portal, sorry.

whatUseek provides results from its own search engine, as well as meta-results from Yahoo!, AltaVista, Excite, and WebCrawler. It groups results by search engine, 10 at a time, listing its own results first, of course.

Meta-Searching

When a search engine feeds a single query to multiple other search engines, it's called *meta-searching*. There are several meta-search sites on the Web, and they're all discussed in Chapter 13, "Kill Two Birds with One Stone at Meta-Search Sites."

The results from whatUseek are pretty good. The site uses Thunderstone (www.thunderstone.com) technology for its searches, which indexes both structured and unstructured data. Thunderstone is one of the most advanced of the current behind-the-scenes search technologies, and it is very effective at keeping out-of-date listings to a minimum.

whatUseek also offers a Web directory under the **Channels** button, as well as Web-based chat and message boards. (It's trying to be a portal, you see—and not just any portal, but the Internet's first multimedia portal!)

Should you use whatUseek? It gives good results, but so do Ask Jeeves! and Google—and they're much less annoying. This next-generation site needs to learn about user-interface expectations before it can be a big hit.

Dig for Information at About.com

About.com (www.about.com) isn't a search engine; it's a directory. And it's a darned good directory, too.

Information on About.com is sorted into more than 600 GuideSites. Each GuideSite is focused on a single topic and includes content (hand-picked Web site listings and reviews, in addition to related news articles), community (chat, message boards, newsletters, and so on), and shopping.

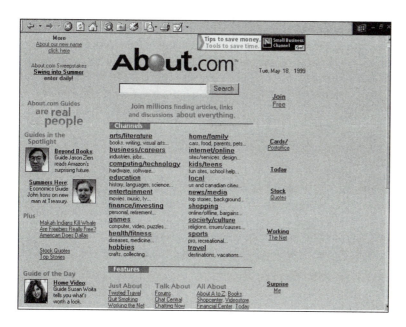

About.com—Click a topic to visit its corresponding GuideSite.

All these activities on a specific GuideSite are managed by the site's Guide. A About.com Guide is a real, honest-to-goodness human being, a subject expert who compiles and manages everything that goes on at his or her assigned GuideSite.

For example, the Guide to About.com's Multimedia Sound GuideSite (mmsound.about.com) is Lorna Brown. Ms. Brown compiles the lists of related sites for the GuideSite, as well as writes a few articles about the topic at hand.

The result of this expert-managed data gathering is that About.com has great information about many topics. In fact, usually you'll find the information you want in

GuideSite's proprietary articles, without ever having to go clicking through a list of matching Web sites.

You use About.com as you would any directory, browsing through its hierarchical list of topics. You can also search through About.com's list of GuideSites to find the one you want.

At the end of the day, About.com doesn't feature any fancy next-generation technology—it relies on the "old technology" of qualified experts assembling the best data available on selected topics. For some reason, that approach seems pretty fresh in today's Internet search environment.

Rely On Your Fellow Users at the Netscape Open Directory

In addition to its standard search service, Netscape Netcenter includes a Web directory called the Netscape Open Directory (`directory.netscape.com`). The Open Directory looks like most other directories, with 15 major browsable categories.

What makes the Netscape Open Directory unique is that its users are its editors. The Netscape Open Directory is the first open content Web directory to harness the knowledge and creativity of volunteer editors, letting users share their Web experiences with other users. With users as editors, the Open Directory has nearly 7,000 contributing editors who have listed close to a half million individual sites.

The Netscape Open Directory—The Internet's largest user-edited directory of Web sites.

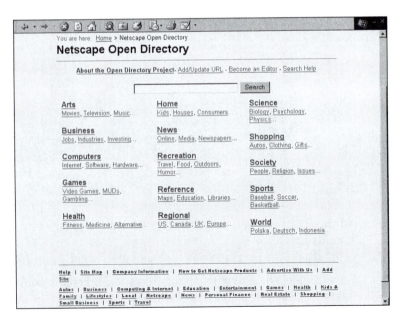

The Netscape Open Directory is actually a continuation of a project originally known as NewHoo. NewHoo's goal was to produce the most comprehensive directory of the Web, by relying on a vast army of volunteer editors. The project continues, largely unchanged (but renamed the Netscape Open Directory), after its acquisition by Netscape.

In addition, Netscape has been actively licensing the Open Directory to other Web sites. At this writing, the Open Directory has been licensed to Dogpile, HotBot, and Lycos. The best implementation is the Lycos Open Directory; they've expanded on the original with additional content and features. (For more information about the Lycos Open Directory, see Chapter 6, "Go Get It at Lycos.")

To look for a particular site in the Open Directory, you can either click the category on the Open Directory page or enter a search phrase in the query box at the top of the page and click the **Search** button. The results page lists the best sites (indicated by a star icon) first and the rest in alphabetic order, and it gives a description of what you'll find there.

Become an Open Directory Editor

To join the Netscape Open Directory project, go to a particular category you'd like to help maintain, then click the **Become an Editor** link and follow the onscreen instructions. You don't have to be an editor to recommend a new URL, however; just click the **Add URL** link on any category page.

G.O.D. Is in the Details

The final next-generation search site has actually been around since 1996. The Global Online Directory (www.god.co.uk)—otherwise known as G.O.D.—is a high-quality Web directory, perhaps the only directory that can truly give Yahoo! a run for its money.

Like Yahoo!, G.O.D. goes for quality over quantity. Its hand-picked listings are stored in an object-oriented database for more accurate results and faster retrieval times.

The latest version of the site, G.O.D. V3, provides a Global Search feature that lets users search for Web sites by country, state, province, county, or city. This "localization" feature will become more important as the World Wide Web switches from being U.S.-focused to being truly worldwide in its composition; users in other countries want results that are more localized, when possible. (It's no surprise that this localization comes from the only major search site based outside the U.S.)

A better directory than Yahoo? G.O.D. only knows.

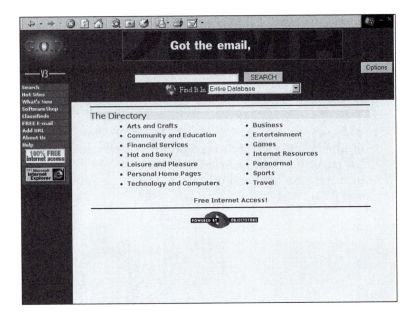

To perform a search on G.O.D., pull down the **Find It In** list and select the region you wish to search. Then enter a normal query into the search box and click the **Search** button. (Alternatively, after you've defined your geographic region, you can also browse through the topic categories on the main page.)

G.O.D. also includes a collection of **Hot Sites**; when you click this link, you see a list of what, in G.O.D.'s eyes, are the best sites on the Web, in no certain order.

Should you let G.O.D. guide your searches? If you're based outside the U.S. and you like Yahoo!, most certainly. In fact, even many U.S. users find that G.O.D.'s way is the right way when it comes to supplanting Yahoo! as their chosen directory.

The Least You Need to Know

➤ Ask Jeeves! lets you ask questions in plain English—and takes you directly to the precise answer.

➤ Google almost always puts the best results first, especially if you're searching for official information.

➤ whatUseek uses multimedia technology to present a visually stimulating interface, in case your searches get too boring.

➤ About.com's expert-managed GuideSites provide a combination of useful articles and hand-picked Web links.

➤ The Netscape Open Directory contains sites by more than 7,000 volunteer users.

➤ G.O.D. is a good directory alternative to Yahoo!, especially for non-U.S. Web users.

Chapter 11

Paying for Information: Subscription Search Sites

In This Chapter

➤ Discover why professional researchers pay good money for their information

➤ Find out whether you need to subscribe to professional research services

➤ Learn all about LEXIS–NEXIS, Dialog, and ProQuest Direct

I might as well say this up front:

If you're a casual Web searcher, if you're searching from your home, or if you don't have an unlimited research budget, you can skip this chapter. (It's short, anyway.)

That's because this chapter deals with professional search services, sites that charge big bucks to let you access their databases of information—sites such as LEXIS–NEXIS, Dialog, and ProQuest Direct.

Most Web searchers will never access these sites. But if you're a professional researcher or you work for a company with a big research budget, you may find something useful here.

Why Would You Use a Professional Search Service?

With so much information available for free on the Web—and accessible via free search sites, such as AltaVista and Yahoo!—why would you choose to use an expensive professional research service?

First, not all information in the world is available on the Internet. Second, no one search engine can find even half the information that *is* on the Web. And third, the information you do find on the Web is often disorganized and unreliable.

Now, that might be fine for you and me, but for professional researchers—whose careers depend on the information they provide—the Internet simply isn't as effective, efficient, or reliable as a professional research service. You might not know this, but an entire group of professional researchers and librarians need better access to more information than what is currently accessible via the Internet—and these researchers and their employers are willing to pay for the privilege.

The professional research services have traditionally not viewed the Internet as competition for their services. They have created vast databases of information, and they maintain these databases in a very organized and easily searchable fashion. The Internet, on the other hand, is a vast database only by default, and nobody maintains anything in any fashion whatsoever. (Perhaps, one might think, that's why information on the Internet is essentially free—you get what you pay for!)

In fact, most professional research services have been slow to embrace the Internet, reserving full access to their databases for their proprietary dial-up services. In other words, they don't want to let in "every man"; they want to maintain the image of providing exclusive, high-quality content that allows them to continue to charge their exorbitant subscription rates.

To answer the question, then, of whether you should avail yourself of these professional research services—probably not, especially if you're searching on your own or on a limited budget. Even if you work for a big corporation that will willingly fund your research activities, try to find what you're looking for on the Web first, and then turn to the pro services.

But if you're a professional researcher, you don't need me to tell you the value of these professional services. (Heck, you probably don't even need to read this book!) You can—and *will*—find information via LEXIS-NEXIS and the like that you'll never find on the Web.

The Big Daddy of Research Services: LEXIS-NEXIS

LEXIS-NEXIS (www.lexis-nexis.com) is one of the oldest, largest, and most respected sources of research information in the world. Since 1966 (as Data Corporation), LEXIS-NEXIS has been supplying customers with vast databases of information, via its traditional dial-up service, CD-ROMs, books, and, most recently, the Web.

When you use LEXIS-NEXIS for your research, you're accessing the following:

➤ 8,700 databases

➤ 2 billion documents, with 6.8 million new documents added each week

➤ 2 trillion characters

➤ 24,871 sources (18,871 news and business sources, and 6,000 legal sources)

134

Remember that the Web itself "only" has 300 million pages and documents. This means LEXIS-NEXIS contains six times as much information as does the Web!

Even though LEXIS-NEXIS has 1.6 million subscribers, it's very much a service for professionals in large corporations. In fact, LEXIS-NEXIS's individual services are clustered into four business units, by customer type: Legal, Business, Government, and Academic.

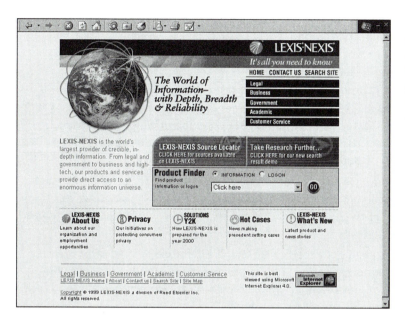

The home page for LEXIS-NEXIS—You can't actually access any information from here; you have to contact the company and arrange a subscription plan first.

Opening a Dialog

Like LEXIS-NEXIS, Dialog (www.dialog.com) has been serving the needs of professional researchers for quite a long time—since 1972. Dialog features access to more than 900 core databases, specializing in the areas of News and Media, Medicine, Pharmaceuticals, Chemicals, Reference, Social Sciences, Business and Finance, Food and Agriculture, Intellectual Property, Government and Regulations, Science and Technology, and Energy and Environment.

Also similar to LEXIS-NEXIS, Dialog aims primarily at corporate customers. Dialog likes to license entire sites for subscription access, with hundreds of desktops per site.

Many ways to access Dialog are available, including its proprietary online dial-up service, a special Lotus Notes-based version, and a new Web service, dubbed DialogWeb. DialogWeb provides access to Dialog's full content and incorporates both Guided Search and Command Search modes. You can find out more about DialogWeb at www.dialogweb.com.

How Much Does It Cost?

You know you're dealing with a professional search service when you can't find pricing information anywhere on its site. For example, look what you get when you click the **Pricing** link on LEXIS-NEXIS:

"LEXIS-NEXIS offers flexible pricing based on transactional, hourly, or flat-rate subscriptions. With over 23,000 news, legal, business and government sources online, subscriptions are highly customizable. For specific pricing information based on your needs, contact the LEXIS-NEXIS New Sales department at `newsales@ lexis-nexis.com` or at 800-227-4908."

In other words, if you have to ask, you probably can't afford it! Be aware, though, that professional research is expensive. Even though subscription plans can get quite complex, expect to pay anywhere from $30 to more than $100 for an hour's worth of searching.

Unless, of course, you can get access to LEXIS-NEXIS for free—which is possible. You may be part of an organization that has its own multi-user license that you can take advantage of. For example, some college libraries offer their students free access to LEXIS-NEXIS. It's worth asking about!

*Dialog's home page— Click the **DialogWeb** link to go to the Web-based service.*

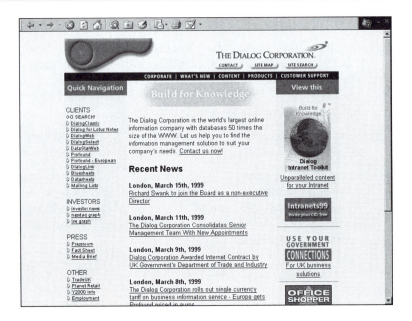

Be a Pro; Use ProQuest Direct

ProQuest Direct (www.umi.com/proquest/) is more of a periodical-based research service than its competitors. The ProQuest collection includes articles from more than 5,000 business, technical, and professional publications, with many available in full-text format.

For professional researchers, ProQuest offers some nice options. Users can search for both text and graphics and retrieve articles in varying degrees of detail, from citations and abstracts to full text and text with graphics. ProQuest Direct even has an optional "children's interface," presumably for installations in K-12 libraries.

Although some Web sites, such as Northern Light, are starting to offer access to periodical databases (for a fee), the largest selection of journals and other periodicals continues to be available at pro sites, such as ProQuest.

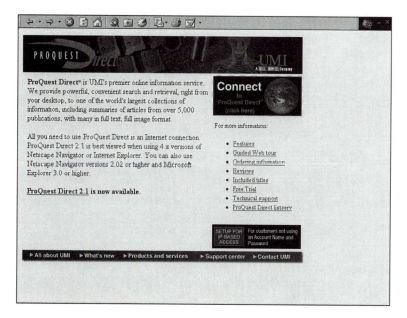

Search for periodical articles at ProQuest Direct.

The Least You Need to Know

➤ Professional research services offer more information and better *organized* information than you can find on the Web.

➤ These services charge a lot for access to their information, and they aim their services at large corporate clients.

➤ The biggest professional research services are LEXIS-NEXIS, Dialog, and ProQuest Direct—all of which now provide Web-based access to their databases.

Chapter 12

Madame Librarian: Online Libraries and Encyclopedias

Before there was the Internet, there were libraries and encyclopedias. When you wanted to look something up pre-Web, you either headed over to the local library or sat yourself down in front of your family's set of encyclopedias.

In a good library, you could find just about anything—books, magazines, journals, newspapers, tapes, you name it. The very best libraries had their own special collections—items that you just couldn't find anyplace else.

A good encyclopedia held its own wonders. Volumes and volumes of concise articles mixed with in-depth features, with enlightening illustrations and beautiful four-color pictures, on just about any topic from A to Z.

Today, you don't have to head to the library to access library resources, and you don't have to buy an entire set of encyclopedias just to read a single article. Today, both libraries and encyclopedias have gone online.

Sorting Through the Digital Stacks of Online Libraries

I find it amazing how quickly libraries have adopted the Internet. Today, it's unusual to find a major public or university library that does not have a Web presence of some kind.

What kind of library sites can you find on the Web? Let's take a look at what you can find, from simple to sophisticated.

The most basic library site simply lists the library's public catalog. This might not sound like much, but it's a great way to see if a particular location has the book you're looking for—*before* you jump into your car and head over there.

Many libraries also let you perform additional tasks through their Web sites. For example, you may be able to renew a book online, without having to return to the branch to get the book "stamped." Or you may be able to request books from other branches to be delivered to a branch closer to your home.

More advanced library sites have some or all of their individual collections online. This can range from digitized texts to full-scale multimedia exhibits. You typically find these types of sites at major university sites and from the very largest public libraries.

Table 12.1 presents some of the most popular library-related sites on the Web. These include the sites of the most innovative public and university libraries—sites that contain lists of other libraries and library resources, and a handful of libraries that exist only on the Internet.

OPAC (*not* OPEC!)

An *OPAC* is an Online Public Access Catalog—in other words, a library's publicly accessible listing of contents.

Table 12.1   Major Library-Related Sites

Site:	URL:	Comments:
Argus Clearinghouse	`www.clearinghouse.net`	A large directory of subject-specific guides created at the University of Michigan
Berkeley Digital Library SunSITE	`sunsite.berkeley.edu`	A vast repository of collections, research tools, and archival information from the University of Berkeley

Site:	URL:	Comments:
CyberStacks	`www.public.iastate.edu/ ~CYBERSTACKS/`	A collection of Internet resources from Iowa State University, categorized using the Library of Congress classification scheme
Digital Library Net	`www.digitallibrary.net`	Links to resources related to digital libraries, including a large listing of online library sites
Electric Library	`www.elibrary.com`	An online research library with access to magazines, newspapers, journals, and other periodicals, in addition to newswires, book, movie, and software reviews, and a complete encyclopedia and dictionary (this is a fee-based site, charging $5.95 per month after an initial free period)
Internet Public Library	`www.ipl.org`	"The first public library of the Internet," with a huge collection of online reference works, hosted by the University of Michigan
Library of Congress	`lcweb.loc.gov`	America's national library online, complete with online collections, texts of many of the Library's publications, and access to bibliographic catalogs and legislative information (THOMAS)
LibrarySpot	`www.libraryspot.com`	The information sweet spot of the best library and reference sites on the Web, a gateway to more than 2,500 libraries around the world
Michigan Electronic Library	`mel.lib.mi.us`	The first virtual library on the Internet, opened in February 1993, built for public libraries in the state of Michigan

continues

Table 12.1   CONTINUED

Site:	URL:	Comments:
My Virtual Reference Desk	`www.refdesk.com`	A family-oriented collection of online reference materials
National Libraries of the World	`www.ifla.org/II/natlibs.htm`	Links to individual countries' national and major libraries
New York Public Library Digital Library Collections	`digital.nypl.org`	Numerous online collections and exhibitions from the NYPL
Public Libraries with WWW Services	`sjcpl.lib.in.us/homepage/PublicLibraries/PubLibSrvsGpherWWW.html`	Links to more than 600 (and growing!) Web sites of U.S. public libraries
School Libraries on the Web	`www.voicenet.com/~bertland/libs.html`	A list of Web pages maintained by K-12 school libraries in the U.S. and around the world
Smithsonian Institution Libraries	`www.sil.si.edu`	Digital collections, electronic journals, and other online services from the Smithsonian Institution
webCATS	`www.lights.com/webcats/`	Major list of library catalogs available on the Web
World Wide Web Virtual Library	`www.vlib.org`	The oldest catalog on the Web, created by Web pioneer Tim Berners-Lee—and the model for Yahoo!'s category-based directory

Finding Older Library Files with Hytelnet

Although many libraries have placed their catalogs on the Web, some libraries still use an older, non-Web standard called *Telnet* to access their OPACs. To access Telnet-based library catalogs, you use a DOS-based utility called *Hytelnet*. You can download a copy of Hytelnet—and find out more information about Hytelnet in general—at `www.lights.com/hytelnet/`.

Why should you add online libraries to your list of research sites? I like library sites for a few reasons:

> ➤ Library sites often provide access to journals and periodicals that you can't find elsewhere.

> ➤ The proprietary collections at the major library sites present unique information in an entertaining fashion.

> ➤ You can use OPACs to streamline your search for hardcopy materials at physical libraries.

A Quick Tour of the Web's Best Libraries

Now let's narrow down our search and take a very quick tour of a half-dozen of the most interesting library sites on the Web.

The Original Online Catalog: The World Wide Web Virtual Library

The World Wide Web Virtual Library (www.vlib.org) is the oldest catalog of the Web. Its pedigree is unparalleled; the Virtual Library was created by Tim Berners-Lee, the creator of the Web itself.

The Virtual Library is essentially a big Web directory, like a proto-Yahoo! This site differs from Yahoo! and other commercial directories, however, in that it is run completely by volunteers, each expert in his or her field. It isn't the biggest directory around, but it has some of the highest-quality listings—and a very academic flavor.

You browse through the Virtual Library the same as you would Yahoo! or any other directory. Just click through the topics and subtopics until you find the links you're looking for.

The First Public Library of the Internet: The Internet Public Library

The Internet Public Library (www.ipl.org) is a project based at the University of Michigan School of Information, staffed by professional librarians with assistance from students and volunteer librarians from around the world. The goal of this project is to create the first public library of the Internet—and they've made good progress toward that goal.

To achieve its goal, the IPL maintains its own collection of reference materials, responds to users' reference-related questions, and evaluates and categorizes Web-based resources. The library also works with other libraries on special projects to determine what will and will not work in the online environment.

The original Web directory—The very academic-oriented World Wide Web Virtual Library.

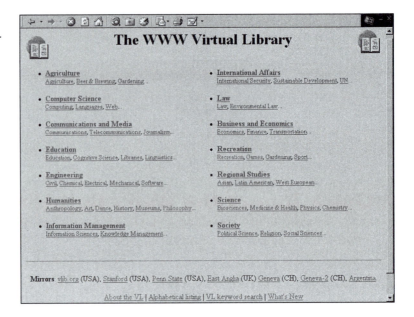

The best way to search the IPL site is to click the **Collections** link on its home page. From there you can choose either to browse or to search a variety of categories, including Ready Reference, Associations, Native Authors, Literary Criticism, Texts, Newspapers, Serials, and Other Text Collections. Special collections exist for Youths and Teens, as well as collections of Librarians' Resources and Great Libraries. In total, the IPL has more than 20,000 individual items in its collections.

Browse through the collections at the Internet Public Library.

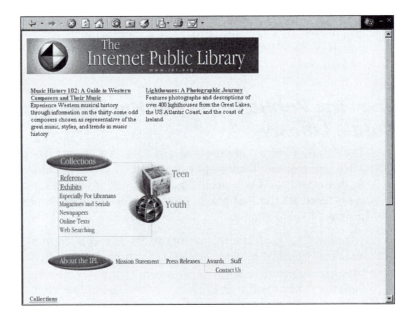

The Premiere College Digital Library: Berkeley Digital Library SunSITE

The UC Berkeley Digital Library (sunsite.berkeley.edu) is one of the Web's largest and most prestigious online libraries. SunSITE, as it's known, not only collects and displays a vast collection of digital content, but it also works with other online libraries to provide information, tools, research, and development support.

What can you find at SunSITE? How about the following collections:

➤ KidsClick! (a database of Internet resources for kids)

➤ Libweb (the single largest directory of library-based Web servers)

➤ The California Heritage Digital Image Access Project

➤ The Emma Goldman Collection

➤ The Librarians' Index to the Internet

➤ The Jack London Collection

➤ The Networked Computer Science Technical Reports Library

➤ The Online Medieval and Classical Library

And that's just a small sampling of what SunSITE offers. Click the **Collections** link to see more of what SunSITE has available.

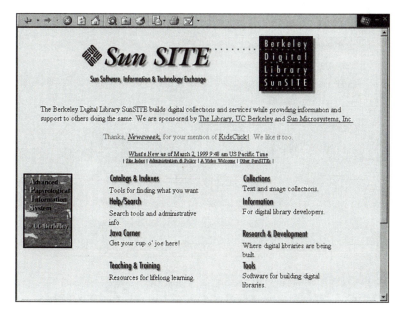

One of the best digital libraries on the Web—UC Berkeley's SunSITE.

The Independent Guide to Web Guides: Argus Clearinghouse

The Argus Clearinghouse (www.clearinghouse.net) was originally created by University of Michigan library staff; today it is one of the premier independent guides to specialized information on the Web. The Clearinghouse is essentially a huge directory to other directories, a collection of reviews and links to the best academic and topic-specific database resources and sites on the Web.

Argus organizes its guides into twelve major categories; you browse through the categories as you would any Web directory. The difference is that Argus provides a well-thought-out review and rating for each of the databases in its listings. (You can also click the **Search/Browse** link to search for specific topics in the Argus Clearinghouse.)

By the way, not all guides and directories make it into the Argus Clearinghouse; this is a fairly exclusive listing. Argus rates its listings on five criteria: level of resource description, level of resource evaluation, guide design, guide organizational schemes, and guide meta-information. Guides are rated on a scale of one to five checks in each category, as well as for the overall guide.

Use the Argus Clearinghouse to look for Web guides to a variety of topics.

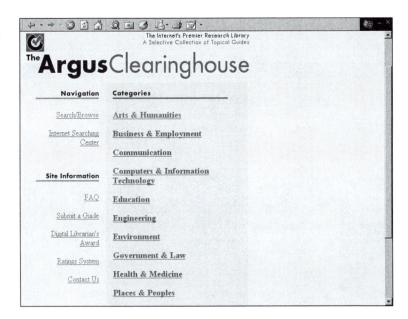

The Nation's Library, Online—The Library of Congress

Now, *this* is a library! The Library of Congress's Web site (lcweb.loc.gov), although huge, provides just a glimpse into the massive collections housed in the nation's library.

What will you find on this Web site? Look for yourself by clicking the **Web Site Map** link. The following is a sampling of what you'll find:

➤ A variety of digital collections and programs, including Religion and Founding of the American Republic; Frank Lloyd Wright: Designs for an American Landscape, 1922-1932; Women Come to the Front: Journalists, Photographers, and Broadcasters During WWII; and The Gettysburg Address

➤ Access to the THOMAS database of current and historical information on the U.S. Congress

➤ American Memory, America's story in words, sounds, and pictures

➤ Current exhibitions

➤ Forms and information from the U.S. Copyright Office

➤ Services for researchers, publishers, educators, students, and the blind and the physically handicapped

➤ Today in History

As gigantic as this site is, it has ambitious plans for further expansion. Today, the National Digital Library Program offers access to key documents, films, photographs, and sound recordings from key periods of the nation's history. By the year 2000, the Library of Congress plans to digitize millions of additional items and make them available on the Internet.

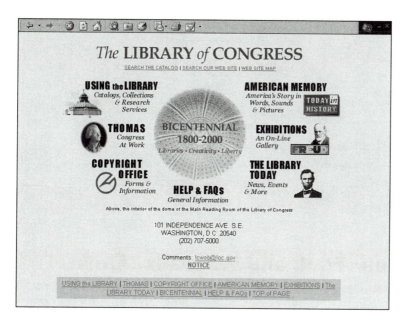

You can either search or browse through the Library of Congress site.

Not All Online Libraries Are Free—The Electric Library

The Electric Library (www.elibrary.com) is a subscription-based online research library run by Infonautics Corporation. This site lets you use plain-English queries to search through full-text articles from thousands of newspapers, magazines, newswires, classic books, maps, photographs, and major works of literature and art.

Although you may balk at the thought of a fee-based library, the Electric Library does a good job of organizing information in a student-friendly fashion. The content is safe and the information up-to-date; it is updated daily via satellite. In fact, this site's target market includes both home users and K-12 schools.

To use the Electric Library, enter your query (in the form of a question) into the search box, select which content you wish to search (magazines, newspapers and newswires, and so on), and click the **Go!** button. When you click the **Search Options** link, you can limit your searches by source type, publication, date, title, and author. The Electric Library returns a prioritized list of results, displaying the document title, source, author, date of publication, size, and grade reading level.

A library you have to pay for—The Electric Library.

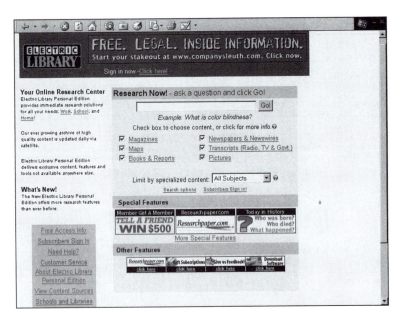

Look It Up in Your Funk and Wagnalls—Online!

An encyclopedia is a great way to look up information. When I was a kid, I used to spend untold hours lying in front of the bookshelf, browsing randomly through the multiple volumes of our family's multi-volume encyclopedia.

148

Today, it's hard to find a print encyclopedia. Most traditional print encyclopedias have migrated to multimedia CD-ROM—and now, some have even made the leap to the Web.

Note, however, that a wide variation exists in what are called online encyclopedias. Some are true online versions of actual print encyclopedias, complete with full-text articles, four-color graphics, and multimedia-enhanced presentations; others are simply Web directories or guides, prettied up with an encyclopedia-like interface.

How do you tell the real online encyclopedias from the imposters? (Not that the imposters are all bad, mind you.) See if you have to pay. The sites with the most proprietary content charge you for it, either on a monthly or yearly subscription basis. The smaller guys don't charge. It's that simple.

That said, Table 12.2 presents some of the more popular online encyclopedia sites along with their relevant information.

Table 12.2 Major Online Encyclopedias

Encyclopedia Site:	URL:	Comments:	Free or Fee?
Encyclopaedia Britannica Online	www.eb.com	Access to the complete text of *Encyclopaedia Britannica*, *Merriam-Webster's Collegiate Dictionary*, the Britannica Book of the Year, and a 130,000-site Web directory. Includes more than 72,000 articles, 10,000 illustrations, and 75,000 definitions	Subscription
Encyclopedia.com	www.encyclopedia.com	Free online encyclopedia with more than 17,000 short articles from *The Concise Columbia Electronic Encyclopedia, 3E*. Presented by the Electric Library	Free
Funk & Wagnalls Knowledge Center	www.fwkc.com	Reference site featuring the *Funk & Wagnalls Multimedia Encyclopedia*, Bridgeman Interactive Art Exhibits, Reuters News Center, and more	Subscription

continues

149

Table 13.2   CONTINUED

Encyclopedia Site:	URL:	Comments:	Free or Fee?
Letsfindout Kids' Encyclopedia	www.letsfindout.com	An online children's encyclopedia from Knowledge Adventure	Free
Microsoft Encarta Online	www.encarta.msn.com	Online version of Microsoft's popular digital encyclopedia	Subscription
My Virtual Encyclopedia	www.refdesk.com/ myency.html	Not a traditional encyclopedia per se; more like a large Web directory, from the My Virtual Reference Desk site	Free

Is it worth subscribing to one of these online encyclopedias? You never know until you try—if you have school-age children, check out one of these sites on a trial basis and see what you think!

The Least You Need to Know

➤ Most traditional libraries allow you to browse their contents online.

➤ Large digital libraries, such as SunSITE and the Internet Public Library, provide complete multimedia collections online.

➤ Major institutions, such as the Library of Congress, are in the process of digitizing their collections for online use.

➤ If you have school-age children, subscription-based online encyclopedias might be an alternative method to provide information for educational use.

Chapter 13

Kill Two Birds with One Stone at Meta-Search Sites

In This Chapter

➤ Discover how meta-search sites can result in more efficient searches

➤ Learn about the most popular meta-search sites

➤ Find out why meta-searches might not always return the best results

One of the problems with today's search engines is that not only do they all work differently, but they all tend to index different parts of the Internet. That is, the 150 million-page index of AltaVista doesn't include all the same sites that are in HotBot's 110 million-page index. Don't ask why; it has to do with the way their different spiders and crawlers work.

You can see this problem by comparing the results of identical queries to different search engines. How often is the number one match at AltaVista the number one match at HotBot or Excite?

If you really want to search the entire Web—or as much of it as is possible—you need to submit your query to multiple search engines. Then, after you have your results from AltaVista, HotBot, Northern Light, and the rest, you can combine and compare the Web page matches from all the engines to get a more complete picture of what is truly available on the Web.

Or you could go to a site that does all that work for you.

Not surprisingly, several sites let you search multiple search engines with a single query, and then combine and organize all the results for you in a single list. These sites are called *meta-search* sites, and they let you do a lot of work in one place.

How Meta-Search Sites Work

Meta-search sites are essentially middlemen. They take your query and deliver it simultaneously to multiple traditional search engines, and then they intercept the multiple results and deliver them back to you—often in a form that compiles the results into a single list.

In my experience, meta-search sites are really good only with simple keyword searches. Because different search sites use different search commands (some use Boolean, some don't, and so on), it's impossible to create a complex query that works the same on every search engine. Although some of the meta-search sites try to interpret more sophisticated queries, they seldom get it right. Therefore, if you want to use a meta-search site, keep your queries simple—and if you need to perform a complex search, skip the meta-search sites!

Should you use a meta-search site? Frankly, I'm not a fan. Although using a meta-search site can be an efficient shortcut for some simple types of searches, I invariably get better qualified results by going directly to the search engines I want to use.

A Meta-Search Site for Names and Addresses

Meta-searches aren't just for Web sites. If you'd like to consolidate your name, address, and phone number searches into a single site, check out The Ultimates (www.theultimates.com). This one site lets you search 25 directories, including WhoWhere, Switchboard, Infospace, and American Directory Assistance, all from a single page. (See Chapters 14 and 15 for more information on searching for street and email addresses.)

Picking a Meta-Search Site

If you do choose to use a meta-search site, be aware that some significant differences exist between the major ones. Some are relatively simple in their operation, you just send your query to the individual sites and they return individual lists of results; others are more "intelligent," trying to interpret your query differently for different sites and combining and compiling the results into a single, more usable list.

In other words, you'll get wildly different results from different meta-search sites—so try before you buy!

Here are some questions you should ask before you choose a meta-search site:

➤ **Which search engines and directories does it query?** Although almost all meta-search sites query the major search engines, some query additional next-generation or specialist search sites—resulting in more possible matches to your query.

➤ **How well does it handle complex queries?** Some meta-search sites attempt to *parse* complex queries to forms that are specific to each search engine it uses. Others simply strip out modifiers and Boolean operators, trying to transform your search into a *lowest-common denominator* query. Still others pass everything you enter onto every search engine, resulting in a lot of garbage in a lot of places. Check the instructions for any particular meta-search site to determine if it handles your queries the way you want them handled.

➤ **How are the results reported?** Some real differences occur here. Some meta-search sites report your results from each search engine individually; others combine the results into a more intelligent single list. Still others actually report results by keywords or phrases. Pick the method you like best.

➤ **Can you customize how and where it searches—or how the results are displayed?** The more flexible meta-search sites let you control which sites are searched, as well as how the results are reported.

More than a dozen meta-search sites are on the Web. The major ones are listed in Table 13.1 along with their key differences and similarities.

Table 13.1 The Major Meta-Search Sites on the Web

Meta-Search Site:	URL:	Searches These Sites:	Results Format:	Other Features:
Dogpile	www.dogpile.com	About.com AltaVista Excite Excite Web Page Guide GoTo.com Infoseek Lycos Lycos Top 5% Magellan PlanetSearch Thunderstone WebCrawler whatUseek Yahoo!	Sorted by search engine; duplicates not eliminated	Also searches Usenet, FTP, various news-wires, stock quotes, Infospace white and yellow pages, maps, and weather

continues

Table 13.1   CONTINUED

Meta-Search Site:	URL:	Searches These Sites:	Results Format:	Other Features:
InferenceFind	www.infind.com	AltaVista Excite Infoseek Lycos WebCrawler Yahoo!	Sorted into subjects (defined by clusters of words or phrases found in results); duplicates eliminated	No other searches available
Internet Sleuth	www.isleuth.com	AltaVista Excite Infoseek Lycos WebCrawler Yahoo!	Sorted by search engine; duplicates not eliminated	Also searches Usenet; includes list of more than 3,000 searchable databases
Mamma	www.mamma.com	AltaVista Excite Infoseek WebCrawler Yahoo!	Consolidates results into single list; duplicates eliminated	Also searches Usenet, MP3, and picture files
MetaCrawler	www.go2net.com/ search.html	About.com AltaVista Excite Infoseek LookSmart Lycos Thunderstone WebCrawler Yahoo!	Consolidates results into single list; duplicates eliminated	Also searches Usenet; includes Channel Searching, which searches specialized Web directories by topic
OneSeek	www.oneseek.com	AltaVista Excite GoTo.com HotBot Infoseek LookSmart Lycos Yahoo!	Displays results one engine at a time or in side-by-side frames; duplicates not eliminated	Also searches Usenet; searches specialized Web directories by topic

154

Meta-Search Site:	URL:	Searches These Sites:	Results Format:	Other Features:
SavvySearch	www.savvysearch.com	About.com AltaVista Direct Hit Excite Galaxy Google GoTo.com HotBot Infoseek LookSmart Lycos Magellan National Directory PlanetSearch Snap Thunderstone User-edited Open Directory WebCrawler Yahoo!	Consolidates results into single list; duplicates eliminated	Also searches specialized Web directories by topic (claims to search more than 200 engines and directories)
Search Spaniel	www.searchspaniel.com	AltaVista Excite HotBot Infoseek Lycos Magellan WebCrawler Yahoo!	Results for each engine are displayed in separate frames within a single browser window; duplicates not eliminated	Also searches Usenet, mailing lists, and downloadable files
SuperSeek	www.super-seek.com	AltaVista Excite HotBot Infoseek LookSmart Lycos Magellan Northern Light Questfinder Search.com WebCrawler Yahoo!	Results for each engine are displayed in separate browser windows; duplicates not eliminated	Selecting all 12 engines, opens 12 separate browser windows on your desktop (!); also includes links to 1,300 specialty Web directories

continues

155

Table 13.1 CONTINUED

Meta-Search Site:	URL:	Searches These Sites:	Results Format:	Other Features:
WebTaxi	www.webtaxi.com	About.com AltaVista AOL NetFind Elibrary EuroSeek Excite Galaxy GoTo.com HotBot Infoseek Inktomi Lycos Lycos Advanced Search Lycos Top 5% Magellan OpenText PlanetSearch Snap WebCrawler whatUseek Yahoo!	Results for each engine are displayed in separate frames within a single browser window; duplicates not eliminated	Standard WebTaxi only searches one engine at a time; click **Supersearch** for cross-engine/ directory searching; also searches Usenet and other specific topics

Another Way to Find Multiple Search Sites

If you don't necessarily want to search multiple sites simultaneously, but you do want access to multiple search sites, each of the following sites list links to all the major (and many minor) search engines and directories, all from a single page:

➤ **Argus Clearinghouse** (www.clearinghouse.net)   A large directory of subject-specific guides, created at the University of Michigan.

➤ **Beaucoup** (www.beaucoup.com)   Lists more than 1,000 search engines and directories.

➤ **Directory Guide** (www.directoryguide.com)   You can search this site for 400 of the top search engines and directories.

➤ **SuperSeek** (www.super-seek.com)   Provides links to 1,300 specialty directories in addition to its meta-search capabilities.

Meta-Tips for Using the Top Meta-Search Sites

The three most popular and powerful meta-search sites are MetaCrawler, Dogpile, and InferenceFind. Let's take a quick look at these sites to see how meta-search sites really work.

Crawling Through Multiple Sites with MetaCrawler

MetaCrawler (www.go2net.com/search.html), part of the Go2Net Network, is the granddaddy of meta-search sites. Developed in 1994, MetaCrawler queries nine other search engines and directories (About.com, AltaVista, Excite, Infoseek, LookSmart, Lycos, Thunderstone, WebCrawler, and Yahoo!), and then organizes the results into a single list, ranked by relevance. In many ways, MetaCrawler is a very typical meta-search site.

When you enter a query into MetaCrawler's search box, you select whether you want to search for **Any** keywords (an OR search), **All** keywords (an AND search), or the exact **Phrase**. You can also use + and – modifiers to include and exclude words and the " " modifier to specify a phrase. Click the **Search** button, of course, to initiate the search.

As with all meta-search engines, these query instructions come with a caveat: Not all search engines used by MetaCrawer support all these modifiers and operators. These modifiers, then, are just suggestions that MetaCrawler uses when trying to tailor your query for each search engine.

To rank the results, MetaCrawler combines the rankings returned by each search engine to generate an overall ranking on a scale of 1 to 1,000. Each result also includes a short description of the site as generated by each of the search engines that mentioned it.

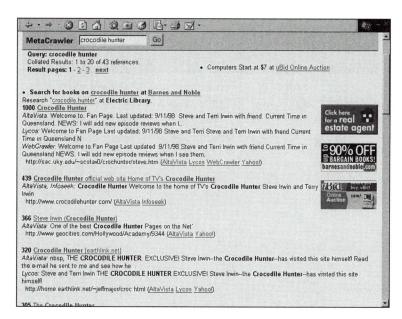

A typical list of search results from MetaCrawler—Results from all nine search engines are compiled and listed in order of importance. (1,000 is a perfect match!)

Searching Smaller Directories with MetaCrawler Channel Search

MetaCrawler also enables you to search a variety of smaller, more specialized search engines and directories. When you click one of MetaCrawler's channel links, you're taken to a *search channel* for that topic. Each search channel incorporates a search function that sends your query to a selected group of topic-specific sites. Note, however, that because these smaller sites do not always specialize in search-engine technology, their results are often less consistent than those found from the general MetaCrawler search.

Dogging the Best Results with Dogpile

Dogpile (www.dogpile.com) is one of the newer meta-search sites. Dogpile's meta-crawler (named Arfie) searches 14 search engines and directories (About.com, AltaVista, Excite, Excite Web Page Guide, GoTo.com, Infoseek, Lycos, Lycos Top 5%, Magellan, PlanetSearch, Thunderstone, WebCrawler, whatUseek, and Yahoo!).

Entering a query is easy; just enter your keywords into the search box and click the **Fetch** button. Dogpile supports the use of Boolean operators AND, OR, NOT, and NEAR, assuming AND if no connectors are present. You can also use " " and parentheses ( ) for exact phrases and word groups.

Remember, of course, that not all search engines support use of all Boolean operators; Dogpile tries to reword your query for those engines that are less than 100 percent compatible.

Although Dogpile supports a large number of search engines, what it does with the results is rather primitive. Unlike MetaCrawler, Dogpile does not combine the results; instead, it lists results from each engine separately (10 at a time), and doesn't eliminate duplicates. In other words, you really don't gain all the potential benefits of a meta-search engine with Dogpile—you might as well query each of the 14 search sites by hand.

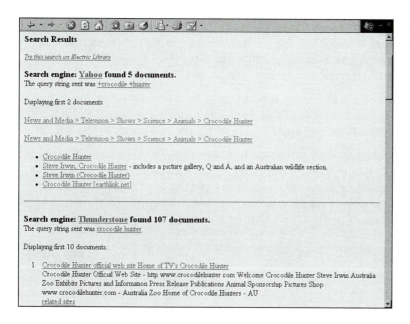

Dogpile's search results, listed engine by engine.

Customize Your Dogpile

When you click Dogpile's **Custom Search** link, you're presented with a form that lets you determine the order in which Dogpile sends your query to its list of search engines. Just choose which search engine you want queried first, second, third, and so on. If you want to exclude a specific engine from your searches, choose the **—skip—** option.

Inferring the Right Results with InferenceFind

MetaCrawler combines its meta-results into one huge ranking; Dogpile presents the results from each engine separately. Believe it or not, a third way exists to present meta-results—and you can find it at InferenceFind.

InferenceFind (www.infind.com) is an interesting critter. It queries only search engines and directories (AltaVista, Excite, Infoseek, Lycos, WebCrawler, and Yahoo!), but then it really works over the results. It merges all the results, removes redundancies, and—this is the neat part—clusters the results into groupings by subtopic.

This clustering is really nothing more than putting similar items together. By grouping results in this fashion, it's easier to see relationships among Web pages that are almost impossible to see in large rankings. If nothing else, you can use the InferenceFind clusters to help you eliminate off-target results!

Searching from InferenceFind's uncluttered home page is very easy—enter your query into the search box and then click the **Go** button. You can use the MaxTime setting to determine how long InferenceFind spends searching; seven seconds is the default.

In terms of modifiers and operators, InferenceFind is honest—it passes your query to each search engine exactly as entered, without trying to "translate" it for different engines. By doing it this way, you can use whatever operators are used by whatever search engines. Note, of course, that because no two search engines use the same modifiers or operators, you're pretty much limited to a straight keyword search.

InferenceFind's search results, grouped by type of site.

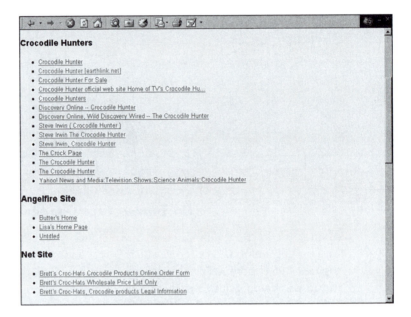

More Meta-Searching, the Software Way

You don't have to use a meta-search site to perform meta-searches; several software programs offer meta-search functions. See Chapter 37, "Let Your Software Do the Searching with Specialized Search Programs," for more information on meta-searching software.

The Least You Need to Know

➤ Meta-search sites send a single query to multiple search engines and directories.

➤ Because different search engines handle queries in different ways, you don't always get as good a result from a meta-search site as you do from going directly to the site itself.

➤ Some meta-search sites group results by search source; others group results by subtopic or keyword; still others combine and compile the results into a single list.

➤ Some of the more popular meta-search sites are MetaCrawler, Dogpile, and InferenceFind.

Part 4

Getting Personal:
How to Find People
and Addresses

*You know how to perform general searches on the general search sites. But what if you're look-
ing for more specific information, such as someone's address or phone number? This part of
the book shows you the personal side of searching, the most effective ways to find information
about people on the Web. Use these chapters when you want to search for street addresses,
phone numbers, email addresses, personal Web pages, and historical family information—or
even someone to go out to dinner with on Friday night!*

Chapter 14

Search for Names, Addresses, and Phone Numbers

In This Chapter

➤ Learn how to look up peoples' street addresses and phone numbers via online white pages directories

➤ Uncover the secret search strategies that will help you find the people you're looking for

➤ Find out how to find out who is registered to a specific phone number—and where they live

➤ Discover some less obvious places to look for people on the Internet

Want to look up an old friend from high school? Wonder whatever happened to a former flame? Need to track down a deadbeat relative?

It's no surprise that one of the more popular types of Web searches involves looking for people—specifically, for people's street addresses and phone numbers.

Although you can search for people using the standard search engines, such as AltaVista or HotBot, chances are you'll find them only if they have their own Web page or are mentioned on someone else's Web page. A much better way to search for people and businesses on the Internet is to use a search engine specifically designed for this purpose.

A Pre-Reunion Reunion

As a personal aside, I used the Internet to locate some old school buddies just before my 20th high school reunion a few years ago; they are people I hadn't heard from in two decades. The search was successful—I was able to contact several of my old friends and spend some quality time with them both before and during the reunion!

Although I used Switchboard for my searches, I could have used a specialized alumni or reunion search site, such as Classmates Online (www.classmates.com), World Alumni Net (www.infophil.com/World/Alumni), or ReunionNet (www.reunited.com).

Picking a White Pages Directory

People listings on the Internet go by the common name of *white pages directories*, the same as traditional white pages phone books. These directories typically enable you to enter all or part of a person's name and then search for his or her address and phone number; in many cases, you can enter the name and a full or partial address to narrow your search.

You definitely want to narrow your search as much as possible. (Just try looking for my name, Michael Miller, without adding any geographic parameters—the list is so long you'll never be able to sort through it!) Enter as much information as you can before you click the **Search** button, and you'll get better results.

Most of the results show you the person's full name, street address, and phone number. Some let you click a link to display a map of that person's neighborhood (a possibly unnerving thought) or to display a list of nearby attractions and businesses. Some even let you send a greeting card or flowers to that person, directly from the search results page!

Just Because It's on the Web Doesn't Mean It's Up-to-Date

Because most Web white pages directories get their information from telephone company listings and traditional white pages phone books, the online listings are only as good and as current as their old-fashioned brethren. That means that some online directories might be three to six months out-of-date—not the kind of instantaneous updating you might expect from Web-based resources—and particularly troublesome if you're looking for the new address of someone who has recently moved.

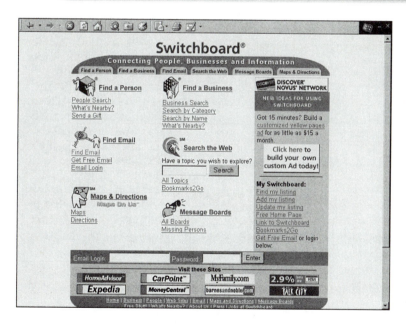

*Switchboard, one of the more popular people searchers on the Web— Click **People Search** to search the white pages directory.*

More than a half-dozen of these white pages directories are present on the Web today. In addition to their capability to search for personal addresses and phone numbers, most of these sites also let you search for personal email addresses (discussed in Chapter 15) and business addresses and phone numbers (discussed in Chapter 19). Table 14.1 lists the major people-search sites on the Web, along with their major features.

Table 14.1   Major Internet White Pages Sites

People Search Site:	URL:	Performs These Types of Searches:	Comments:
411Locate	www.411locate.com	White pages, email, yellow pages, maps, and directions	Not associated with the former Four11 directory (which is now part of Yahoo! People Search)
AnyWho	www.anywho.com	White pages, yellow pages, maps, and directions	A service of AT&T; offers a unique "sounds like" option for "fuzzy searching" of names
Bigfoot	www.bigfoot.com	White pages, email, yellow pages	Basic search only searches by name; click Advanced Search Options for full search capabilities
InfoSpace	www.infospace.com	White pages, email, yellow pages, maps, and directions	Used as a "behind the scenes" people-search engine by many Web portals
International White and Yellow Pages	www.wajens.no	White pages, yellow pages	Individual and business phone listings from around the world—the best site for non-U.S. lookups, from a Norwegian Web site (hence the .no domain name!)
Switchboard	www.switchboard.com	White pages, email, yellow pages, maps, and directions	Includes "What's Nearby?" feature that lists attractions and businesses near the selected address
WhoWhere	www.whowhere.lycos.com	White pages, email, yellow pages, maps, and directions	Part of the Lycos Network
Worldpages	www.worldpages.com	White pages, email, yellow pages, maps, and directions	Includes comprehensive listings of non-U.S. names and addresses
Yahoo! People Search	people.yahoo.com	White pages, email, yellow pages, maps, and directions	Formerly known as Four11; now part of Yahoo!

Which of these sites should you use? Actually, they all function in much the same manner and return pretty much the same results—it's as though most of them feed off the same universal database. Personally, I tend to use either InfoSpace or

Switchboard, but that's more a matter of habit than of deliberate choice. You're probably okay using any of the major sites listed here—just pick the one you feel most comfortable with.

Tips for Searching the White Pages

Whichever white pages directory you're using, some general tips will help you find the people you're looking for:

➤ The more information you enter, the better the results. At the very least, enter a last name and a state (two-letter abbreviation, please). Follow this strategy if you know exactly who you're looking for and have a good idea where they live.

➤ Conversely, the less information you enter, the broader your results. Follow this strategy if you don't have a clue who or what you're really looking for.

➤ If you can't find the person you're looking for, it's either because you entered their information incorrectly, they don't live where you think they live, they moved, or they have an unlisted number.

➤ If you know only part of an item, enter that part. For example, if you're looking for someone named Sherry, enter sherry. If you're not sure whether she goes by Sherry or Sheryl, enter sher. If you're not sure of her first name—but you know it begins with an "s"—enter s. If you don't remember her first name at all, leave the First Name field blank. If the site uses wildcards (check its online Help file, as usual), add a wildcard after the last part of the name you know (sher* or s*, using the above example).

➤ Remember, many women don't list their phone numbers using their full first name—try searching by their first initial, instead.

➤ Many married women don't list their phone numbers with their own name, preferring either to list their husband's name only or to list *both* their names, husband first. If you're looking for a married woman, try looking for her husband, or for lastname, husband and wife.

➤ If you're not sure precisely where someone lives, enlarge your search area. Many of these sites let you select an option to search surrounding towns and regions within a larger metropolitan area; use it!

➤ Don't hesitate to check out each site's advanced search options, where available—often, that's the only place you'll find features such as the metro area search.

Consolidate Your People Searches at a Meta-Search Site

If you'd like to consolidate your name, address, and phone number searches into a single site, a small number of meta-search sites consolidate searches from multiple white pages sites onto a single page. The two most popular meta-search people searchers are

➤ **The Ultimates** (www.theultimates.com) This is one of my favorite search sites, period; it does meta-searching for white pages, yellow pages, and email. For white pages, it searches AnyWho, InfoSpace, Switchboard, WhoWhere, Worldpages, and Yahoo! People Search.

➤ **PeopleSearch** (www.peoplesearch.net) This meta–white pages site searches AOL NetFind, Canada411, Database America, InfoSpace, Internet Address Finder, MIT, Switchboard, WhoWhere, and Yahoo! People Search.

Use The Ultimate White Pages to search six white pages directories simultaneously.

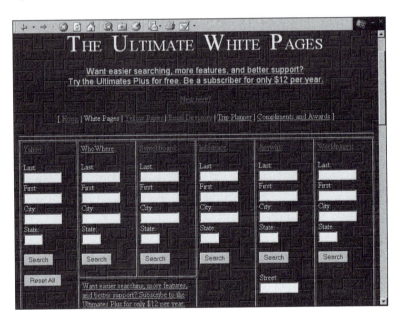

When You Don't Know Who You're Looking For: Perform a Reverse Lookup

If you know a phone number but not a name or address, many of these sites let you conduct a reverse search to find out who is connected to that phone number—and where they live. A dedicated site exists just for reverse phone number lookups, imaginatively titled the Reverse Phone Directory, at www.reversephonedirectory.com.

To perform a reverse search, just enter a valid phone number (including area code). When you click the **Search** button, you'll see the name and address that matches that phone number.

Protecting Privacy

To protect personal privacy, unlisted numbers are not accessible in any of the major white pages directories—and they won't let you do a reverse search from an unlisted number, either.

Look Up the Code!

Want to find out just where a particular area code is? Try FoneFinder (`www.primeris.com/fonefind/`), which lets you enter an area code or phone number and it returns the city, state, and country where that area code operates. Want to check a zip code for a particular area or address? Try the United States Postal Service Zip Code Lookup and Address Information site, at `www.usps.gov/ncsc/`.

When All Else Fails: Other Places to Look for People

A few more places exist that you might not have thought of to look for other Internet users. When all else fails, give these a try.

Ask for Help with People Finder

People Finder (`www.peoplesite.com`) is a Web service that lets you look for people by posting messages publicizing your search. On this site, you **Post a Search**—essentially, post a note on an electronic bulletin board. People access the site, read the notes, and (ideally) help the posters find the people they're looking for.

Notes are filed into one of several categories, such as Friends, Relatives, Genealogy, Veterans, and Loves. Pick the category that best describes your search and cross your fingers that someone browsing this site can help you out!

Hire a Private Dick

If you've exhausted all these means and still can't find who you're looking for, you might check businesses that offer to track down missing people—for a fee. These businesses, essentially Web-based private detective services, use a variety of activities to track down missing persons, perform background checks, and carry out other investigative services.

For example, Find a Friend (`www.findafriend.com`) offers nine search methods to track down friends and relatives, ranging from a last known address search to a national deceased file search, at prices ranging from $20 to $50. Other similar services

171

are Lost Friends (www.lostfriends.com), Infochecks (www.infochecks.com), and 1-800-U.S. Search (www.1800ussearch.com). Use these private detective services when your other searches come up blank—and, of course, when it's worth the money to locate the person you're looking for.

The Least You Need to Know

➤ Web-based white pages directories let you search for people's street addresses and phone numbers.

➤ Most of the white pages sites work pretty much the same; the most popular sites include InfoSpace, Switchboard, and Yahoo! People Finder.

➤ You can perform reverse lookups to find out who is registered to a specific phone number and where they live.

➤ Several meta-search sites exist for white pages lookups, including The Ultimates and PeopleSearch.

➤ Other places to look for people include Usenet newsgroups, instant messaging directories, the AOL membership directory, and online private investigators.

Chapter 15

Search for Email Addresses

In This Chapter

➤ Find out why no universal repository of email addresses is available on the Internet

➤ Discover the most popular email directory sites

➤ Uncover the secret search strategies that help you find the email addresses you're looking for

Looking up names, street addresses, and phone numbers online is relatively easy because that practice is well established—the huge database of names, addresses, and numbers already exists in the offline world. (It's called a telephone directory!) Looking up email addresses, however, is not quite as easy—because no central directory of email addresses exists.

What, you say? Surely a universal directory of email addresses must be available!

Wrong. Sorry.

Every Internet service provider, every commercial online service, almost every Internet domain server issues and controls its own email addresses. Think about that—that's hundreds of thousands of different "gatekeepers," each assigning its own addresses, each keeping its own individual directories. To date, no effort has been successful in getting every single assignor of email addresses to cooperate with every other service or server, thus no central repository of every single email address exists.

Check This Out

SNIFF SNIFF

The One Surefire Way to Find Someone's Email Address:

Ask them for it!

Not that there aren't Web sites you can use to look up email addresses. Unfortunately, these so-called email directories can list only those email addresses that they know about—which typically means addresses provided by major Internet service providers and (in some cases) commercial online services. In addition, many individual sites and domains (such as university servers) let you search for individual email addresses *on their sites*. But no single site exists that consolidates all this disparate information for you to access.

Picking an Email Directory

All that said, this doesn't mean you should give up your search before you get started! Some of the sites that offer email directory services are quite good, all limitations noted, and are worth checking out if you need to find someone's email address.

Many of these email directory sites also offer white pages services (discussed in Chapter 14, "Search for Names, Addresses, and Phone Numbers") and yellow pages services (discussed in Chapter 19, "Search for Businesses"). All let you enter a name or part of a name as your query; some let you enter other information as well, such as phone number, city and state, or company name.

Let me alert you ahead of time—you probably won't like what comes up. Just do a search on my name, Michael Miller, and you'll find thousands of different email addresses—how in the world will you know which one belongs to this particular Michael Miller? (For that reason, I see no need for "unlisted" email addresses—it's just too easy to hide in plain sight!)

Yahoo! People Search's Advanced mode allows some of the narrowest searches for email addresses.

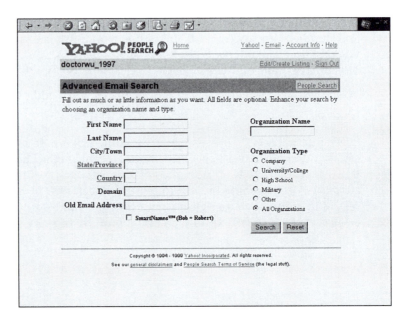

Table 15.1 lists some of the more popular email directories on the Internet.

Table 15.1   Web-Based Email Directories

People Search Site:	URL:	Search Criteria Allowed:
411Locate	www.411locate.com	Search by name, phone number, or company name
Bigfoot	www.bigfoot.com	Search by name only in basic search; click **Advanced Directory Search** to search by city and state
Email Address Book	www.emailbook.com	Search by name only
InfoSpace	www.infospace.com	Search by name, city, state, or country
Internet Address Finder	www.iaf.net	Search by name, organization, or domain
Mailtown	www.mailtown.com	Search by name or city
Switchboard	www.switchboard.com	Search by name only
WhoWhere	www.whowhere.lycos.com	Search by name only in basic search; click **Advanced** to search registered WhoWhere users by city, state, country, school, interests, groups, or profile
World Email Directory	www.worldemail.com	Accepts any freeform search criteria
Worldpages	www.worldpages.com	Search by name or keyword
Yahoo! People Search	people.yahoo.com	Search by name or domain in basic search; click **Advanced** to search by city, state, country, domain, old email address, organization name, or organization type

Which of these sites should you use? More than one is my advice, because the listings in various directories tend to be nonduplicative. That said, if you want the most powerful search, go to Yahoo!'s People Search and use the Advanced mode—it has the most search parameters of any email directory site.

Not Every Directory Is a Big Directory

Be aware that some email directory sites search only for email addresses that users have manually entered into their own proprietary directories. Although that results in some highly qualified listings (people had to deliberately enter their own information), the quantity of listings often leaves something to be desired.

Tips for Finding Email Addresses

Here are some tips you can use to improve your odds of finding the email address you're looking for.

Not Sure of the Name?

If you're not sure of a name (for example, is it Rick or Richard?), most directories let you use the * wildcard. For example, if you want to search for someone whose first name starts with the letter R, enter R*. Such a search returns any name starting with R, including Rick and Richard, as well as Robert and Rudolph.

Search More Than One Directory

Even though many email directories aggregate addresses from many sources to create rather large listings, no single directory lists every possible email address. For every one email address returned, dozens more may exist that are not listed.

In addition, thousands of new email addresses are issued daily—and thousands more older addresses get cancelled. It's hard for any site to keep up with this level of email "churn." So, if you can't find the person you're looking for at one directory, try another!

Use a Meta-Search Engine

Because no single email directory includes every single email address, try using a meta-search engine to search multiple email directories simultaneously. One of the better meta-mail sites is my.email.address.is (my.email.address.is), which searches America Online, Bigfoot, Internet Address Finder, Switchboard, InfoSpace, WhoWhere, World Internet Directory, and Yahoo! People Finder. For a global meta-mail site, check out MESA MetaEmailSearchAgent (mesa.rrzn.uni-hannover.de),

176

which queries Bigfoot, Internet Address Finder, and Yahoo! People Finder, in addition to non-U.S. directories such as Populus, SwissInfo, and suchen.de.

Do the University Search

If you're looking for a college student or a faculty member, the best place to look is on that university's Internet site. Check out the College Email FAQ (`www.qucis.queensu.ca/FAQs/email/college.html`) for some very detailed information on how to find email addresses for undergraduate and graduate students, faculty, and staff at various colleges and universities worldwide.

Search for Posters in Usenet Newsgroups

You can use DejaNews (`www.dejanews.com`) to search for the email addresses of people who have posted Usenet newsgroup articles. See Chapter 25, "Search for Usenet Newsgroup Articles," for more detailed instructions on how to search the DejaNews site.

Note, however, that many people who post in newsgroups do not use their real names, preferring aliases instead. It's hard to search for someone who's using an alias!

Why All the Secrecy?

You might wonder why posters to Usenet newsgroups wouldn't want to reveal their identities along with their opinions. In a few cases, the reasons might be obvious, such as people posting inappropriate material. However, Usenet is known as a fertile ground for spammers to collect email addresses for sending junk email. So savvy users usually disguise their real addresses.

Sometimes, however, they simply add the word "nospam" to the address, as in "joeblow@nospam.aol.com." Just remove the "nospam" and you have the right address.

Search for Instant Messagers

If you have the ICQ instant messaging program installed on your computer, you can use it to search for other users of the ICQ service—and given the fact that more than 16 million people use ICQ regularly, that's a large base of users to search through! Go to ICQ's home page (www.icq.com) to search through the ICQ PeopleSpace directory. You can search based on name, location, special interest, or other criteria.

If you use ICQ's competitor, AOL Netscape Instant Messenger, you can perform a similar search of Instant Messenger users.

Search AOL Subscribers

Another good source of email addresses—tens of millions of them, actually—is the list of subscribers to America Online. This is surprisingly useful because many AOL members aren't listed in other, more traditional Internet directories or databases.

If you're an AOL member, you can search for other AOL members by clicking the **People** button, selecting **Search AOL Member Directory**, and entering your query in the Member Directory dialog box. If you're not a subscriber—sorry, AOL only lets members search for other members.

Search Hotmail Subscribers

Hotmail (www.hotmail.com) is the largest provider of free Web-based email, with millions of members. If you're a Hotmail subscriber, you can search the Hotmail Member Directory to locate other Hotmail subscribers. Just click the Hotmail Member Directory link at the top of your In-Box page and go from there; you can search by first name or last name, and you can focus your search to members in specific countries.

If you're not a Hotmail subscriber, you don't have access to this directory. (But since a Hotmail account is free, why not join just so you can search through their member lists?)

Find Old Email Addresses

One problem with trying to find email addresses is that people change addresses very frequently. Change jobs, get a new email address. Change Internet service providers, get a new email address. Move to a new city, get a new email address.

How do you keep track of all these changing addresses?

Several sites purport either to track email address changes or to notify others when your address changes. These sites include the following:

➤ EmailChange.com (www.emailchange.com)

➤ EmailFinder (www.emailfinder.com)

➤ Find mE-Mail (www.findmemail.com)

Find Celebrity Email Addresses

Want to find the email address for your favorite celebrity? Then check out Chip's Celebrity Home and Email Addresses (www.addresses.site2go.com), which has one of the larger lists of supposedly valid celebrity email addresses.

Another site to look at is Celebrity Email (www.celebrityemail.com). This site lists email addresses for some celebrities, but its unique feature is that it lets you enter a message to your celebrity of choice, and then it sends the message on your behalf, using either email or snail mail.

Beware, however, that people sometimes use email addresses designed to resemble celebrity names, either as a tribute or for fraudulent purposes.

The Least You Need to Know

➤ No universal repository of email addresses exists—which means it is very difficult, if not impossible, to be certain of finding any individual email address on the Internet.

➤ Numerous email directories exist on the Internet, although none of them list every email address currently in use.

➤ The most popular email directories include Bigfoot, InfoSpace, and Internet Address Finder; the most powerful email search engine is Yahoo! People Search's Advanced mode.

➤ To increase your odds of finding an email address, search multiple directories or use a meta-search engine such as my.email.address.is.

Chapter 16

Search for Personal Web Pages

In This Chapter

➤ Discover which sites list or let you search for personal Web pages

➤ Learn about the largest home-page community sites on the Web

➤ Uncover the secret search strategies that will help you find the personal home pages you're looking for

I am continually amazed at the number of people who are creating their own personal Web pages. It seems like every other person with an Internet connection is staking out a home on the Net!

These personal Web pages range from amateurish to highly professional. Some creators use the built-in forms and templates to add their pages to so-called home-page communities; others use professional HTML editing software (such as Microsoft FrontPage) to build slick and sophisticated pages that rival those from commercial Web sites. Some users even pay for their own domain name to put their own stamp on their personal pages.

(By the way, that's what I did. Check out my personal pages at www.molehillgroup. com—created with Microsoft FrontPage—and leave me an email to tell me what you think!)

Because of this proliferation of personal pages, you have another place to look for people on the Internet.

Searching for Home-Page Directories and Search Engines

How do you find personal home pages on the Web? First, you can search for them using a general search engine or directory; just enter the person's name into AltaVista or Yahoo! and see what you get.

This approach is a little broad, however, especially when Web sites are available that specialize in either listing or finding home pages created by individuals. Some of these sites are proprietary directories where users have to manually list their sites; others are search engines fine-tuned to find personal pages.

Table 16.1 lists some of the major home-page search sites on the Web, and you can see an example site, WhoWhere, nearby.

Table 16.1   Personal Home-Page Search Engines and Directories

Site:	URL:	Comments:
One Nation Worldwide	www.onww.com	Directory of personal pages links
Personal Home Page Directories	www.bltg.com/people/	Directory of personal pages links
Personal Pages Worldwide	www.utexas.edu/world/personal/index.html	Links to collections of personal pages at colleges and universities worldwide
Student Homepages	www.westegg.com/students/	Lists student pages from more than 300 colleges
Student.com Personal Page Direct	www.student.com/feature/ppd	Searches personal pages of college students across U.S. by school
The Meeting Place	www.nis.net/meet/	Links to personal home pages, by special interest categories
WhoWhere	homepages.whowhere.com	Search engine and directory—the best place to search across the entire Web

Of all these directories and search engines, my personal recommendation is WhoWhere (homepages.whowhere.com). WhoWhere lets you browse personal pages and collections of personal pages by category, as well as search by keyword (a person's name or interests, for example).

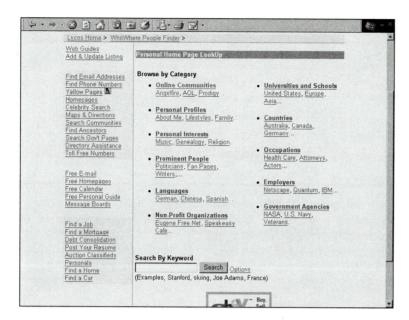

The WhoWhere Personal Home Pages Directory— the best general search engine on the Web for personal home pages.

WhoWhere is also good for searching the member directories of individual home-page communities. Just click the **Online Communities** link and select the community (AngelFire, GeoCities, and so on) you wish to search. You can then browse through the members of that community by location or by interest.

Go Directly to the Source: Search the Home-Page Communities

Many, many sites allow users to post their personal Web pages. Most Internet service providers offer this service, as well as many commercial online services and Web portals. In addition, many educational institutions, from K-12 to college, let their students create their own Web pages—as do many large businesses.

That said, the most popular sites for personal home pages are the so-called *home-page community* sites, such as GeoCities and Tripod. These sites exist solely to host personal Web pages—and they do it for free, making their money by selling advertising on the site. Some of these sites have millions of members, making them good places to look for specific personal home pages.

Table 16.2 lists some of the more popular home-page communities on the Web.

Table 16.2   Major Personal Home-Page Communities

Home-Page Community:	URL:
AngelFire	www.angelfire.com
GeoCities	www.geocities.com
Hometown AOL	hometown.aol.com
iVillage Personal Home Pages	pages.ivillage.com
The Globe	www.theglobe.com
Tripod	www.tripod.com

Most of these communities have some facility to let you either search or browse through the home pages of their community members. For example, as you can see in the illustration, GeoCities puts its search box right at the top of its home page—just enter a member name, select the **GeoCities** option, and click the **Find** button.

Search for member home pages directly from the GeoCities home page.

Creating Your Own Home Page

You can create your own home page in two basic ways: use the tools and templates provided by a home-page community, such as GeoCities, or use a professional HTML program (such as FrontPage) to create your own pages, and then post them to a home-page community or other hosting site. Either option is fairly easy to do because even the most advanced HTML software programs include templates and wizards that help beginning users get started. Whichever way you proceed, you need to follow the instructions from your hosting site to make sure your pages get posted properly.

If you want to obtain your own personal domain name (so that your Web page address reads www.*myaddress*.com), check first with your Web page hosting service; most services and ISPs can do all the legwork for you. You can also use a separate registration service, such as Register.com (www.register.com), or you can register directly with the official InterNIC Registration Services site (www.internic.net). Bear in mind that, although posting a Web page is often free, fees are associated with registering a domain name.

Tips for Personal Home-Page Hunting

➤ If you don't know where to start, start with the WhoWhere Personal Home-Pages Directory (homepages.whowhere.com). This is simply the most comprehensive home-pages search engine and directory on the Web.

➤ If you want to search the home-page communities directly, start with GeoCities (www.geocities.com), which is the biggest. Next in size are Tripod and AngelFire, followed by The Globe and iVillage.

➤ If you know which online service or Internet service provider is used by the people you're looking for, you can always look there. For example, if they're AOL members, chances are their home pages are on the Hometown AOL site (hometown.aol.com). If they get their service through EarthLink, search the EarthLink community of Web pages at www.earthlink.net. (Just look at a person's email domain name—the part after the "dot"—to see who the ISP is. For example, the address mmiller@earthlink.net indicates that I get my Internet service from EarthLink.)

➤ If you're looking for a college student's home page, go directly to that college's Web site—most college sites let you search for pages created by their students.

➤ If you want to use one of the major search sites to search for an individual's personal home page, add the words **personal home page** to your query, to help narrow the results.

➤ Don't forget, you can often find people by searching on their interests. For example, if I create a personal home page that mentions my interest in animation art, searching on **animation art** can turn up my personal page.

The Least You Need to Know

➤ Millions of personal home pages are on the Web, created by individuals just like you and me.

➤ You can use a variety of directories and search engines to search for specific personal pages; the best place to start searching is WhoWhere.

➤ All the major home-page communities, such as GeoCities and Tripod, let you search through the millions of personal Web pages on their sites.

Chapter 17

Search for Your Family's Roots

In This Chapter

➤ Learn which Web sites can help you advance your genealogical research

➤ Find out about FamilySearch, a Web site from the Mormon Church that contains a huge amount of genealogical data

➤ Discover Usenet newsgroups and email mailing lists where you can search for others with your surname

➤ Uncover the secret search strategies that help you find the family information you're looking for

Genealogy is both fun, important, and a really big deal. By one count, over 19 million families are in the process of researching and documenting their roots, and the Internet is a great source of information for this process.

Thousands of Web sites are devoted to genealogical research, and a tremendous amount of information is available online. You can find things like surname databases, the Social Security death index, some directories of public records, and tons of other links and data.

The Internet, however, can't be your *only* source of information. For example, many physical records of value to a researcher are not yet available on the Internet. These include birth certificates, marriage certificates, death certificates, land grants and warrants, census records, and military records—all public records, but none accessible via the Internet at this point in time.

So, while researching your family's roots can be very time-consuming (but fun!), you can get a lot of help with the information you can find when searching the Internet!

Searching for Genealogy Resources on the Web

The first places to turn in your genealogical research are the general Web search engines and directories. Sites such as AltaVista and Yahoo! list a large number of sites containing genealogical information. In addition, you can always do a search on your family's surname to turn up personal Web pages from individuals who might help you in your research.

Beyond these basic resources, a large number of genealogy-related sites are available on the Web—so many that it can be somewhat overwhelming. Interestingly, the vast majority of these sites are run by amateur genealogists and include both general information as well as information specific to their family lineage. Some of these sites are remarkably comprehensive and informative, and they are definitely worth checking out, such as Cyndi's List, shown here.

Cyndi's List of Genealogy Sites—a must-see amateur site with one of the largest lists of genealogy-related resources on the Web.

Also, a number of commercial genealogy sites are available; some are free and others are fee-based. Because genealogy is big business, these sites are good first-stops on your search for genealogical information; they contain informative articles and vast databases of information. Ancestry.com, shown here, is one example.

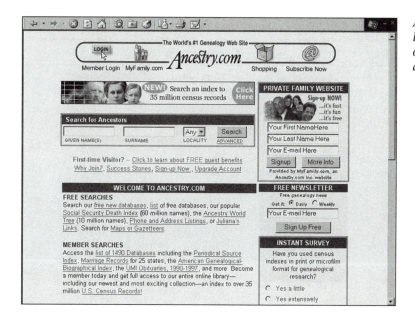

Ancestry.com, one of the largest commercial genealogy sites, has many useful databases and indexes.

Table 17.1 lists some of the larger and more popular amateur and commercial genealogy-related sites on the Web.

Table 17.1 Genealogy Sites on the Web

Site:	URL:	Comments:
Ancestry.com	www.ancestry.com	One of the largest genealogy sites on the Web; includes an index of 35 million census records, a 60-million name Social Security death index, the Ancestry World Tree (10 million names), and 1,490 other databases; some services accessible to members only
Common Threads	www.gensource.com/ common/	A large, searchable database of surnames
Cyndi's List of Genealogy Sites on the Internet	www.cyndislist.com	A marvelous, award-winning amateur site with more than 41,600 genealogy-related links, sorted into more than 100 categories (such as Adoption, African-American, Books, Cemeteries & Funeral Homes, Heraldry, The Middle East, Personal Home Pages, and Wills & Probate)

continues

Table 17.1 CONTINUED

Site:	URL:	Comments:
Family History Research Register	symbiosis.uk.com/ fhistory/	A searchable surname registry containing almost 50,000 names
FamilySearch	www.familysearch.org	A massive collection of genealogical information gathered by the Mormon Church—*recommended*
Genealogical Research at the National Archives	www.nara.gov/ genealogy/genindex.html	Presents all the resources and research tools available at the U.S. government's National Archives and Records Administration (NARA), including immigration records, naturalization records, Civil War records, WWI records, passport applications, and more
Genealogy Home Page	www.genhomepage.com	Good general listing of genealogy resources
Genealogy Online	www.genealogy.org	A full-service genealogy site, including online chat and a surname database
Genealogy Resources on the Internet	members.aol.com/ johnf14246/internet. html	An amateur site listing a variety of Internet-based genealogy resources including mailing lists, Usenet newsgroups, FTP sites, Web sites, Telnet sites, and so on
Genealogy.com	www.genealogy.com	A genealogy supersite with various directories, Social Security death index, and a variety of news and informational articles
Rootsweb	www.rootsweb.com	The Internet's oldest genealogy site, with a large surname list, downloadable files, and lists of related mailing lists
Vital Records Information	www.vitalrec.com	Helpful information on how to obtain U.S. records vital to genealogical research—including birth, death, and marriage certificates—in all 50 states

I suggest you visit several of these sites and browse through the links from these sites to other genealogy sites, as well. *Somewhere* in this mass of information is the data you're looking for!

FamilySearch: A Really Big Deal in Genealogical Research

There's a new site on the Web that has genealogists going ga-ga. ("It's really breathtaking" and "It's going to change the way we do business" are two quotes from a recent article about the site.) The site, managed by the Church of Jesus Christ of Latter-Day Saints, is called FamilySearch, and it promises to revolutionize genealogical research on the Internet.

FamilySearch (www.familysearch.org) presents several one-of-a-kind collections that have not been widely available up until now—and they're all free to the public. Among the church databases either already online or slated to go live soon are:

➤ **Ancestral File**, with 35 million names organized by family.

➤ **Family History Library Catalog**, with more than two million rolls of microfilm and hundreds of thousands of books and maps.

➤ **International Genealogical Index**, with 285 million names extracted from public records.

➤ **SourceGuide**, containing more than 150 research outlines, a glossary of word meanings, and a Catalog Helper to help you find the best subjects when searching a catalog.

In addition, the site includes links to literally thousands of other relevant Web sites, and collaboration mailing lists maintained by other FamilySearch users.

Serious genealogists have been accessing the Mormons' data for some time, through their 3,200 Family History Centers located around the world. But this is the first time that their massive collection of information has been available to a wider audience, over the Internet. This site is truly a treasure trove for those serious about documenting their family histories.

Searching Usenet Newsgroups for Genealogy Data

Another source of genealogical data is Usenet. Usenet newsgroups let you post and read articles about specific topics; a large number of newsgroups are devoted to genealogical topics. (See Chapter 25, "Search for Usenet Newsgroup Articles," for more information on using and searching through Usenet newsgroups.)

Table 17.2 presents a list of genealogy-related newsgroups.

Table 17.2   Genealogy-Focused Usenet Newsgroups

Newsgroup:	Description:
alt.adoption	For adoptees, birthparents, and adoptive parents
alt.genealogy	General genealogy topics
alt.scottish.clans	General discussions about Scottish clans
alt.war.civil.usa	General discussions about the Civil War era
dk.historie.genealogi	Dutch genealogy
fido.eur.genealogy	European genealogy
fido.ger.genealogy	German genealogy
fr.rec.genealogie	French genealogy
no.slekt	Norwegian genealogy
no.slekt.etterlysning	Norwegian relative/ancestor searches
rec.heraldry	General discussions about heraldry
sfnet.harrastus.sukututkimus	Finnish genealogy
soc.genealogy.african	African genealogy
soc.genealogy.australia+nz	Australian and New Zealand genealogy
soc.genealogy.benelux	Benelux genealogy
soc.genealogy.britain	British genealogy
soc.genealogy.computing	Genealogical computing and Internet resources
soc.genealogy.french	French genealogy
soc.genealogy.german	German genealogy
soc.genealogy.hispanic	Hispanic genealogy
soc.genealogy.ireland	Irish genealogy
soc.genealogy.italian	Italian genealogy
soc.genealogy.jewish	Jewish genealogy
soc.genealogy.marketplace	Commercial genealogy programs and services
soc.genealogy.medieval	Medieval genealogy
soc.genealogy.methods	Genealogical methods and resources
soc.genealogy.misc	General genealogical discussions
soc.genealogy.nordic	Nordic genealogy
soc.genealogy.slavic	Slavic genealogy
soc.genealogy.surnames	Surname queries
soc.genealogy.surnames.britain	British surname queries
soc.genealogy.surnames.canada	Canadian surname queries
soc.genealogy.surnames.german	German surname queries
soc.genealogy.surnames.global	Global surname queries

Table 17.2   CONTINUED

Newsgroup:	Description:
soc.genealogy.surnames.ireland	Irish surname queries
soc.genealogy.surnames.misc	Surname queries for regions not covered elsewhere
soc.genealogy.surnames.usa	American surname queries
soc.genealogy.uk+ireland	General United Kingdom surname queries
soc.genealogy.west-indies	Caribbean genealogy
soc.history.moderated	General historical discussions

You can use these newsgroups to discover general information or to ask specific questions pertaining to your own family search. (Note, however, that some of these are foreign-language newsgroups—which is great when you're researching your pre-U.S. ancestry, but problematic if you don't speak the language!)

Don't Forget the Mailing Lists!

Mailing lists are similar to Usenet newsgroups, but take place via normal email correspondence. You have to subscribe to a mailing list to receive messages from other members. You can find a list of genealogy-related mailing lists both at Rootsweb (www.rootsweb.com/~maillist/) and Genealogy Resources on the Internet (users.aol.com/johnf14246/gen_mail.html). Remember that you can sometimes subscribe to a digest, or collection of messages, rather than receiving many separate messages.

Tips for Successful Genealogy Searches

As you start searching for family-specific and general genealogical information on the Internet, keep these tips in mind:

➤ **Work backward**   As you're researching your family history, it's best to start with yourself and then work backward in time—it's a lot easier than trying to pick the right immigrant with your surname from thousands of likely candidates!

➤ **Search for surnames**   Use the databases at commercial genealogy Web sites, the mailing lists at Rootsweb (www.rootsweb.com/~maillist/), or targeted Usenet newsgroups to search for others with your family's surname.

➤ **Check for variations**   Back in 1790, the U.S. Census listed 3,661 different surnames, but these surnames encompassed 20,051 spelling variations—which means, of course, that you should research not only your proper surname, but also any logical variations on that surname. For example, the letter "a" in your name could show up as either "ai" or "ae"; the letter "s" could turn into "sc" or "z." Make sure you've thought of all variations before you start your search!

➤ **Look for the vital records—on and off the Internet**   Some of the best data comes from public records, such as birth certificates, marriage certificates, and death certifications—few of which are available on the Internet, unfortunately. (You have to use more traditional means—such as letter writing and phone calls to public officials—to obtain these types of documents. However, you can always search the Internet to find the right address or phone number.)

➤ **Create your own home page**   One last way to augment your genealogical research is to create your own personal Web page. This way, others who are doing similar research can find you—just as you might be looking for them!

Expand Your Search with Genealogy Software

A plethora of genealogy software programs is available to help you on your trip through your family tree. Some of the more popular packages include the following:

➤ Ancestral Quest

➤ Ancestry Reference Library

➤ Family Tree Maker

➤ Generations

➤ Master Genealogist

➤ Parson's Family Origins

➤ Ultimate Family Tree

You can find many of these products at your local computer software store or online at the Ancestry.com online store (www.ancestry.com/software/index.htm).

The Least You Need to Know

➤ You can use traditional search engines and directories to search for others with your surname, as well as to search for general genealogical information.

➤ Some of the best genealogy sites are run by amateurs, such as Cyndi's List of Genealogy Sites.

➤ Of the full-service commercial genealogy sites, the most popular are Ancestry.com, Genealogy.com, Genealogy Online, and Rootsweb.

➤ You can also use select Usenet newsgroups and email mailing lists to search for others with your surname

Chapter 18

Search for Love

In This Chapter

➤ Discover why online personal ads are an increasingly popular way to meet new people

➤ Learn which sites are the most popular for online romance

➤ Uncover the secret search strategies that will help you find an interesting date—or the love of your life—and see through the phonies

Searching the Internet is a lonely activity. It's you, your PC, and lots and lots of data somewhere on the Internet. That's all.

Except...

The Internet is actually a great way to meet people. The age-old concept of personal ads has found a new home—online. Using typical search functions, numerous sites exist where you can both place and browse through personal ads from other Internet users. Whether you're looking for a pen pal, a casual date, a more intimate relationship, or something more long-lasting, you can find that special person through an online personal ad.

Get Personal: The Best Personals Sites on the Web

Three types of personals sites are available on the Web:

➤ **Full-service singles sites**   These sites, such as Swoon and Flirt, offer complete communities for singles, including news, information, message boards, chat rooms, informative articles, and (last but not least) personal ads. These sites typically do not have the largest quantity of ads available for browsing and may not always be organized by locality.

➤ **General classified advertising sites**   These sites, such as Yahoo! Personals and Classifieds 2000 (shown here), offer a variety of types of classified advertisements, from apartment rentals to snow blowers to personals. Although these sites are always organized by locality, they're also totally nonmoderated. That, combined with high traffic, results in a large number of ads to browse, but also includes a lot of sex-spam and irrelevant postings.

➤ **Dedicated personal ad sites**   These sites do nothing but personal ads. Some are free, some charge fees; some are general interest, some are organized by special interest; some are organized by locality, some are not. In general, these sites have the highest-quality, most-qualified ads.

Getting ready to search the personal ads at the Classifieds 2000 Personals site.

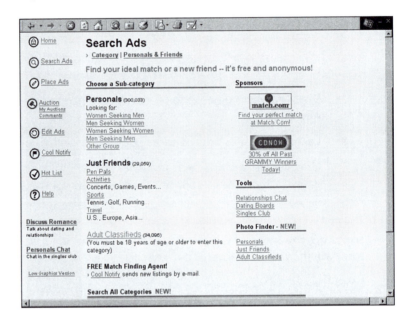

It's tough to say that one kind of site gives you better results than another. The higher quality of the dedicated sites is often counterbalanced by the larger number of listings coming through the classified ad sites. In my personal experience, I've arranged dates with people whom I met at all three kinds of sites, so it's kind of a toss-up—give each one a spin and see what you think!

To help you find the right site to search, Table 18.1 lists some of the more popular sites for personal ads.

Table 18.1   Web Sites for Personal Ads

Site:	URL:	Comments:
Classifieds 2000 Personals	www.classifieds2000.com	Free personal ads (click the **Personals and Friends** link); includes separate Adult Personals category
CyberMatch Worldwide	www.cmww.com	Fee-based personal ads, all with photos
Flirt	www.flirt.com	A "romance channel" with fee-based personal ads for singles
Friendfinder	www.friendfinder.com	A network of fee-based personals sites for various types of singles; includes the basic Friendfinder site (for all singles), SeniorFriendFinder (for the 50+ community), OutPersonals.com (for gays), and Adult Friend Finder (for more sexually oriented encounters, at the separate adult.friendfinder.com address)
Internet Personals	www.montagar.com/personals/	Free personal ads
Lovecity	www.lovecity.com	Fee-based personal ads
Match.com	www.match.com	Fee-based personal ads
Matchmaker	www.matchmaker.com	A network of fee-based sites focused both on locality and on interest (Christian Connection, Teen Talk, College Connection, Silver (>40), Gay/Lesbian lifestyles, Nudist lifestyles, and so on)
MeetMeOnline	www.meetmeonline.com	Free personal ads
Netscape Netcenter Personals	digitalcity.netscape.com/personals/	Free personal ads
One and Only Internet Personals	www.one-and-only.com	Free personal ads
Romance Makers	www.romancemakers.com	Free personal ads
Swoon	www.swoon.com	A "dating, mating, and relating" site, complete with free personal ads
Webpersonals	www.webpersonals.com	Includes three fee-based sites: Avenia (for straight men and women), Manline (for gay males), and Womanline (for gay females)
Yahoo! Personals	personals.yahoo.com	Free personal ads

Flirt, a fun site for young singles—offering much more than just personal ads.

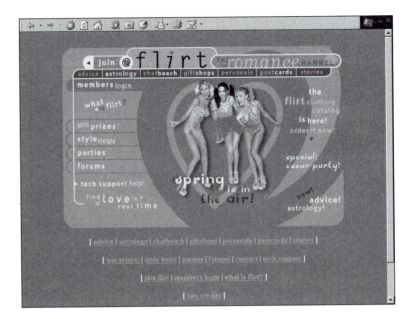

Tips and Strategies for Finding Someone to Love—Online

The following are some tips to keep in mind when you access online personal ads:

➤ **Watch out for sex-spam**   On the sites that offer free ads, you'll find a lot of ads for sex sites masquerading as personal ads. This sex-spam is highly annoying but easily identifiable. Typically, the ad offers something just too good to be true (an 18-year-old girl looking for hot sex with fat, 50-year-old men, for example), and often includes a link to another site. If the personal ad reveals the email address of the poster, the message usually requests that replies not go to that address. Although some legitimate advertisers do have their own personal Web pages (and link to them in their personal ads), most of these links are to fee-based sex sites—*not* to real people!

➤ **Qualify the advertisers**   In general, the sites that charge membership or listing fees offer better-qualified lists of potential dates or mates, although the fees often result in a smaller selection of advertisers. The more classified ad sites, such as Yahoo! and Classifieds 2000, typically have a lot of listings but contain a lot of noise and sex-spam.

➤ **Beware of hidden fees**   Some sites let you browse or even list your ads for free, but start in with the fees when you actually want to contact someone. Don't get suckered!

BTW, Just What Do All Those Darned Abbreviations Mean?

When you first start reading the personal ads, you'll see a lot of acronyms and abbreviations. If you don't know what they mean, you could end up with a very surprising date! Here's a short list of the more common abbreviations:

Abbreviation:	Means This:
S	Single
D	Divorced
F	Female
M	Male
W	White
B	Black
H	Hispanic
A	Asian
C	Christian
Bi	Bisexual
G	Gay
n/s	Nonsmoker
l/s	Light smoker
n/d	Non-drinker
l/d	Light drinker
d/d free	Drug- and disease-free
TAN	Tested AIDS negative
HPTW	Height proportionate to weight
LTR	Long-term relationship
ISO	In search of

If you see a listing, for example, that reads "SWPF HPTW ISO n/s GAM for LTR," it means that a single, white, professional female, whose height is proportionate to her weight, is in search of a nonsmoking, gay, Asian male for a long-term relationship. (Undoubtedly as costars of a wacky new sitcom!) Easy, isn't it?

➤ **Browse locally, if possible**   Really, most people don't want to find out that their perfect match lives 500 miles away. Use the parameters within a given site to narrow your search to people in your specific region. Some sites provide lists of major cities that you can click to browse ads for that locality.

➤ **Play it safe**   It's best to be cautious when corresponding with and ultimately meeting people you find through online personal ads. For example, you don't have to give out your real email address; on many sites you can elect to send your replies anonymously, or you can use an alternative email address (see the next tip). Withhold personal information such as your address and phone number until you are sure you trust the other person—which could be after several offline meetings. If you decide to physically meet someone after corresponding with them, choose a public place during the daytime and make sure one of your friends knows where you are. *Don't* meet someone at his or her home on the first date—keep it public, keep it casual, and always have an "escape" planned if things don't turn out as you'd like.

➤ **Use an alternative email address**   If you don't want to give out your normal email address, use one of the free, Web-based email services (such as HotBot, at www.hotbot.com) to create a second email address under an assumed name. This way no one can trace your email address back to you and your real physical address.

Above all, take it easy and have fun. Don't set your hopes too high—chances are the next ad you respond to will not be your soulmate, although it could be someone who might lead to an interesting and enjoyable casual date or a lengthy and entertaining exchange of email.

Online Chat—A Live Alternative to Personal Ads

Another place to meet people online is on an online chat room or channel. These services let you engage in real-time "conversation" with other users, via text messages sent live to other users in the channel. Learn more about online chat in Chapter 26, "Search for Mailing Lists and Chat Rooms." The cautions I listed earlier still apply, of course.

The Least You Need to Know

➤ Three types of sites contain personal ads: full-service singles sites, general classified-ad sites, and dedicated personal-ad sites.

➤ The most popular sites for classified ads include Classifieds 2000 Personals, Flirt, Matchmaker, One and Only Internet Personals, and Yahoo! Personals.

➤ If you know all the codes, search the right sites, confine your search to local ads, and take the proper precautions, making a date with someone you met online can be fun and safe.

Part 5

Getting Down to Business: How to Find Business and Financial Information

Sure, you can find business information through the general search sites. But if you want really detailed business information—including historical financials and the inside poop on management moves and insider trading—then you have to go to some business-specific Web sites that store a ton of important corporate information. This part of the book shows you how to hunt for that important business information—and how to hunt for job openings at those businesses!

Chapter 19

Search for Businesses

In This Chapter

➤ Discover why all Web Yellow Pages aren't created equal (although many are!)

➤ Learn how to expand your search beyond the Yellow Pages sites

➤ Uncover the secret search strategies that will help you find the business you're looking for

Most businesses today have a Web presence. Even those businesses that don't have their own Web pages are listed in various Web-based business directories, which means it's fairly easy to find basic information about just about any company—online.

Some users go right to AltaVista or Yahoo! to search for companies, even if all they need is the company's phone number or address. *Wrong!* Traditional search engines and directories actually won't return this simple information. (They will direct you to the company's corporate Web pages, if they exist, but sometimes company sites don't make contact information easy to find, if they list it at all.) Here's some important advice: If all you want is a phone number or address, don't go to AltaVista or Yahoo!—instead, use one of the many Yellow Pages directories available on the Web.

Web-based Yellow Pages are offshoots of traditional printed Yellow Pages. They list businesses by location and by category, just like those old yellow phone books do. If you want a phone number or address, these sites are the best places to look.

If you want more detailed information about a company, however, *then* turn to one of the larger search sites. In fact, if you want really detailed information about a company, you may even want to turn to one of the financial sites I describe in Chapter 20, "Search for Financial and Market Information."

But you don't need to use a nuclear weapon to kill a fly. For simple information, use a simple site!

Table 19.1 Popular Business Yellow Pages Directories

Yellow Pages Site:	URL:	Search by Name?	Search by Address?
411Locate	www.411locate.com	Yes	No
Ameritech Yellow Pages	yp.ameritech.net	Yes	Advanced mode only
AnyWho	www.anywho.com	Yes	Yes
At Hand Network Yellow Pages	www.athand.com	Yes	No
BellSouth Real Yellow Pages	yp.bellsouth.com	Yes	No
Bigbook	www.bigbook.com	Yes	Advanced mode only
Bigfoot	www.bigfoot.com	Yes	No
BigYellow	www.bigyellow.com	Yes	Advanced mode only
Excite Yellow Pages	yellowpages.zip2.com	Yes	No
GTE SuperPages	yp.gte.net	Yes	Advanced mode only
InfoSpace	www.infospace.com	Yes	No
International White and Yellow Pages	www.wajens.no	Yes	No
SMARTpages	www.smartpages.com	Yes	No
Switchboard	www.switchboard.com	Yes	Yes
U.S. West Dex	yp.uswest.com	Yes	No
WhoWhere	www.whowhere lycos.com/YellowPages/ yp.html	Yes	No
Worldpages	www.worldpages.com	Yes	No
Yahoo! Yellow Pages	yp.yahoo.com	Yes (via keyword search)	No
Zip2	www.zip2.com	Yes (via keyword search)	No

Let Your Fingers Do the Searching in the Yellow Pages

Regardless of whether a business has its own Web page, its basic business information—phone number and street address—will be listed in one of the many Yellow Pages directories on the Internet. These directories work more or less like traditional printed Yellow Pages—in most cases you can look up a business either by category or by business name.

Table 19.1 lists some of the more popular of these Yellow Pages sites, and you can see two of them (AnyWho and Bigfoot) illustrated.

Search by City/State?	Search by Category?	Comments:
Yes	No	An independent directory
Yes	Yes	A service of Ameritech
Yes	Yes	An independent directory
Yes	Yes	A combined service of all the regional Bell directories
Yes	Yes	A service of BellSouth
Yes	Yes	A service of GTE—identical to GTE Superpages
Yes	Yes	Reroutes searches to regional Bell directories
Yes	Yes	A service of Bell Atlantic
Yes	Yes	A custom version of Zip2
Yes	Yes	A service of GTE—identical to Bigbook
Yes	Yes	An independent directory; also includes a separate search for businesses near a specific address
Yes	Yes (via keyword search)	The only site that lists businesses outside North America
Yes	Yes	A service of Southwestern Bell, Pacific Bell, and Nevada Bell
Yes	Yes	An independent directory; includes optional wizard driven "Guided Search"
Yes	Yes	A service of U.S. West
Yes	Yes	Reroutes searches to regional Bell directories
Yes	Yes (via keyword search)	Listings for both U.S. and Canada
No	Yes (via keyword search)	Organized by category with minimal searching
Yes	Yes (via keyword search)	An independent directory

AnyWho lets you search by the greatest number of parameters.

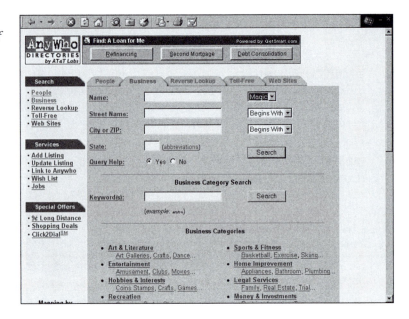

Bigfoot reroutes your search to one of the regional Bell company directories.

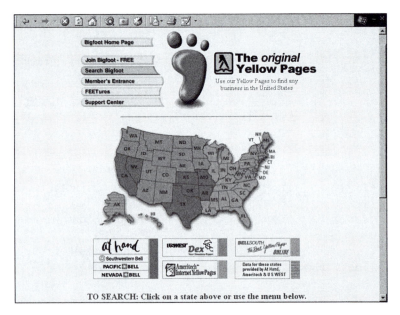

Although some of these sites search through the same directories (the regional Bell sites lie in the background for At Hand Network, Bigfoot, and WhoWhere, for example), some major differences exist among these sites. For example:

➤ AnyWho and Switchboard are the only sites that let you search by street address.

➤ InfoSpace and Switchboard let you look for businesses located *near* a specific address.

➤ Yahoo! Yellow Pages doesn't use traditional search forms, instead it presents hierarchies of business categories similar to the standard Yahoo! home page; or you can search for businesses in your area by zip code.

➤ International White and Yellow Pages is the only site that includes listings outside North America—it's a true global directory.

Which Yellow Pages site should you use? If you're happy with your current printed Yellow Pages directory, use the site associated with your local phone company. (For example, if you're in California, go to the SMARTpages site run by Pacific Bell.) Otherwise, shop around—some sites do get updated more frequently than others, and some include different categorization of business types. Differences do exist in the results from site to site!

Other Places to Look for Businesses on the Internet

If you want to find more specific business information—such as a list of business-to-business firms in a specific category or the Web site address of a corporation—you may want to search some other sites. (These sites don't include as much information as the financial sites I discuss in Chapter 20, however—so flip ahead to that chapter if you really want to delve into a business's financial performance.)

Table 19.2 lists some of these alternative business search sites.

Table 19.2   Other Sites for Business Information

Site:	URL:	Comments:
BizProLink	www.bizprolink.com	A business-to-business portal
Business and Technology Research Library	www.brint.com/interest.html	A good compilation of resources of value to the business research professional
CompaniesOnline	www.companiesonline.com	From Dun & Bradstreet, a comprehensive listing of more than 100,000 private and public companies—*recommended*
FindLinks	www.findlinks.com	Industry-specific Web links
Inter-Linked Communications	www.inter-linked.com	Links to commercial and business-related Web sites

continues

211

Table 19.2 CONTINUED

Site:	URL:	Comments:
Pronet	pronet.ca	International directory of businesses
U.S. Business Advisor	www.business.gov	Links to business-related information and services available from the U.S. government
Web100	www.metamoney.com/w100/	Lists the largest U.S. and international corporations, along with relevant information and links to their Web sites
World Trade Search	world-trade-search.com	Directory of and for import/export businesses

Tips on Finding Businesses on the Web

When you're searching for businesses on the Web, consider the following advice:

➤ If you want only a business's street address or phone number, use one of the major Yellow Pages sites.

➤ If you're searching a Yellow Pages site and aren't sure of the specific name of a particular business category, look for a "top categories" link to display an alphabetic list of "official" Yellow Pages categories.

➤ If you want to get the official line about a company directly from the company itself, use a traditional search engine to find the company's Web site. After you find the company's official site, look for an "about us" or "corporate information" link for company-supplied information.

➤ If you want detailed and impartial financial information about a company, turn to Chapter 20, "Search for Financial and Market Information" for more particulars.

➤ If you want to look for press releases from or about a company, check out the PR Newswire site (www.prnewswire.com). This site includes both recent press releases and a huge press-release archive.

➤ If you want to look for news about a company, turn to Chapter 32, "Search for Archived News Articles," for help on finding both current and older news stories on the Web.

➤ If you can't find any information about a company anywhere, try Dun & Bradstreet's CompaniesOnline site (www.companiesonline.com). It might not have much information, but it often has listings for companies that simply don't show up anyplace else.

The Least You Need to Know

➤ Numerous business Yellow Pages directories are available on the Web, many run by the traditional Bell Yellow Pages companies; the At Hand Network Yellow Pages combines all these directories into one official site.

➤ Some of the more popular independent Web Yellow Pages are AnyWho, InfoSpace, and Switchboard.

➤ If you want detailed official information about a business, use a traditional search engine to access the company's official Web site; don't use traditional search engines just to look for phone numbers!

➤ If you can't find a business anyplace else, search the CompaniesOnline site from Dun & Bradstreet.

Chapter 20

Search for Financial and Market Information

In This Chapter

➤ Discover which financial sites offer the right information for your research needs

➤ Find the most popular sites on the Web for online investing

➤ Uncover the secret search strategies that will help you find the financial information you're looking for

In the old days (pre-Web), if you wanted investment advice, you had to pay a financial advisor some big bucks. Today, however, you can search the Web to find financial advice of every conceivable flavor, and you can use the Internet to research financial options, track stock performance, and even buy and sell stocks and other securities.

After you start searching, you'll quickly discover a veritable plethora of Web sites devoted to dispensing financial information and advice. Most of the full-service sites offer similar services: stock quotes, portfolio tracking, company news, historical financial information, and even message boards where users can discuss the latest financial rumors. Other sites are more specialized, focusing just on mutual funds or in-depth company info.

In any case, it's easy to find all the online financial information you can digest, and you probably won't even have to pay for most of it!

You Get What You Pay For

Even with all the free financial resources you can find on the Web, you still might want to invest in professional, personalized financial advice. Given the old saying that a fool and his money are soon parted, remember that the Internet lets you part with your money even more quickly than you could in the old, pre–Web days!

Searching for Stock Quotes and Other Financial Information

If you search for financial information on a traditional search site, you will be overwhelmed by the results. Hundreds, and perhaps thousands, of commercial sites are dedicated to providing financial advice and information of one sort or another. In addition, many ordinary search sites let you retrieve a stock's current price if you just enter its ticker symbol. With all these sites staring you in the face, where should you start?

Which site or sites you end up using depends a lot on you—the amount and types of information you need, the kind of investing you do, and the amount of time you want to put into this activity.

For most users, one of the many full-service sites (Motley Fool, Quicken.com, Yahoo! Finance, and so on) provides more than enough information; which of these you choose is mostly a matter of personal preference. For more active investors, however, you may need to visit several more specialized sites to obtain all the information you need.

Table 20.1 lists some of the more popular and robust finance-oriented sites on the Web.

Table 20.1   Web Sites for Financial and Corporate Information

Site:	URL:	Comments:
Annual Reports Library	www.zpub.com/sf/arl/	Collection of more than 1.45 million annual reports from corporations, foundations, banks, mutual funds, and public institutions
Armchair Millionaire	www.armchairmillionaire.com	General information about saving and investing, from iVillage
Bank Rate Monitor	www.bankrate.com	All the latest rates in one place—for auto loans, mortgages, CDs, and so on
BigCharts	www.bigcharts.com	Up-to-date financial charts of all shapes and sizes
CNNfn	cnnfn.com	Full-service finance site from the CNNfn cable financial network
CompaniesOnline	www.companiesonline.com	From Dun & Bradstreet, basic listings for more than 100,000 public and private businesses
Company Sleuth	www.companysleuth.com	Free service that searches the Internet for inside information on the companies you select—including new patents and trademarks, SEC filings, earnings estimates, analyst ratings, insider trades, and so on; *recommended*
ConsumerInfo.com	www.consumerinfo.com	Fee-based site that provides personal credit reports
Corporate Information	www.corporateinformation.com	Excellent search site for Web-based information on both public and private companies
Dun & Bradstreet	www.dnb.com	Good source of information on smaller, nonpublic companies
Hoovers Online	www.hoovers.com	Detailed corporate news, financial, and other information; *recommended*

continues

Table 20.1   CONTINUED

Site:	URL:	Comments:
invest-o-rama!	www.investorama.com	Full-service finance site
InvestorLinks	www.investorlinks.com	Massive directory of links to financial information and Web sites
Microsoft Investor	investor.msn.com	Full-service finance site from Microsoft
Morningstar	www.morningstar.net	Mutual fund-oriented site
Motley Fool	www.fool.com	Full-service finance site; great message boards
Multex	www.multexnet.com	Fee-based site providing a massive database of company and industry research reports
PC Quote	www.pcquote.com	Full-service finance site
Quicken.com	www.quicken.com	Full-service finance site from Intuit, the publisher of Quicken software
QuoteCom	www.quote.com	Full-service finance site
SEC EDGAR Database	www.sec.gov/edgarhp.htm	Official corporate financial filings, including quarterly reports, annual reports, and IPO filings
Yahoo! Finance	quote.yahoo.com	Full-service finance site, from Yahoo!

If you don't know where to start, two sites serve as good portals to the financial Web. InvestorLinks (www.investorlinks.com) is a huge directory of links to other financial sites; Corporate Information (www.corporateinformation.com) functions as a kind of index to the financial Web. Both sites are good "home pages" in your search for corporate data.

Tips for Fine-tuning Your Financial Search

Surfing through all these financial sites, I often find that no single site has all the information I need. Instead, I visit a collection of sites that together offer fairly complete views of just about any public company I choose to research.

Let me share my online financial research strategy with you.

A Fool and His Money Are Soon Started at The Motley Fool

I tend to start my research at a good full-service financial site. If it's simple information I'm looking for, these types of sites have it in droves and make it easy to find.

For my money, one of the best full-service sites is The Motley Fool (`www.fool.com`). The Fool is a great site for numbers, news, charts, and (especially) rumors. I find the key metrics here more reliable than on many other sites, and The Fool provides a good summary of key numbers and ratios for all U.S.-based public companies.

If you're a beginning investor, you should find the basic information on this site top-notch. The Fool is known for its investment advice, and it's hard to fault its record.

Also, this is without a doubt the best site on the Net for rumors and opinions—just check out the discussion boards for the real buzz. (For what it's worth, the message boards at Yahoo! Finance—`quote.yahoo.com`—are also quite lively.)

Start your financial search at The Motley Fool, an informative and opinionated site.

Get the Straight Poop at Hoover's Online

When you want to move beyond the standard financial data, the full-service sites sometimes let you down. When you want more in-depth information, it's time to turn to a more professional site, such as Hoover's Online (`www.hoovers.com`).

Hoover's is probably the most comprehensive site on the Web for in-depth financial information; the site specializes in providing detailed financial and operating information about publicly traded corporations. Some of the info here is free, some is fee-based, but you'll find a lot of good basic data on almost any public company.

For most public companies, you can find the following information:

➤ Company capsule (basic info)

➤ Company profile (history, operating info)

➤ Financials (basic, in-depth, and historical)

➤ Earnings estimates

➤ Comparative data with related companies

➤ Research analyst reports

➤ Annual reports and SEC filings

➤ News and press releases

You might have to click around a bit to find the specific information you're looking for—and you will have to pay for some of it—but if you're a serious investor, Hoover's is the best place to start. (And there's now a version of Hoover's for British companies; Hoover's Online UK can be found at www.hoovers.co.uk.)

Go to Hoovers Online for in-depth financial information on any publicly traded company.

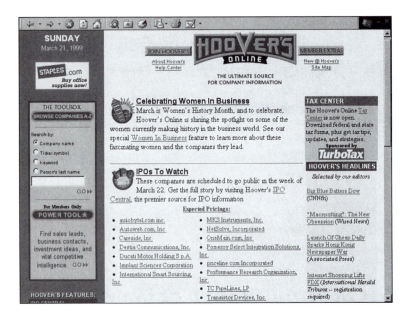

Search for More Information with Corporate Information

When I can't find what I'm looking for on Hoovers, I turn to Corporate Information (www.corporateinformation.com). This site specializes in corporate research on publicly traded and privately held companies.

220

Corporate Information contains a massive index, organized by country, of other sites offering financial information. The site also links to market research reports, accounting policies, court decisions, and so on, that might be related to the specific company you're researching.

Get Notified Automatically with Company Sleuth

Company Sleuth is my latest favorite Internet service. Here's how it works:

First, you go to the Company Sleuth Web site (www.companysleuth.com) and register. During registration, you tell the site which companies you're interested in tracking.

After you've registered, you'll receive an email from Company Sleuth in your inbox every morning. This email lists all the companies you selected, and informs you of any new activity relating to that company—news articles, patent filings, insider trades, analyst reports, earnings estimates, even messages about the company on key financial bulletin boards. To view any particular item, all you have to do is click the related link within the HTML email.

This is simply the best, the easiest, and the most comprehensive way to track company information that I've ever seen. Whether you're tracking competitors or companies you've invested in, Company Sleuth tells you virtually *everything* the company is doing—every morning, automatically.

Find the Official Financials in the SEC EDGAR Database

If you're looking for a company's official SEC filings, the only place to look is the SEC EDGAR Database (www.sec.gov/edgarhp.htm). This isn't a pretty site, but it is the best place to go for quarterly and annual financial filings, as well as IPO filings.

Get Advice from the Analysts at Multex

When you've collected enough data and what you really need is advice, head to Multex, The Online Investment Research Network (www.multexnet.com). This is a fee-based site that offers analyst reports on individual companies—and on entire industries. (And they also offer a 30-day free trial, in case you want to nose around before you ante up.)

Here you'll find more than a million full-text research reports on more than 15,000 companies from countries around the world. These reports come from more than 400 of the world's leading brokerage firms, investment banks, and independent research providers. It's quality stuff and well worth the money.

If It's Not a Public Company, Try Dun & Bradstreet

What if you're looking for information on a private company, not a publicly traded one? Your choices narrow considerably in the private world; Hoover's, The Motley Fool, and the like simply don't track nonpublic companies.

One of the best sites for information on smaller private companies is Dun & Bradstreet (www.dnb.com). You won't always find a lot of information—most private companies tend to guard their data religiously—but if it's there, chances are D&B has it.

When All Else Fails, Search Companies Online

If you simply can't find any information anywhere else, go to Companies Online (www.companiesonline.com). This site is run by Dun & Bradstreet and lets you search not only for publicly traded companies, but also for private companies. You won't find much information on any single copmany, but chances are you'll find *something*.

Investing Online—The Best Online Brokerages

If you're looking for financial information on the Web, chances are you're already an active investor. If you want to do your investing online, an increasing number of online brokerages let you buy and sell securities right from your personal computer. Some of these firms even offer special services just for day traders.

To save you the search, Table 20.2 shows some of the more popular online brokerage firms and their Web sites.

Table 20.2   Major Online Brokerages

Brokerage:	URL:
1800daytrade.com	1800daytrade.com
Accutrade	www.accutrade.com
Charles Schwab	www.eschwab.com
Datek	www.datek.com
Discover Brokerage Direct	www.dbdirect.com
DLJdirect	www.dljdirect.com
E*TRADE	www.etrade.com
Fidelity Web Xpress	webxpress.fidelity.com
Investex Securities Group	www.investexpress.com
InvesTrade	www.investrade.com
Net Investor	www.netinvestor.com
ProTrade Securities	www.protrade.com
Quick & Reilly	www.quick-reilly.com
SURETRADE	www.suretrade.com
Waterhouse Securities	www.waterhouse.com

Note that fees and services vary wildly from firm to firm, so be sure to shop around for the combination that best suits your investment style. If you want a little more help picking out an online brokerage firm, check out the rankings at Gomez (www.gomez.com)—this site will give you the straight poop about which site is best for different types of investors.

Home-Buying Information Online

The biggest financial investment most people make in their entire lives is their home. Numerous home-buying resources are available on the Internet, many of which provide mortgage rate information and—in many cases—direct access to mortgages online. Some of the more popular sites include the following:

➤ Homebuyer's Fair (www.homefair.com)

➤ Home Shark (www.homeshark.com)

➤ LoanGuide (www.loanguide.com)

➤ Microsoft HomeAdvisor (homeadvisor.msn.com)

➤ QuickenMortgage (www.quickenmortgage.com)

➤ Realtor.com (www.realtor.com)

➤ Today's Mortgage Information (www.hsh.com)

For further details, see the *Complete Idiot's Guide to Buying and Selling a Home Online*, coming soon.

The Least You Need to Know

➤ You can find financial data on practically any public company online—somewhere.

➤ If you're looking for general financial information and stock quotes, The Motley Fool is one of the better sites to search.

➤ If you need more in-depth financial information, try searching the Hoovers Online site.

➤ If you need a directory to all the financial sites on the Web, try searching either InvestorLinks or Corporate Information.

Search for Jobs

Searching for a job has never been easier, now that many employers are using the Web as a key recruiting device. You can find job postings from hundreds of thousands of firms with just a few keystrokes and sort through the jobs you want based on the criteria you select. For that matter, you can let the Web do the searching for you. Leave your online résumé at one or more of these career-oriented sites, and potential employers will be sending *you* email about positions they have open that match your qualifications.

Searching for Job Listings

Dozens of sites exist on the Web where you can look for jobs—or where employers can look for you after you post your online résumé. Many of these sites let you post your résumés at no charge; most charge employers either to place ads or when positions are filled.

Table 21.1 lists some of the more popular online job sites.

Table 21.1   Jobs and Careers on the Web

Site:	URL:	Comments:
4work	www.4work.com	An easy-to-use search engine that lets you search for jobs by state and keyword
CareerBuilder Network	www.careerbuilder.com	An all-purpose job search site for job seekers and employers
CareerMosaic	www.careermosaic.com	One of the oldest and largest full-service career sites with a variety of career-related resources as well as standard job-wanted services
CareerPath	www.careerpath.com	One of the largest job search sites on the Web with listings from most major U.S. newspapers
CareerSite	www.careersite.com	An all-purpose job search site, complete with "virtual agents" and "virtual recruiters" to match employers with potential employees
HeadHunter.NET	www.headhunter.net	An all-purpose site specializing in middle- and upper-management positions
HEART Career.com	www.career.com	An all-purpose job search site for job seekers and employers
Hot Jobs	www.hotjobs.com	A great site for technical and computer-oriented positions
Job Options	www.joboptions.com	Formerly E-Span, one of the oldest job-search sites on the Web for job seekers and employers
jobfind.com	www.jobfind.com	A full-service career-oriented site with job listings, career news, and corporate profiles
JobWeb	www.jobweb.com	A student-oriented career site from the National Association of Colleges and Employers
Monster.com	www.monster.com	One of the Web's largest sites for job listings
NationJob	www.nationjob.com	An all-purpose job-hunting site for job seekers and employers
Online Career Center	www.occ.com	Featuring job listings and career-oriented news
Recruiters Online Network	ipa.com	A site that compiles services from more than 20,000 recruiting firms

Which of these many sites should you use for your job search? It depends on what kind of job you're looking for.

If you're just out of college, use JobWeb. If you're looking for a technical job, try Hot Jobs. If you just want to browse the largest number of job listings, go to Monster.com. In other words, check out each site—browse the listings, kick the tires—and see if it offers a lot of listings for the kind of jobs that you're specifically looking for.

Looking for a Monster Job at Monster.com

The largest job search site on the Internet is Monster.com (`www.monster.com`), with a massive job-listing database and lots of other useful information and services. Because most job-search sites work in a similar fashion, let's take a quick look at how you can search for jobs on Monster.com.

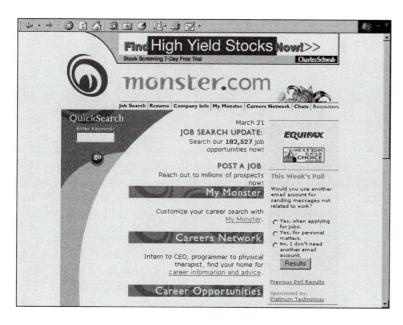

Monster.com, the largest career site on the Web— and one of the best places to start your job search.

Searching Monster.com for Jobs

A quick job search on Monster.com is really easy. Just enter one or more keywords describing the job you want into the QuickSearch box on the home page, and then click the **Go** button. Monster returns all matching jobs, listed in reverse chronological order (in other words, newest jobs first).

QuickSearch isn't the best way to search, however, as it doesn't let you fine-tune your search for little things, such as where you want to work, geographically. For a more powerful search, you have to click the **Job Search** button on Monster's home page.

Now you have some options from which to choose! You can use the pull-down boxes to select one or more locations, professions, and industries that you're interested in— as well as use keywords to better describe the job you want. Click the **Search Jobs** button to start the search.

Make Multiple Selections

To select more than one item in a pull-down list, hold down the **Ctrl** key while you click the items you want.

Monster's Search Results page tells you how many jobs were found that match your search criteria. Jobs are listed by date posted, location, job title, and company name; the most recent jobs posted appear at the top of the list. To fine-tune these results, enter one or more keywords into the search box and click the **Subsearch** button. To see the actual job posting, click the job title.

When the full job posting appears, follow the on-screen instructions for how to contact the employer about this job. Many listings let you email the employer or the hiring agency; or you can apply for the job online by clicking the **Apply Online** link.

Posting a Résumé at Monster.com

One way to find a job is for you to look for an employer; another way is to have potential employers look for you. Monster.com, like most job-search sites, lets you post your résumé online, where it can viewed by potential employers.

You Gotta Join!

To use all of Monster.com's services, such as emailing potential employers or applying online, you first have to register. (This is the case with many of the job search sites.) Registration is free, but a little time-consuming.

All you have to do is click the **Resume** link on Monster's home page. When the Submit Resume page appears, fill in all the appropriate information (name, email address, street address, telephone number, and so on) and answer all the questions on the form shown here. In the section headed Type or Paste the Body of Your Resume in Plain Text or HTML, you can either type your résumé by hand or cut and paste text created in a word processing pro-

gram. (Cutting and pasting is preferable—not only is it easier, but it also lets you take advantage of your word processor's spell check function.)

1.	Please enter your contact information:	

Name

Email Address

Street Address

City

Country/State

Zip or Postal Code

Telephone Number

Fax Number

2. Are you willing to relocate?

⊂ Yes   ⊂ No   ⊂ Maybe

Please enter any comments regarding relocation:

3. What type of job are you looking for? Please select all that apply.

☐ Full Time   ☐ Part Time   ☐ Permanent   ☐ Contract

4. What is your minimum compensation requirement? Please complete all that apply.

$ [____] per year $ [____] per hour

5. What is your highest level of education?

High School ▾

Just fill out the form to create a résumé on Monster.com.

Make It Plain...

When you enter or paste text into the text box, you have to remove *all* formatting, such as boldface and italic. You also have to use your return key at the end of each line because the text box doesn't have "auto-wrap" capabilities. In addition, your Tab key does not function at all in this text box, so you'll have to remove all the tabs in your document—use the spacebar to insert extra spaces, if needed.

When you click the **Submit this resume now!** button, your résumé is entered in the Monster.com database, where it can be browsed by potential employers. You'll be notified by email if and when any potential employers wish to contact you.

The daily email you'll start receiving from Monster.com includes a link to a part of the site called My Monster. My Monster is a personalized page that contains all your personal information, including the potential jobs found by the "agent" that searches the Monster.com database every day. Once you're a Monster.com member, you might want to go directly to my.monster.com, rather than hitting the Monster.com home page first every time you visit.

229

...Or Pretty It Up with HTML

If you know basic HTML formatting, you can boldface, italicize, and otherwise format the text in your résumé. If you submit your résumé in HTML, be sure to place the <HTML> tag at the very start of the résumé and the </HTML> tag at the end; then use normal HTML codes as appropriate (such as <B>*text*</B> to boldface text or <I>*text*</I> to italicize text). If you want to include hyperlinks to other Web pages, be sure to include the full http:// address. If you don't know HTML, don't bother with it!

Tips for Better Online Job Searches

Wherever you focus your online job search, some tips follow that will help you find a better job, faster.

➤ **Check out the other ads**   Before choosing a site to host your own job-wanted ad, check out the other ads on the site. Are there plenty of ads similar to the position you're looking for? If so, you've probably found the right site. (Birds of a feather, and all that.) If not, you could be stuck on a site that is of no interest to your potential employers. It pays to search around and find the right site for your occupation.

➤ **Use the right keywords**   Most sites let you fine-tune your search by using keywords. In the job search world, keywords should describe your technical and professional experience. Examples of good keywords include UNIX, programmer, SAP, sales, COBOL, human resources, ORACLE, FORTRAN, marketing, advertising, and so on.

➤ **Write a punchy résumé**   First, make it short—nobody wants to read a long résumé. Second, use bullets instead of block paragraphs for most of your text. Third, remember that you're selling yourself, so use your marketing skills—use power words and active voice. Fourth, develop a strong objective or job description—and make sure it's truly descriptive of what you want to do! And fifth, get straight to the point—describe what you can do for their company, in terms of how much money you can save or make for them based on your skills and experience.

Write a Better Résumé

You can pick up résumé–writing advice at most of the general job search sites, or check out the JobStar (`jobsmart.org/tools/resume/`) or Resume Writing (`www.10minuteresume.com`) sites for more tips.

➤ **Be anonymous**   If you want to be absolutely, positively sure that your current employer can't trace a job-wanted ad back to you, don't use your work email address and don't use your normal email address! Instead, create a new email address (under an untraceable name) using one of the many Web-based email services, such as Hotmail (`www.hotmail.com`).

➤ **Don't forget to search Usenet**   In addition to the career-oriented Web sites discussed in this chapter, you can also find positions posted on many Usenet newsgroups. Look for job postings in vocation-specific newsgroups or in special *.jobs newsgroups. (These are generally region-specific listings; for example, you would find jobs in Minnesota listed in the mn.jobs newsgroup.) One of the better ways to search newsgroups for job listings is to use the DejaNews site (`www.dejanews.com`); see Chapter 25, "Search for Usenet Newsgroup Articles," for more information.

➤ **Do your research first**   If you find a firm that interests you, use the Web (and in some cases, the resources available on the job search site) to research the company *before* your interview. In addition, don't forget to call human resources directors, talk to current and former employees of the company, and scan the company's Web site for more information.

The Least You Need to Know

➤ Many employers are using the Internet to post job listings and look for potential employees.

➤ Monster.com has the most job postings of any career–oriented Web site.

➤ Most job sites let you search for jobs and post your résumé for potential employers, as well.

Part 6

Getting a Bargain: How to Find Things for Sale

Did you know that you can find just about anything you've ever wanted for sale somewhere on the Internet? Whether you're looking for a deal on the latest computer hardware or trying to find a rare copy of some collectible item, it's probably out there on the Web—if only you knew how to find it! This part of the book shows you how to find items that individuals have for sale on the Internet, whether through online classified ads or via online auctions. Use these chapters to find that one thing you've been looking to buy—but couldn't find before!

Chapter 22

Search for
Online Auctions

In This Chapter

➤ Discover why online auctions are the hottest sites on the Web today

➤ Find out which auction sites are best for your specific needs

➤ Learn how to search for items on eBay, the Web's largest auction site

➤ Uncover the secret search strategies that will help you find—and win—the item you're looking for on any online auction site

All kinds of people are turning to online auctions to find all kinds of things that were costly or difficult to find before. It doesn't matter whether they're looking for a rare, 1922 Hamilton pocket watch or a retired Chilly the Polar Bear Beanie Baby, whether they're devoted to a hobby or a collection, or even running a small retail business— millions of people are using online auction sites today, and usage is growing at a mind-boggling rate.

It's fair to say that the hottest trend on the Internet today is online auctions. These immensely popular sites let individual users sell all types of merchandise to the highest bidders. Bidding is often automated; bidders can place both a minimum and a maximum bid and then have the computer software automatically increase their bid amounts if their minimum offer gets outbid by other users.

When it comes to searching for merchandise to bid on, however, you're faced with two problems: searching for the right auction site and searching for the right merchandise within a single auction site. Given that hundreds of individual auction sites exist and that the largest sites have hundreds of thousands of items for sale on any given day, you can sense the magnitude of the problem.

Interested in Online Auctions? Then Read the Book!

The topic of online auctions is so interesting that I just wrote a book about it! If you want to know more about online auctions—which ones to use and how to be a successful seller or buyer—then check out my new book, *The Complete Idiot's Guide to Online Auctions*, available at the same place you bought this book. (If you like, you can read more about this book—and other books I've written—at my personal Web site. Just go directly to www.molehillgroup.com/bibliogr.htm for a complete list of all my written works.)

Searching for the Top Auction Sites

How do you pick the right auction site? Some sites specialize in computer equipment and other sites specialize in sports collectibles; some sites specialize in collectibles and other sites specialize in fine wine. But the vast majority of auction sites really don't specialize in anything, offering auctions in categories ranging from antiques to Beanie Babies to PEZ dispensers to Zippo lighters.

With all these sites to choose from, how do you choose?

It would be tempting to just direct you to eBay, the largest site, and be done with it. But as the other sites pick up steam, you can sometimes find better bargains away from the market leader.

That said, Table 22.1 lists some of the top, all-purpose auction sites on the Web today.

Table 22.1 Top Online Auction Sites

Site:	URL:	Comments:
Amazon.com Auctions	auctions.amazon.com	The new auction site from the popular online book-seller
Auction Universe	www.auctionuniverse.com	One of eBay's major competitors in the general auctions arena—use the Auction Universe Network (www.aun.com) to access local auctions across the country

Site:	URL:	Comments:
AuctionPage	www.auctionpage.com	Free general auctions
CityAuction	www.cityauction.com	Local auctions worldwide
Classifieds 2000 Auctions	www.classifieds2000.com	A large and growing free auction site; click the **Auctions** link to enter
eBay	www.ebay.com	Far and away the largest and most popular general auction site on the Web— *recommended*
FirstAuction	www.firstauction.com	An up-and-coming general auction site
Onsale atAuction	www.onsale.com	Large, general auction site
uBid	www.ubid.com	A large auction site specializing in computer equipment
Up4Sale	www.up4sale.com	Free general auction site
WebAuction	www.webauction.com	One of the best auctions specializing in computer equipment
Yahoo! Auctions	auctions.yahoo.com	Large, free general auction site

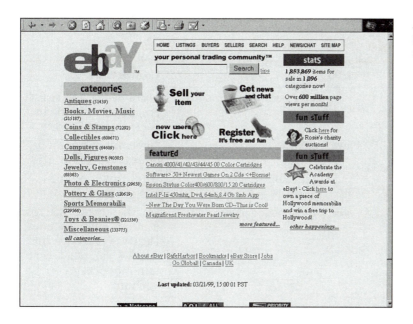

Do your bidding at eBay, the largest auction site on the Internet.

Most of these sites work in similar fashion. You can browse through their topic categories by clicking specific links, or you can search for items using their built-in search engines. After you locate an item, bidding works pretty much the same from site to site—you enter both a minimum and a maximum amount you're willing to bid and let the auction software take over the process from there.

Some differences exist between the sites. Some sites charge a fee to list items; some don't. Some offer additional services (such as escrow and shipping); some don't. Some sites have millions of members (which means more competition for items—but it also means more items for sale); some don't.

Nose around a site before you decide to use it. Browse or search through the listings and check out the fees and policies. Find the site that has the merchandise you want and that you're comfortable with, and settle in for some auction fun!

Meta-Searching Multiple Auction Sites

When you venture outside of eBay, Auction Universe, or any other large, general-purpose auction site, how can you find that item you'd like to bid on—or the site on which it might be listed?

The answer is simple—use a meta-auction site. These sites serve as directories to hundreds of other auction sites, and (in many cases) they let you search across multiple auction sites for particular items. Some even let you manage all your bids and auctions directly from their sites!

Table 22.2 lists some of the more popular meta-auction sites.

Table 22.2   Meta-Auction Sites

Site:	URL:	Comments:
Auction Watchers	www.auctionwatchers.com	Multiple-auction search engine specializing in computer equipment
AuctionInsider	www.auctioninsider.com	Directory of hundreds of online auction sites
Auctions Online Supersite	guestservices.hypermart.net	Directory of online auction sites
Bidder's Edge	www.biddersedge.com	Searches auctions across multiple sites; includes DealWatch service that notifies you when certain products go on auction

Site:	URL:	Comments:
BidFind	www.bidfind.com	Multiple auction listing and multi-site search engine
Lycos Auctions Search	www.lycos.com/auctions/	Multiple-auction search engine from Lycos

Use BidFind to search for items across multiple auction sites.

Use these meta-auction sites with a degree of caution, however, especially if you're searching for individual items across multiple sites. Quite frankly, not all of these search engines catch all the items that are really up for bid. That's partly because different auction sites use different search parameters (the old meta-search buggedy-boo) and partly because some of these meta-auction sites haven't quite got all the bugs worked out yet. Just keep your eyes open is all I'm saying.

Searching for Stuff on eBay

Let's get right down to it—eBay (www.ebay.com) is the largest auction site on the Web—no questions asked. If you want to browse through the largest selection of merchandise up for sale, this is the place to go. (So go there now!)

Now that you're here, how do you search through the 1.5 million items that are up for bid on eBay on any given day? You could browse through the merchandise categories on eBay's home page, but given the huge number of categories, this could take forever—besides, you're never quite sure if all sellers have picked the right categories for their merchandise.

239

Some Interesting Facts About eBay

Want some cocktail party conversation? Then whip out these interesting items:

➤ eBay has more than 2.1 million registered users.

➤ On any given day, eBay has more than 1.5 million individual items for sale.

➤ The average visit to eBay is 27 minutes—an eternity for Web site visits.

➤ Since its launch in 1997, eBay has logged more than 48 million items for sale, with more than 179 million bids made.

A better solution is to use eBay's built-in search engine.

A simple search box is available on eBay's home page, but I prefer to use the more powerful Search page that is displayed when you click the **Search** link (*not* the **Search** button!). When you do, you'll see the screen shown next.

Use this search form to search for items for sale on eBay.

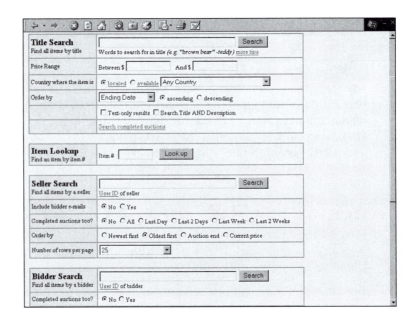

eBay's search page lets you search by the following criteria:

➤ Title keywords (the best place to start searching—just enter words describing the item you're looking for)

➤ Price range

➤ Country where the item is either located or available (good for bidders outside the U.S.)

➤ Item number (all eBay items are assigned a unique number—if you know the item's number, this is the best way to go directly to the listing)

➤ Seller ID (lists all items from a given seller)

➤ Bidder ID (lists all items bid on by a given bidder)

➤ Completed searches (lists only those auctions that are already over)

In addition, this form lets you sort your results by ascending or descending auction ending date, bid price, or search ranking (how well the item matched your query). I like to display my results by ending date, with expiring auctions listed first—that way I know which items have to take priority in my bidding activities.

To get the best results from your eBay searches, you need to know which commands and operators you can use in the various search boxes. These commands are used almost exclusively in the Title box to help modify your keywords and fine-tune your searches. Table 22.3 lists the commands you can use when searching on eBay.

Table 22.3   eBay Search Commands

To Do This:	Use This Command:	Example:
Search for part of a word	*	`bat*`
Search for either word	(word1,word2)	`(batman,robin)` Note: Both words have to be enclosed in the parentheses, and there should be *no space* after the comma
Search for either word	@0	`@0 batman robin` Note: No comma between words
Include at least two of the words	@1	`@1 pez furbie plate` Note: No comma between words
Search for an exact phrase	" "	`"batman pez dispenser"`
Must include a word	+	`batman +pez`
Must exclude a word	–	`batman -pez`
Include a year or number	#	`#1972`

The Automatic AND

If you enter more than one word into a query with no operator between them, eBay assumes you want to look for both words and automatically inserts an AND between the words.

Note that eBay does not support the use of Boolean operators—if you type an AND or an OR into your query, eBay treats them as keywords and searches for them!

Let's quickly put together a sample search using some of these commands. Suppose you want to search either for PEZ dispensers or original artwork concerning anything related to Batman—including Batgirl, the Batmobile, the Batcave, and so on. To perform that search, you would use this query:

```
bat* (pez,art)
```

Another example: Suppose you want to look for all rare coins issued in 1955. You'd use this query:

```
coin #1955
```

And so on.

Tips for Winning Online Auctions

Now you know how to search for items you want to bid on. How do you make sure you have the winning bids? Just follow this advice:

➤ **Narrow your search**   For some of the more popular categories on big sites such as eBay, thousands of items are listed. If you do a search on beanie baby, you'll be overwhelmed by the results; narrow your search within these large categories to better describe the specific item you're looking for.

➤ **Don't bid on the first thing you see**   Probably several other items on that auction site are similar to the first item you saw—is the first one really the one you want, or the best deal? Just because it's an auction doesn't mean you can't shop around!

➤ **Don't bid blind**   Make sure you know the true value of an item before you offer a bid. Look around at other auctions of similar items; what prices are they going for? Be informed, and you won't bid too high—or too low.

➤ **Check out the seller**   Most auction sites provide feedback ratings for their sellers and bidders. Make sure the seller of a particular item has a good feedback rating—and avoid those who don't.

➤ **There are other fish in the sea**   In 99.9 percent of the auctions, that one-of-a-kind item really isn't one of a kind, so if you don't get this one, you'll get the chance to bid on something very similar sometime soon. Which means, of course, that it's okay to lose a few auctions here and there!

➤ **Bid early**   Establish yourself as a player by making an early bid. If it's a rare item, you can also preempt other bidders by bidding early—and high.

➤ **Bid late**   Make sure you track the final hours of bidding on the items you really want so that you aren't outbid at the last minute. In fact, one of the most effective "unofficial" tactics involves waiting until the very last second to place your bid; by *sniping* the other bidders, no one has time to outbid your last-minute offer!

➤ **Scare off your opponents**   If your bid gets topped mid-auction, quickly come back with a higher bid. Aggressive bidding can often frighten off inexperienced bidders.

➤ **Be disciplined**   Set a maximum price you're willing to pay for an item, and *don't exceed it!* It's just too easy to get caught up in the excitement of a fast-paced auction—know when to say no!

The Least You Need to Know

➤ Online auction sites let you bid on merchandise offered for sale by other individuals.

➤ Meta-auction sites let you search for items for sale on multiple auction sites.

➤ Most bidding is automated—you enter a minimum and a maximum bid, and the auction software handles the rest.

➤ eBay is the largest auction site on the Web, with more than 1.5 million items up for bid on any given day—and it's the logical first choice to start searching for the items you want.

Search for Things on Sale

The Internet is overrun with things for sale. Whether you want new merchandise from an online retailer or used goods from an individual, literally millions of items are available to choose from—on thousands of sites.

If you want new stuff, how do you find the best online retailer that carries the specific items you're looking for? Better yet, how do you find the best prices on what you want to buy?

If you want used stuff, how do you find that one classified ad that's offering what you want to buy? And which sites have the best selection of online classifieds?

You can answer all those questions with one word, of course: *search!*

Is It Safe to Shop?

Most online retailers are as reputable as most "bricks-and-mortar" retailers. Just to be safe, look for the following features on any shopping site:

➤ A *secure server* that encrypts your credit card information

➤ Good contact information—email address, street address, phone number, fax number, and so on

➤ A stated returns policy and satisfaction guarantee

➤ A stated privacy policy that protects your personal information

This begs the question about how safe it is to give out credit card information over the Internet. Frankly, having purchased stuff off the Net for years, I'm tired of this question! Quit being paranoid—providing your credit card information to a secure Web site is much safer than handing your credit card to a complete stranger dressed as a waiter in a restaurant, or giving it over the phone. I am unaware of any documented case of anyone having his or her credit stolen while buying something off the Web. In addition, all major credit card companies limit your liability if your card gets stolen, whether that's on the Web or in the so-called real world. Bottom line: Don't worry about it.

(If you can't help worrying about it, however, look into *The Complete Idiot's Guide to Protecting Yourself Online*, by Preston Gralla.)

Searching for Online Retailers

Online shopping has arrived. It seems that everyone is buying something online—so-called *e-tailing* isn't just for geeks anymore.

Where do you look for the best online retailers? You can use the traditional search engines, and you'll get okay results. But a handful of specialized sites aggregate hundreds of online retailers into large, searchable directories—and, in some cases, even let you search for specific items across multiple sites and track down the best prices on the items you're looking for. You can see an example of one, Bottom Dollar, following the table.

Table 23.1 lists some of the best sites to use to search for online retailers and merchandise.

Table 23.1   Shopping Search Sites

Site:	URL:	Comments:
Acses	www.acses.com	Compares prices on books, CDs, and movies
BizRate	www.bizrate.com	Offers lists of online merchants, complete with actual consumer rankings of various sites
BookBlvd.com	www.bookblvd.com	Compares prices on books
Bottom Dollar	www.bottomdollar.com	Shopping search engine for books, electronics, flowers, gifts, computer hardware and software, movies, music, office products, sporting goods, toys, video games, and more
Buyer's Index	www.buyersindex.com	Shopping search engine listing 12,000 shopping sites and mail-order catalogs
Catalog City	www.catalogcity.com	Index to major mail-order catalogs and online merchants
Compare.Net	www.compare.net	No shopping here, but lots of buyer's guides for electronics, cars, computers, home appliances, and more
ComparisonShopping.net	www.comparisonshopping.net	Links to sites that compare prices across multiple sites on books, air fares, credit cards, life insurance, and mortgages
Excite Shopping	www.excite.com/shopping	Topic-oriented index of shopping sites, from Excite

continues

Table 23.1 CONTINUED

Site:	URL:	Comments:
HotBot Shopping Directory	shop.hotbot.com	Topic-oriented index of shopping sites, as well as the Shopping Bot shopping search engine, from HotBot
Public Eye	www.thepubliceye.com	Site collects public satisfaction reports to rate online merchants
ShopFind	www.shopfind.com	Shopping search engine that indexes more than 3,000 shopping sites
Yahoo! Shopping	shopping.yahoo.com	Topic-oriented index of more than 2,700 shopping sites, with online ordering, from Yahoo!

Use Bottom Dollar to find what you want to buy—click a merchandise category, and then use that category's search engine to look for specific items.

Most online retailers have their own custom search engines that let you search through the merchandise for sale on their sites. For example, Amazon.com (www.amazon.com) lets you search for books by book title, author name, book format, category, publisher, ISBN, or date of publication. (You might have even found this book there!) Make sure you read the instructions on each site to learn how to maximize the results from your queries of that site.

What To Do If You Get Ripped Off, Online

If you've had a bad experience with an online retailer, you're not alone. Several organizations and Web sites exist that you can contact to help you out or that let you file a complaint. These sites include

➤ Better Business Bureau (www.bbb.org)

➤ Internet Advocacy Center (www.consumeradvocacy.com)

➤ National Consumer Complaint Center (www.alexanderlaw.com/nccc/cb-intro.html)

➤ National Consumers League (www.natlconsumersleague.org)

➤ National Fraud Information Center (www.fraud.org)

Searching Through the Online Classifieds

Sometimes the stuff you want isn't available in a store. Sometimes you want to buy something secondhand, from a private individual. Sometimes you want to search through the classified ads.

Searching the classifieds is easier online than it is in the world of paper and ink, at least in my opinion. Although you can browse through the listings in a given category the same as you do when you read a newspaper's classified ads, with online classifieds you have the much more powerful option of searching for exactly the item you want. (Try that with a newspaper!)

Of course, before you can perform your search, you need to know where to search. Table 23.2 lists some of the major classified ad sites, as well as several sites that let you search across multiple classifieds sites. You can see one of them, Excite's Classifieds 2000, nearby.

Table 23.2   Major Online Classified Ad Sites

Site:	URL:	Comments:
AdAmerica	www.adamerica.com	Classified ads from newspapers across the U.S.
Classifieds 2000	www.classifieds2000.com	One of the largest, free classified ad sites on the Web, owned by Excite—*recommended*
Directory of Free Classified Ad Sites	www.windsorbooks.com/adsites/	The site's title describes it all…
ePages Classifieds	www.ep.com	A network of more than 10,000 online classified ad and auction sites
Free Classified Ads	www.freeclassifiedlinks.com	Links to dozens of smaller classified ad sites
Recycler.com	www.recycler.com	Large listing of free classified ads
Yahoo! Classifieds	classifieds.yahoo.com	One of the largest, free classified ad sites on the Web, from Yahoo!

Search the ads at Classifieds 2000, one of the largest classifieds sites on the Web—and it's free!

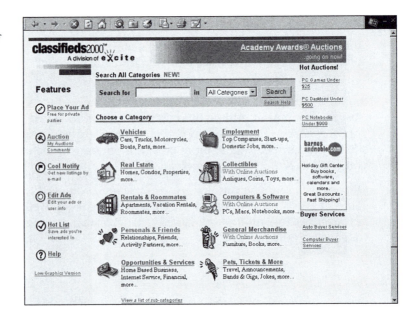

250

Protecting Yourself When Buying Via Online Classifieds

Dealing with an established online retailer is one thing, but buying from an unknown individual is something else completely. What guarantees do you have that the person on the other end of that email address isn't going to rip you off?

First, get all the important information in advance—not just an email address, but the person's real name, address, and phone number. Then, if you want full protection, use an online *escrow service*. An escrow service acts as a neutral third party between the buyer and seller, holding the buyer's money until the seller's goods are delivered and found to be satisfactory.

The following are some of the more popular Internet-based escrow services:

➤ *i-Escrow* (`www.iescrow.com`)

➤ TradeMaker (`www.labx.com/escrow.htm`)

➤ TradeSafe (`www.tradesafe.com`)

You can also use escrow services to protect yourself when you buy items from online auction sites.

Don't Forget Usenet!

In addition to the dedicated classified ad sites, several Usenet newsgroups exist where you can find items for sale and list items of your own. These include

➤ alt.ads.forsale

➤ alt.ads.forsale.computers

➤ alt.art.marketplace

➤ alt.collecting.beanie-babies.forsale

➤ alt.forsale

➤ alt.marketplace.* (several groups are within this hierarchy)

➤ alt.commerce.computers.forsale

➤ biz.marketplace.* (several groups are within this hierarchy)

➤ misc.forsale.computers.* (several groups are within this hierarchy)

➤ misc.forsale.non-computer

➤ us.forsale

➤ us.forsale.computer

➤ us.forsale.misc

In addition, if you do a search for newsgroups containing the words `forsale`, you'll find lots of regional newsgroups with items for sale. Also, if you search for the word `marketplace`, you'll find a lot of merchandise-specific newsgroups.

To find out more about searching Usenet newsgroups, turn to Chapter 25, "Search for Usenet Newsgroup Articles."

The Least You Need to Know

➤ Online shopping is completely safe—and a great way to find specific items.

➤ Numerous sites help you find individual online retailers—or search across multiple sites for specific items.

➤ Another way to buy things online is through online classified ads, such as those offered at the Classifieds 2000 site.

➤ You can also look for items for sale in specific Usenet newsgroups.

Part 7

Getting Technical: How to Find Computer-Related Stuff

It's no surprise that there is a ton of computer-related information on the Internet—after all, it's because of computers that the Internet exists! Whether you're looking for troubleshooting information or downloadable computer files, Usenet newsgroup articles or topic-specific chat rooms, the computer-related stuff you're looking for is somewhere out there on the Internet. This part of the book shows you where to look for specific types of computer stuff, so use these chapters to hunt for files, articles, and archives on the Net!

Chapter 24

Search for Solutions to Technical Problems

In This Chapter

➤ Discover the "tech portals" that provide a universe of technology-related news and information

➤ Learn the secret of obtaining free information from expensive market-research firms

➤ Uncover the best sites to help you solve your computer-related problems

The Internet was born as a technical infrastructure. Its backbone runs on highly technical equipment, managed by highly technical people, using highly technical software and protocols. You even use the most technical equipment in your home or office (your personal computer) to access the Internet via a technical connection.

Let's face it, the Internet is technical.

So, it should come as no surprise that the very-technical Internet is also a great place to find technical information. All the techies who built the Internet—and who composed almost all its early user base—put a ton of technical info online, and it's all available for your searching convenience.

Searching for Anything Technical: The Tech Portal Sites

If you like the "all you can eat" approach to technical information, check out one of the major "tech portals" that provides daily computer and Internet news, software and hardware product reviews, and, in some cases, Web-based training classes. Whether you want to scope out the features of the newest PCs, find out what Microsoft is up to this week, or just get some tips to improve your Internet use, these are the sites to visit.

How do you find the information you want after you access a tech portal? Fortunately, most of these sites have search boxes or search links right on their home pages. Typically, you can either browse through the various sections of the site or use the built-in search engines to search directly for information.

Table 24.1 lists the major Web tech portals.

Table 24.1 Tech Portal Sites

Site:	URL:	Comments:
CMPnet	www.cmpnet.com	Resources for technical professionals from the CMP magazine group (*BYTE, InformationWeek, Windows Magazine*, and so on)
CNET	www.cnet.com	One of the top full-service tech portals, with links to tech news, file downloads, and how-to information—*recommended*
EarthWeb	www.earthweb.com	A network of sites targeting developers and IT professionals; sites include Developer.com, HTMLGoodies, Gamelan (for Java programmers), Y2Kinfo, and ITKnowledge
IDG.net	www.idg.net	News and resources from the IDG family of magazines (*PC World, MacWorld, InfoWorld*, and so on)
Internet.com	www.internet.com	Internet and Web developer news and resources, from the company that runs the InternetWorld trade shows
TechWeb	www.techweb.com	Tech news and resources, associated with CMPnet
ZDNet	www.zdnet.com	A portal that combines all the technology news and information from Ziff-Davis Publishing magazines (*PC Week, PC Magazine*, and so on); also features ZD University Web-based training

My favorite tech portal is CNET. I find that CNET—and its network of related sites—has the freshest and the most in-depth technology information available anywhere, online or off. This is a site I always visit first thing in the morning, every day.

CNET's network of sites, which are all accessible from the bottom of the CNET home page, include

➤ **CNET.com** (www.cnet.com)   The main site that links to all other sites; it also includes product reviews and tech industry perspectives.

➤ **ActiveX.com** (www.activex.com)   A library of development tools and controls for ActiveX programmers.

➤ **Builder.com** (www.builder.com)   A central source of information for Web page development and Web site administration communities.

➤ **Computers.com** (www.computers.com)   The most comprehensive source for computer hardware reviews.

➤ **Download.com** (www.download.com)   A popular and powerful site for finding and downloading computer files (discussed in Chapter 27, "Search for Files to Download").

➤ **Gamecenter.com** (www.gamecenter.com)   With news, reviews, tips, and downloads for the PC gamers and videogamers.

➤ **News.com** (www.news.com)   Simply the best site on the Net for technology news.

➤ **Search.com** (www.search.com)   A basic search engine powered by Infoseek.

➤ **Shareware.com** (www.shareware.com)   A large library of shareware programs and utilities for downloading.

➤ **Shopper.com** (www.shopper.com)   A good site for determining where to buy computer products online.

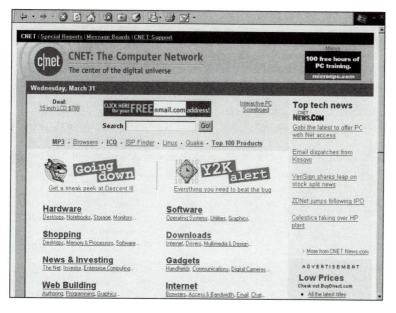

If you visit only one technology-oriented site, visit CNET—and its related News.com tech news site.

Searching for Up-to-the-Minute Technology News

If current technology news is what you're looking for, most of the major tech portals have their own news sites or pages. In addition, several other sites offer news of interest to the technology aficionado or investor.

Table 24.2 lists the major sites for tech news on the Web.

Table 24.2 Technology News on the Web

Site:	URL:	Comments:
CNET News.com	www.news.com	Probably the best daily computer-industry news, period—on the Net or otherwise; *recommended*
Computer News Daily	computernewsdaily.com	Consumer-oriented tech news, from the *New York Times* syndicate
Forbes Digital Tool	www.forbes.com	Lots of tech-industry news of value to investors
The Industry Standard	www.thestandard.net	Technology business news, with some good editorial commentary
New York Times Technology	www.nytimes.com/yr/mo/day/tech/	The daily technology section from the *New York Times*, online
Red Herring	www.herring.com	Technology business and investing news, from *Red Herring* magazine
SiliconValley.com	www.mercurycenter.com/svtech/	High-tech news from the *San Jose Mercury News*, the hometown newspaper of Silicon Valley—lots of news is reported locally first
Upside Today	www.upside.com	Daily business-oriented tech news from *Upside* magazine, good for Silicon Valley investors

Site:	URL:	Comments:
Wired News	www.wired.com/news/	Trendy tech news, from the *Wired* magazine folks
ZDNet News	www.zdnet.com/zdnn/	Tech news with a decidedly technical flavor, well-suited to the IT professional

Searching for Market Research and Analysis

There are a plethora of market research firms who conduct ongoing surveys and analyses of the technology industry. This research is of interest to industry insiders, of course, and of vital importance to investors in technology stocks.

How to Get Expensive Research—for Free!

Most of this tech-industry research is expensive—it costs literally hundreds and thousands of dollars to purchase an original research report! However, you can often access summaries of this research for free—just by clicking the site's "press release" link. These press releases—which don't cost a single penny to read!—typically contain the highlights of the research, as well as most of the key data points.

Table 24.3 lists the major technology research sites on the Web.

Table 24.3 Technology-Related Market Research Sites

Site:	URL:	Comments:
Computer Industry Almanac	www.c-i-a.com	Mainly a sales site for its expensive publication, but the press release links include most of the highlights for free

continues

Table 24.3 CONTINUED

Site:	URL:	Comments:
Computer Intelligence Infobeads	`www.ci.infobeads.com/INFOBEADS/Pages/Main/MAIN.ASP`	A great source for tech-industry statistics and analysis; although most of the CI site costs money, click the **Goldberg's Insider** link for tons of free information—*recommended*
Dataquest	`www.dataquest.com`	Well-known technology market research firm; incorporates the Gartner Group
Forrester Research	`www.forrester.com`	Tracks all kinds of Internet and technology hardware trends; click the **Press Resources** link for the free info
GVU Center's WWW User Survey	`www.cc.gatech.edu/gvu/user_surveys/`	An annual survey of Web usage trends, from the Georgia Institute of Technology
International Data Corporation	`www.idcresearch.com`	Good source for global hardware sales statistics; click the **Press Releases** link for the free stuff
Media Metrix	`www.mediametrix.com`	Tracks Web site usage; monthly free stats on top Web sites
NUA Internet Survey	`www.nua.ie/surveys/`	A great compilation of surveys and research from around the Web—one of the first places to look for tech-industry research—*recommended*
PC Data	`www.pcdata.com`	Tracks top-selling PC software; top 10 lists are always free

Searching for Troubleshooting and Repair Information

What do you do if your computer punks out on you? What happens if you try to install a new piece of hardware and all your old hardware quits working? What are your options when Windows freezes and displays an obtuse error message?

First—don't panic!

Second—turn to one of the many sites on the Web that specializes in providing solutions to computer-oriented problems.

Searching for Problems

Most of these sites let you search their databases for articles related to your specific problem. When you enter your query, try to be as precise as possible—if you have a problem with Outlook Express not deleting messages, don't just search for `outlook express`; search for `outlook express deleted messages`. If you don't narrow it down, it'll return articles about every single problem related to the piece of software in question—which, given the number of bugs in today's programs, can simply be overwhelming!

Table 24.4 lists the major sites to turn to if you have computer-related problems.

Table 24.4 Technology Troubleshooting Sites

Site:	URL:	Comments:
Annoyances.org	`www.annoyances.org`	Effective solutions to Windows 95/98 annoyances
informIT	`www.informit.com`	New site from Pearson Education and Macmillan Computer Publishing (the owners of Que, who published this book) that lets you read complete libraries of computer books online— both on a free and on a subscription basis
ITKnowledge	`www.itknowledge.com`	A complete online library for the IT professional, from EarthWeb
Kim Komando's Komputer Klinic	`www.komando.com`	Online help from the popular tech-radio show host
Microsoft Knowledge Base	`support.microsoft.com/ servicedesks/ directaccess/`	Click the **Search Support Online** to enter the Knowledge Base, where you can search for official solutions to problems you may have with any Microsoft product
PcTips.com	`www.pctips.com`	Articles and forums offering online help for all major software and operating systems platforms

continues

Table 24.4   CONTINUED

Site:	URL:	Comments:
Techni-Help	www.freepchelp.com	Free online help from a group of self-professed computer nerds; includes links to other tech-support–oriented sites
TechSupportSites	www.techsupportsites.com	A huge directory of links to all the major tech-support resources on the Internet; essentially a vendor directory with more than 1,000 links—*recommended*
Tom's Hardware Guide	www.tomshardware.com	A great PC hardware site, lots of info on souping up your system
ZDNet Help	www.zdnet.com/zdhelp/	Tips, tricks, secrets, downloads, and FAQs to help you solve computer-related problems, from Ziff-Davis Publishing

Go to the Manufacturer!

If you're having problems with a particular piece of hardware or software, one of the best places to go for help is the manufacturer's site! Most manufacturer sites have tech-support links, which often include downloadable fixes, patches, drivers, answers to common problems, and links to forms that let you contact the manufacturer directly with your own specific problem. For a good list of manufacturer tech-support sites, check out the TechSupportSites site (www.techsupportsites. com).

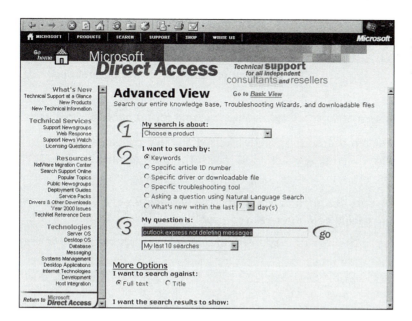

The best place to solve your Microsoft problems—the Microsoft Knowledge Base.

Chances are you have several Microsoft programs installed on your personal computer: Windows, Office, and the like. If you ever have problems with any of these Microsoft products—and if you haven't yet, you will—the best place to turn is to Microsoft's internal database of technical support questions and answers, the Microsoft Knowledge Base. The following is what you need to know to search the Knowledge Base:

➤ Which product you're having the problem with.

➤ What you want to search by (keywords, article ID number, and so on—I recommend you choose the Keywords option).

➤ Your question (enter as you would a query to any major search engine).

➤ Search against Full Text or Title—choose the Full Text Option.

Click the **Go** button and the Knowledge Base returns a list of articles, written by Microsoft's technical support staff, that are purportedly related to your problem at hand. Now, chances are not all the articles will be pertinent—the Knowledge Base has a pretty lousy search engine, actually—but chances are that at least *one* of the articles can lead you in the right direction to get your system up and running again.

The Least You Need to Know

➤ Use a tech portal, such as CNET, to search for general technology-related information.

➤ Go to a tech-news site, such as News.com, to search for technology news.

➤ Go to a tech-research site, such as NUA Internet Surveys, to search for technology-industry market research (and search the press releases for free information).

➤ Access a tech-support site, such as Microsoft's Knowledge Base, to search for solutions to your specific computer-related problems.

Chapter 25

Search for Usenet Newsgroup Articles

In This Chapter

➤ Discover what Usenet is and what newsgroups are

➤ Find out how to use Deja.com to search newsgroups for important information

➤ Learn to use Deja.com's unique but powerful search commands to narrow your search results

A Usenet newsgroup is an electronic gathering place for people with similar interests. Within a newsgroup, users post messages (called *articles*) about a variety of topics; other users read these articles and, when so disposed, respond. The result is a kind of ongoing, freeform discussion in which dozens—or hundreds—of users participate.

Newsgroups are great sources of information. Of course, because there are over 20,000 active newsgroups, you won't be able to track the flow of messages in all of them all the time, so you'll need a way to search them for the information you want.

All About Usenet

Usenet is the largest and oldest existing online community in the world. Predating the World Wide Web—but using the Internet's basic infrastructure—Usenet is a collection of more than 30,000 online discussion groups, organized by topical hierarchy. Usenet utilizes a technology called NNTP to propagate messages between dedicated Usenet servers all around the world. For more information about Usenet, read the Usenet FAQs at Deja.com, located at `www.deja.com/info/usenet_faq.shtml`.

Searching for a Place to Search—and Finding Deja.com

Normally, you use a program such as Outlook Express, Netscape Messenger, or NewsXPress to subscribe to newsgroups and browse through individual newsgroup articles. This is fine if you're trying to participate in an individual newsgroup community, but it just doesn't cut it if you're power searching for specific information across multiple newsgroups. For that, you need a more powerful tool—a true Usenet search engine.

Most of the major search sites include an option to search newsgroup articles. Many of these sites don't actually do the searching themselves. Instead, they use the newsgroup search engine provided by Deja.com—the only site you need for your own personal newsgroup searches.

Deja.com (`www.deja.com`)—formerly known as DejaNews—lets you search Usenet newsgroup articles for particular topics you're interested in—or search newsgroup posters for particular people you're interested in. Deja.com then searches all the newsgroups on Usenet for what you want and returns the results in a form that you'll find very familiar.

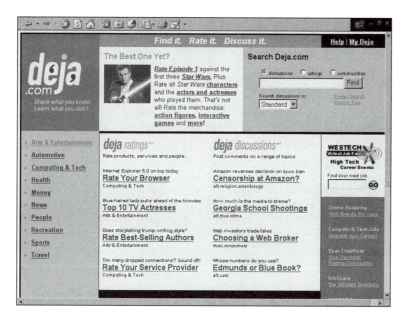

*Deja.com—ignore all this portal-type stuff and click the **Power Search** link for the best Usenet search engine on the Web.*

Newsgroups, Discussions, and Communities—Which Is Which?

Deja.com has started using some confusing language on its site. For some reason, Deja.com now refers to Usenet newsgroups as *discussions* (and they used to refer to them as *forums*, if you want to get even more confused). So when you see a link to forums, it means newsgroups. But if you see a link to *communities*, this is *not* a link to newsgroups—it's a link to some homegrown message boards and personal Web pages Deja.com runs on its site. Deja.com communities are not Usenet newsgroups—don't confuse them!

In addition, Deja.com now includes a feature it calls *Ratings*. They're encouraging their users to offer their opinions and comments on various products, places, and people, and promoting the site as "the best place to learn what others think." In *my* opinion, they've diluted what was special about the old DejaNews, and I give them a lower rating than they had before.

Searching for Information Across Newsgroups

There's lots of stuff on Deja.com's home page, and my advice is to ignore almost all of it. Instead, click the **Power Search** link to go directly to Deja.com's powerful newsgroup search engine.

Getting ready to search the Usenet archives from Deja.com's Power Search page.

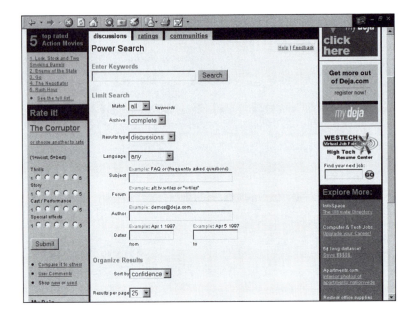

From the Power Search page, here's how you search for specific information in the Usenet newsgroup archives.

1. Enter your query into the **Enter Keywords** box. Your query is used to search both the subject and the text of all newsgroup articles.

2. Select whether you want to match **All** or **Any** keywords.

3. Select which Archive you want to search: **Complete** (contains all the newsgroups), **Standard** (excludes the Adult archive), **Adult** (searches only newsgroups containing adult content), **Jobs** (searches only those newsgroups that feature job postings), or **For Sale** (searches only newsgroups focusing on items for sale). Generally, you should use the **Complete** option unless you have a more specific search in mind (for jobs, something to buy, or something kinky).

4. Pull down the **Results Type** list and select **Discussions** (which is what Deja.com calls newsgroups).

5. If you want to limit your search to articles written in a specific language, select that language from the **Language** pull-down list.

6. If you want to limit your search to articles with certain words in their subject lines, enter those keywords into the **Subject** box.

268

7. If you want to limit your search to specific newsgroups, enter those newsgroups into the **Forum** box.

8. If you want to limit your search to articles posted by a specific user, enter that user's email address in the **Author** box.

9. If you want to limit your search to articles posted within a specific time period, enter those dates in the **Date** boxes.

10. In the **Results** section, select whether you want to sort results by Confidence, Subject, Forum, Author, or Date.

11. Select how many results to display on a page.

12. Click the **Search** button to begin the search.

Deja.com offers one of the most powerful and versatile search engines available on the Web. Unfortunately, although it's powerful, it's rather nonstandard. So pay close attention to the commands listed in Table 25.1—Deja.com does things a little differently from what you're probably used to.

Table 25.1   Deja.com Search Parameters

To Do This:	Use This Command:	Example:
Search for part of a word	*	mon*
Search for a complete phrase	" "	"monty python"
Search for both keywords (AND)	&	monty & python
Search for either keyword (OR)	|	monty ¦ python
Exclude a word (NOT)	&!	monty &! python
Search for words *near* each other (within 5 characters)	^	monty ^ python
Search an alphabetical *range* of words *NOTE: Don't confuse braces {} with parentheses () used to group items together*	{}	{monkey monty}
Search only for items from a specific author	~a	~a me@molehillgruop.com
Search only within a specific newsgroup	~g	~g alt.art.theft
Search only within the subject of an article	~s	~s (monty python)
Search only for articles posted on a specific date	~dc *yyyy/ mm/dd*	~dc 1998/02/14

After you've started your search, Deja.com automatically retrieves a list of newsgroup articles (from a variety of newsgroups) that match your search criteria. This page not only lists matching articles, but also lists the top newsgroups pertaining to your

269

search. For each matching article, Deja.com includes the article's date and subject, which newsgroup (forum) the article appeared in, and the author of the article. Click the subject link to read the text of the article.

Reading Newsgroup Articles

When you click an article on the results page, you display the entire text of the article. From here you can do a number of things (in addition to just reading the article, of course).

Reading a newsgroup article—and linking to additional articles and information.

Click to access all articles in this newsgroup.

Click to view all messages in the current thread.

Click to privately email the author of this article.

Click to reply to this article publicly.

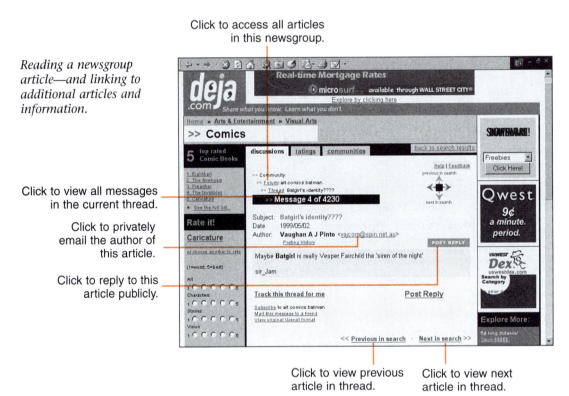

Click to view previous article in thread.

Click to view next article in thread.

➤ Display all current articles in this article's newsgroup by clicking the **Forum** link.

➤ View all articles in the current message thread by clicking the **Thread** link.

➤ Read the previous message in this thread by clicking the **Previous in Search** link.

➤ Read the next message in this thread by clicking the **Next in Search** link.

➤ Reply to this message (publicly) by clicking the **Post Reply** link.

➤ Reply to the author of this message (via private email) by clicking his or her email address.

➤ View other articles posted by this author by clicking the **Posting History** link.

➤ Return to your list of search results by clicking the **Back to Search Results** link.

➤ View a page of user ratings related to this article's topic by clicking the **Ratings** tab.

➤ View Deja.com's user communities related to this article's topic by clicking the **Communities** tab.

Thread Your Subjects

A thread is a collection of newsgroup articles on the same subject. Each subsequent post to a thread is in response to a previous article.

Use Deja.com for All Your Newsgroup Needs

In addition to its search capabilities (and all the ratings and community crud cluttering up its home page), Deja.com can actually be used to read newsgroups on a regular basis. The best way to do this is to use the **My Deja** function. Just click the **My Deja** link on the site's home page, and then use the **Subscribe to a New Forum** link to personalize the list of newsgroups that appear on your My Deja page. (You can also add other functions to your My Deja page, of course, such as a calendar, Web-based email, and other typical portal stuff.)

The Least You Need to Know

➤ Usenet newsgroups are topic-oriented online message boards.

➤ Messages in newsgroups are called *articles*; articles are *posted* to newsgroups by *authors*.

➤ To search Usenet newsgroups, use Deja.com.

➤ Deja.com includes powerful but unique search commands to help you narrow your search.

Chapter 26

Search for Mailing Lists and Chat Rooms

In This Chapter

➤ Learn how to search for topic-specific email mailing lists

➤ Discover how Internet Relay Chat works—and where you can find directories of chat networks, servers, and channels

➤ Find out how to locate other users for instant messaging

In addition to the Usenet newsgroups discussed in the last chapter, there are several other forums for communicating with other Internet users who are interested in similar topics. Those methods include email mailings, chat channels, and instant messaging services.

Where do you find these things on the Internet? Read on and find out.

Searching for the Right Special-Interest Email Mailing Lists

Email mailing lists are similar to Usenet newsgroups in that they both serve as gathering places for people with similar interests. The main difference is that mailing lists tend to be a little more organized and focus on more specific topics, whereas newsgroups are open forums in which anyone can participate. Most mailing lists have fewer members than many newsgroups, because mailing lists must be moderated by a single individual. Newsgroups, as most people discover quite quickly, don't have much moderation at all!

Another big difference between newsgroups and mailing lists is that newsgroups are centralized—it's easy to obtain a list of newsgroups and easy to join the ones you like. Mailing lists, on the other hand, are run by individuals—called *list managers*—off of their own individual computers. There's no centralized organization, and pretty much anybody who wants to can start up their own mailing list.

The way mailing lists work is that you first have to find out about the list, and then you email the list manager to let you subscribe, and then—either daily, weekly, or whenever—you'll receive (via email) a batch of messages from other mailing list members. Naturally, you can also send email messages to the rest of the group.

But where can you get a list of these mailing lists? Table 26.1 lists some of the more popular Web sites that maintain these "lists of lists."

Table 26.1   Mailing List Directories on the Web

Site:	URL:
Liszt	www.liszt.com
Publicly Accessible Mailing Lists	www.neosoft.com/internet/paml/
The List of Lists	www.catalog.com/vivian/interest-groupsearch.html
Topica	www.topica.com

Use Liszt to search for mailing lists—and Usenet newsgroups and IRC Chat channels.

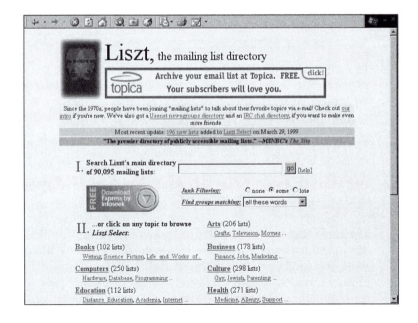

274

Most of these sites let you search for specific mailing lists, and some let you browse the lists by topic. My personal favorite list search site is Liszt; it's currently tracking more than 90,000 mailing lists. Liszt also has sites that list Usenet newsgroups (www.liszt.com/news/) and IRC Chat channels (www.liszt.com/chat/, discussed later in this chapter), so it's a good all-in-one site for these kinds of searches.

Because new mailing lists are created every day, return to these sites often for new listings.

How to Subscribe

To subscribe to an email mailing list, you must send email to the list manager noting that you want to become a member. You have to follow a particular format in your message, however. The most common format is to enter the email address of the mailing list in the **To** field of your message; enter the word SUBSCRIBE in the Subject field; then enter SUBSCRIBE *listname firstname lastname* as the message's text. If you want to cancel a mailing list subscription, send a similar message to the list with UNSUBSCRIBE as the subject and UNSUBSCRIBE *listname* as the message text. Because some mailing lists may work a little differently, be sure to read and follow the specific instructions for each particular mailing list—you can find the instructions on Liszt and most of the other "lists of lists" sites.

Searching for the Right Online Chat Channel

Chatting online is one of the most popular—and time-consuming—online activities. There are more than 35,000 chat channels on hundreds of different chat servers on more than two dozen chat networks. Where do you find this information?

Table 26.2 lists some of the better sites that offer directories of all these chat networks, servers, and channels.

Table 26.2   Chat Directories on the Web

Site:	URL:
IRC Networks and Server Lists	`www.irchelp.org/irchelp/network.html`
Liszt's IRC Chat Directory	`www.liszt.com/chat/`
Saint's List of IRC Networks and Servers	`www.geocities.com/~saintslist/`

Of these sites, I'm a Liszt fan. It's an easy-to-use site and has one of the larger lists of chat channels. My advice is to start there and branch out to the other sites only if you can't find what you're looking for.

More Than One Kind of Chat

The most popular type of Internet chat is *Internet Relay Chat* (IRC). IRC runs on more than two dozen separate networks (nets). Each net has its own group of *servers*, based at various locations around the world. And each net also has its own group of *channels*, organized by topic—some of the larger nets have more than 10,000 channels active at any given time! The largest nets are EFnet (the original IRC net), Undernet, IRCnet, DALnet, and NewNet. When you run your chat program (such as mIRC, found at `www.mirc.com`), you first choose which net you want to use, then you connect to a server on that net, and then you join one or more chat channels. I won't even go into Microsoft's Comic Chat (which runs on only a handful of Microsoft chat servers), the Web-based chat rooms that you find on most portal sites, or the proprietary chat rooms on AOL and other online services. That's just too much chat to chat about! (For a good primer on IRC, check out `www.irchelp.org`.)

Searching for Other Instant-Messaging Users

There is yet another method of online communication that is faster than newsgroups or mailing lists and more private than chat channels. *Instant messaging* lets you send short electronic messages back and forth to other online users, in real-time, without the need to enter a public chat room.

276

Searching for ICQ Users

The most popular instant messaging program, with more than 16 million users, is called *ICQ* (say it out loud—it stands for "I seek you"). ICQ, downloadable for free from www.icq.com, lets you send messages to other ICQ users, engage in private chat sessions with other ICQ users, and even send and receive files to and from other ICQ users, all in real-time. ICQ will even let you keep lists of your favorite users and notify you when they're online.

Where do you find other ICQ users to message with? Easy—you search for them with ICQ Power Search. Just go to www.icq.com/search/ and use the People Search section. You can look for users by first name, last name, email address, or ICQ Nick Name.

You can also search for ICQ users from within the ICQ program itself. When you click the **Add Users** button, you see the Find/Add Users window. From here, select the **Find Users** tab and search for users in one of several ways:

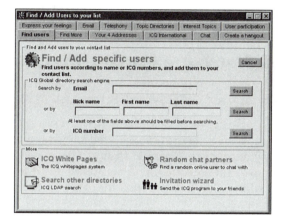

Search for other ICQ users by name, number, or address.

➤ **ICQ Global Directory Search Engine**   This section lets you search by email address, Nick Name, first name, last name, or ICQ number. Just enter your search parameters and click the appropriate Search button.

➤ **ICQ White Pages**   Search the ICQ directories by interests, background, affiliation, profession, and other similar parameters.

➤ **Random Chat Partners**   Find other ICQ users, randomly. (It's a great way to meet people you weren't looking for!)

➤ **Search Other Directories**   Search for users in more than a dozen online directories. (Unfortunately, these directories list *all* users, including many who aren't ICQ users.)

277

Invite Your Friends

If you're an ICQ user and an online friend *isn't*, then click **Invitation Wizard** in the **Find/Add Specific Users** window to send a copy of the ICQ program to your friend.

In addition, you can select other tabs in this window to display several more narrow types of searches. For example, select the **ICQ International** tab to find users by language or by country.

Searching for AOL Netscape Instant-Messenger Users

The number two instant messaging program is AOL Netscape Instant Messenger. (Download the program for free from `home.netcenter.com`; just click the **Instant Messenger** link.)

Unfortunately, Instant Messenger doesn't have a Web site where you can search for their users; you can, however, search for other Instant Messenger users from within the program. Just pull down the **People** menu and select **Find a Buddy Wizard**. This launches a special wizard that lets you look for other users either by name, address, location, or email address.

The Instant Messaging Monopoly

Both ICQ and AOL Netscape Instant Messenger are owned by America Online— and when you throw in AOL's proprietary Buddy List instant messaging system, just about all the instant messaging in the online world is owned by one company!

278

The Least You Need to Know

➤ Search for email mailing lists at Liszt or Topica.

➤ Search for chat networks, servers, and channels at Liszt.

➤ Search for ICQ users at the ICQ Power Search page—or from within the ICQ program itself.

➤ Search for AOL Netscape Instant Messenger users from within the program with the Find a Buddy Wizard.

Chapter 27

Search for Files to Download

In This Chapter

➤ Discover how easy it is to find and download files from the Internet

➤ Learn which are the top three download sites

➤ Find out why you should use virus protection software if you do a lot of file downloading

The Internet is a huge repository for computer files of all shapes and sizes, from utilities that help you better manage your disk drive to full-featured email and newsgroup programs. There are hundreds of thousands of these programs available *somewhere* on the Internet; if you can find them, you can download them to your computer.

There are three major Web sites that serve as either directories of or search engines to huge online software repositories. I'll talk about those sites pretty much exclusively in this chapter because if you can't find the files you want on these sites, they're probably not available!

The Least You Need to Know About Downloading

The Internet is filled with files, utilities, pictures, and programs—and most of them are free. But before you can use any of them, you first have to know how to download them.

Fortunately, all the major sites make downloading fairly easy. There are some variations to the process, but overall, it's pretty straightforward. In a nutshell, all you have to do is the following:

1. Create a special download directory on your computer's hard drive.

2. Find and download the software you want from one of the major download sites.

3. If the software was compressed (generally in a Zip file), decompress (or "unzip") the software, using a utility such as WinZip. (You can download a copy of WinZip from any of the major download sites—don't worry, it doesn't come zipped itself!)

4. Install the software. Installation instructions are usually included somewhere on the download information page or in a readme file included with the file download. In most cases, installation involves running a file named setup.exe or install.exe; after the setup program launches, follow the onscreen instructions to complete the installation.

5. Delete the original compressed (Zip) file.

Find Files Anywhere with Download.com

The other two download sites discussed in this chapter are actually huge repositories of files. CNET's Download.com (www.download.com), on the other hand, doesn't include a single file on its site. What it does include are links to and descriptions of more than 20,000 of the best software programs available for downloading from the Internet. This is the site to go to if you're unsure about downloading, because the Download.com team does the evaluation and categorization for you.

Use Download.com to search for files anywhere on the Internet.

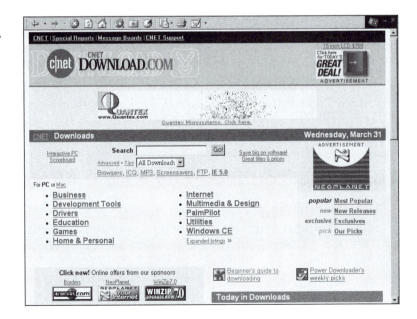

There are several ways to access the files listed on Download.com, including

➤ **Browse by category**   The categories include Business, Development Tools, Drivers, Education, Games, Home and Personal, Internet, Multimedia and Design, Utilities, PalmPilot, and Windows CE; click the **Expanded Listings** link to view subcategories within these major categories.

➤ **Browse by special lists**   Download.com breaks some of its listings into special categories—Most Popular, New Releases, Exclusives, and Our Picks.

➤ **Search**   Use the **Search** box at the top of the home page to enter your query, then click the **Go** button. If you know the name of the file you want to download, enter the filename as your query. If you just want to search for a certain type of software (for example, an IRC client), then enter that as your query. (You can also conduct a more selective search by clicking the **Advanced Search** link.)

After you've found the file you want to download, read its description and download instructions, and then click the **Download now** link. This automatically starts the download via the best available download site. (Remember, none of these programs are on CNET itself; all CNET does is link to other servers where the programs are stored.)

Download.com Versus Shareware.com

CNET actually operates two download sites—Download.com and Shareware.com (www.shareware.com). Both sites enable you to find and download software programs from numerous sites around the Internet, and both offer a reliability guide to point you toward the best download location. The difference is that Shareware.com allows you to search more sites for software (250,000 files as compared to 20,000 for Download.com), but the results are edited. The Shareware.com files are not categorized, and the file descriptions are provided by third parties and typically don't include all the information that you find on the Download.com descriptions. My advice is to start with Download.com; then if you don't find the file you want, give Shareware.com a try as your second CNET download site.

Search the Shelves of the ZDNet Software Library

The ZDNet Software Library (`www.zdnet.com/swlib/`) is just what it says it is—a huge library of software provided by Ziff-Davis' ZDNet Web service. As with Download.com, there are three ways to find files here:

➤ **Browse by category**   The categories listed down the left side of the page include Games, Internet, Utilities, Home and Education, Small Business, Graphics and Multimedia, Development, Win 95/98/NT, and Demos.

➤ **Browse by special lists**   ZDNet breaks some of its listings into special categories—What's New, Reviewer's Picks, and Most Popular. In addition, there are links to special software libraries for Macintosh, PalmPilot, and LaunchPad software.

➤ **Search**   Use the **Search** box at the top of the home page to enter your query, then click the **Search** button. (You can also conduct a more advanced search by clicking the **Options** link.)

Search the huge ZDNet Software Library for files to download.

After you find the file you wish to download, click its link to display a full-page description. To download the file, click the **Download Now** button.

Freeware and Shareware

Many of the program files you find online are available free of charge; these programs are called *freeware*. Other programs can be downloaded for no charge, but they require you to pay a token amount to receive full functionality or documentation; these programs are called *shareware*. Both types of programs are in contrast to the stuff you buy in boxes at your local computer retailer, which is *commercial software*.

Download Till the Cows Come Home at Tucows

The other "big dog" in downloading sites is actually a big *cow*—Tucows. Tucows (www.tucows.com) is one of the oldest repositories of software on the Internet, serving up software downloads since 1993.

Put a Sock in It

If you wondered, Tucows stands for The Ultimate Collection Of Winsock Software. Just what is Winsock software, you ask? Well, Tucows was one of the first program repositories on the Net, and as such, it specialized in Internet-related programs. A Winsock program was an early Internet connection program, providing *Windows sockets*—hence, Winsock. Today, what goes for a Winsock is already built into Windows; back then, Windows wasn't Internet-ready.

Like Download.com and the ZDNet Software Library, you can either browse through Tucows or search for files. Tucows's browsing is a little different, however, because it is operating-system based. That is, instead of starting out by software category, you first click the operating system you're using. *Then* you can click through the different categories of software within the repository.

Tucows's search function has the same operating system bias. Yes, you enter your query into the **Quick Search** box, but then you select your operating system from the pull-down list—and only then do you hit the **Search** button. (To use "any word" and "either word" search parameters, click the **Options** link.)

Because Tucows has such a large user base, it actually mirrors its collection on multiple servers around the world. You will be prompted for your location so your query can be directed to a server near you for faster downloading. After you find the software you want, downloading it is a simple matter of clicking the **Try Now** link next to the software listing.

Tucows may not have the most detailed program listings, but the "four-cow" rankings are always on the mark, and downloading is quite fast. Because of this, Tucows is a good site for the more experienced file downloader.

Other File Repositories

If you can't find what you want at one of the big three download sites, you might want to try searching one of these other file repositories on the Web:

➤ FileMine (www.filemine.com)

➤ FilePile (filepile.com)

➤ Jumbo (www.jumbo.com)

➤ Shareware Place (www.sharewareplace.com)

➤ WinSite (www.winsite.com)

Downloading Via FTP

All the software libraries listed in this chapter are Web-based. You may also find repositories of files on the Internet that are not hosted on Web sites, but instead require the use of an *FTP* program for downloading. FTP (which stands for File Transfer Protocol) is an older technology still used by some sites; in some cases, FTP downloads might be a tad faster than downloads from Web sites. Note that you don't have to have a separate FTP program to access FTP sites—you can use your Web browser as a quasi-FTP client! Just enter ftp:// and the FTP site's address into your browser's address box, and the contents of the FTP site will appear in your browser window.

One Last Thing—Protect Your Computer Against Viruses

Computer viruses are programs that harm your computer in some fashion. Some are more annoying than harmful, but others can destroy the contents of your computer system and render it useless. You can protect yourself from viruses by being careful about what you put on your machine and by running antivirus software regularly.

Unfortunately, files on the Internet can be easily infected with viruses. The best prevention is to download files only from major download sites (such as those discussed in this chapter), because unknown files from unknown sites pose the highest risk.

If you download files from the Internet, you should install an antivirus program on your computer. This program checks your system for viruses each time your system is booted. To be safe, you should download any programs from the Internet to a separate directory and scan them with the antivirus program before you run the new programs on your system.

You can find several popular antivirus programs at your local computer software retailer—or at any of the download sites discussed in this chapter. My favorites are McAfee VirusScan (a free version is included with Microsoft Plus! 98) and Norton AntiVirus.

The Least You Need to Know

➤ Downloading files from the Internet is relatively automated, although you may need an unzip program (such as WinZip) to decompress zipped files.

➤ The three main sites for file downloading are Download.com, ZDNet Software Library, and Tucows.

➤ All these sites scan their files for computer viruses; if you download from any other sites, however, you should use virus-checking software for protection.

287

Chapter 28

Search for Pictures and Graphics

In This Chapter

➤ Learn all about the different graphics file formats found on the Web

➤ Discover which sites have the best search engines customized for finding images

➤ Uncover the best collections of images available on the Web

Have you ever needed or wanted to find a picture of a red sports car? Or of a particular supermodel or celebrity? What about a digital copy of a painting by Rembrandt?

How do you find particular images on the Internet? One way is to search for them, using special image search engines fine-tuned to find pictures, graphics, and photographs. Another way is to visit one of the many image archive sites where you can browse through directories of images available for downloading.

We'll take a look at both kinds of sites.

What Kinds of Images Are Available on the Web?

Before we get going, it helps to know what you're looking for. Table 28.1 lists the various image and movie file formats you're likely to find on the Web.

Table 28.1 Image and Movie File Formats

File Format:	Description:
.bmp	A simple graphics format (abbreviation for "bitmap") that is the default format for Windows desktop backgrounds
.gif	A popular Web-based graphics format (pronounced "jif"). GIF files can include transparent backgrounds (so a Web page background can show through) and can include multiple images for a simple animated effect
.jpe	An alternate file extension for JPG graphics files
.jpg	Another popular Web-based graphics format (pronounced "jay-peg"). JPG files are often slightly smaller in size than comparable GIF files
.mov	A video format (for "QuickTime Movie") used for video clips
.mpg	A video format (pronounced "em-peg") used for video clips
.pcx	An older graphics format (pronounced "pee-see-ex") not normally used on Web pages. PCX files can be used as desktop backgrounds for more recent versions of Windows
.pdf	A file type from Adobe that lets you view pages on your screen exactly as you'd see them on paper. (PDF stands for Page Definition Format)
.png	A newer graphics format (pronounced "ping") designed to ultimately replace the GIF format—although it's not yet widely used
.qt	An alternate file extension for QuickTime Movie (.mov) files
.ram	A video format (for "RealMovie") designed for real-time streaming video feeds
.rm	An alternate file extension for either RealAudio or RealMovie files
.tif	A graphics format (pronounced "tif") not widely used on Web pages. TIF files are popular with professional desktop publishers

Search the Web for Images

Normal Web search engines do a poor job of finding image files—they're text-based engines, after all. When you're searching for images, you want a search engine that incorporates technology that in some way indexes a *description* of the image.

Fortunately, there are several such image searchers available—as well as other sites that manually catalog images found on the Net. Table 28.2 lists some of these image search sites.

Table 28.2 Image Search Sites

Site:	URL:	Comments:
About.com Web Clip Art Links	webclipart.about.com	Great collection of links to hundreds of clip art sites
AltaVista Photo & Media Finder	image.altavista.com	Tracks more than 17 million photos, video, and audio clips—one of the best image searchers on the Web; *recommended* (see Chapter 4 for more detailed information)
Amazing Picture Machine	www.ncrtec.org/picture.htm	Indexed and searchable collection of graphical resources
Arthur	www.ahip.getty.edu/arthur/	ART media and text HUb and Retrieval System from the Getty Information Institute, powered by the AMORE engine; indexes 30,000 images on 300 Web sites
Clip Art Review	www.webplaces.com/html/clipart.htm	Links to dozens of clip art sites on the Web, organized by category
Clipart Directory	www.clipart.com	Links to more than a hundred free and commercial clip art sites
Lycos Image Gallery	www.lycos.com/picturethis/	Serviceable search engine for picture and sound files (see Chapter 6 for more detailed information)
NCrtec Good Photograph and Image Sites	www.ncrtec.org/tools/picture/goodsite.htm	Large collection of links to other image sites; part of the Amazing Picture Machine site
WebSEEk	www.ctr.columbia.edu/webseek/	Browse the catalog by category or search the Web for videos, color photos, grayscale images, or graphics; from Columbia University
Yahoo! Image Surfer	ipix.yahoo.com	Good (but not great) directory of photographic images (see Chapter 3 for more information)

Many of these sites let you browse by image category (animals, business, and so on); some let you search by keyword. Some of these sites are directories that have cataloged images at other sites; some are true search engines that have indexed images on the Web. The reality is that you will find very little overlap among these sites, so you may have to go to multiple sites to find the exact image you want.

Don't Forget the Newsgroups!

There are tons of Usenet newsgroups that specialize in posting images of various types. Granted, many of these newsgroups are erotic in nature, but there are also a handful of non-sex picture newsgroups available. Look in the `alt.binaries.pictures.*` hierarchy for the groups that focus on pictures.

Search for Dedicated Image Libraries

There are also sites that specialize in providing a database of images of various sorts for your personal or professional use. Table 28.3 lists some of the major image libraries on the Internet.

Table 28.3   Image Libraries on the Web

Site:	URL:	Comments:
art.com	`www.art.com`	Expansive site with several different fee-based galleries—includes more than 100,000 great works by famous artists
Art Today	`www.arttoday.com`	Massive fee-based archive of more than 750,000 clip art and photographic images—*recommended*
Barry's Clip Art Server	`www.barrysclipart.com`	Large collection of free GIF and JPG images
ClipArtConnection	`www.clipartconnection.com`	Good collection of free clip art

Site:	URL:	Comments:
ClipArtNow	www.clipartnow.com	Fee-based collection of clip art
Corbis	www.corbis.com	Great collections of high resolution photographs; owned by Bill Gates—but still *recommended*!
Icon Bank	www.iconbank.com	Huge database of icons for Web designers
Mediabuilder	www.mediabuilder.com	Free database of icons, animation, and Web-page backgrounds
Smithsonian Photo Archive	photo2.si.edu	Huge archive of photographic and digital images from the Smithsonian Institution

Some of the best photographs on the Internet are available at Corbis.

Many of these libraries or archives are free; others charge for each download. The commercial sites, such as Art Today (www.arttoday.com), are generally worth it, providing much larger, better-organized archives of higher-quality images.

Don't Steal the Art!

Many image files on the Web are copyrighted and cannot legally be used without payment for permission. Although it's probably okay to download a graphics file for use on your personal computer (assuming the Feds aren't going to raid your house looking for illegal pictures), using graphics without permission for commercial use—for a newsletter or a personal Web page, for example—is definitely a legal no-no.

The Least You Need to Know

➤ There are a variety of image file types to be found on the Internet; the two most popular file types are JPG and GIF.

➤ Use a special image search engine to search for graphics files on the Web; one of the best is the AltaVista Photo & Media Finder.

➤ You can also find images in dedicated image libraries; many of the better image libraries—such as Art Today—charge for downloads.

Chapter 29

Search for Music and Sounds

In This Chapter

➤ Learn about all the different audio file formats available on the Web

➤ Find out where you can download MIDI song files on the Web

➤ Discover why MP3 audio is revolutionizing the music industry—and where you can find MP3 files for downloading

Downloading sound files is a big thing—especially music files. The Internet is a huge resource for sound files of all types, from simple WAV files for Windows system sounds, to complex MIDI files favored by musicians, to the new MP3 files that provide near-CD quality sound for music collectors.

But before you can download a sound file, you have to find it—and the best way to find something is to search for it.

What Types of Audio Files Can You Find on the Web?

Before we start searching, we'll do a quick overview of the types of sound files we'll be searching for. Table 29.1 lists the various audio file formats you're likely to find on the Web.

Table 29.1   Audio File Formats

File Format:	Description:
.au	An audio format (abbreviation for "audio") that originated on the Sun and NeXT computer systems.
.mid	An audio format (abbreviation for MIDI—the Musical Instrument Digital Interface format used by professional musicians) used for longer music-based audio clips.
.mp3	An audio format that uses data compression to reduce digital sound files by a 12:1 ratio with virtually no loss in quality. The result is a high-quality, small file size version of a digital original; MP3 files are often used to make hard-disk copies of music from compact discs. (The file extension itself is short for MPEG Layer 3, the technology behind the file format.)
.ra	An audio format (abbreviation for RealAudio) designed for real-time streaming audio feeds.
.rm	An alternate file extension for either RealAudio or RealMovie files.
.snd	An audio format (abbreviation for "sound") similar to the AU format; not widely used on the Web.
.wav	An audio format (pronounced "wave") used on many Web pages as well as for Windows system sounds.

Searching for Regular Audio

If you're looking for general audio files, there are only a handful of specialized search engines you can use.

The best general audio searcher, in my opinion, is the AltaVista Photo & Media Finder (`image.altavista.com`). This search engine scans the Web for about a dozen different media formats—including WAV and RealAudio files—and has already indexed more than 17 million audio and image files. (For more information on the AltaVista Photo & Media Finder, see Chapter 4, "Scale the Heights of AltaVista.")

The other major general audio search engine is the Lycos Image Gallery (`www.lycos.com/picturethis/`), which—as the name implies—tends to do better at finding pictures than sounds. Still, this search engine will find WAV, AU, and RA files fairly easily. (For more information on the Lycos Image Gallery, see Chapter 6, "Go Get It at Lycos.")

Searching for MIDI Files

MIDI, the acronym for *Musical Instrument Digital Interface*, is the audio format of choice for professional musicians, allowing them to digitally record and play back music. But most computer sound cards come with basic MIDI capabilities, and many

Web sites and videogames use MIDI files for background music. In fact, I like to browse the Web while playing select MIDI song files in the background, using Windows' built-in MIDI player!

There are tons of sites that provide libraries of songs in MIDI format; some of the most popular ones are listed in Table 29.2.

Table 29.2   MIDI Song Libraries

Site:	URL:
Classical MIDI Archives	`www.prs.net/midi.html`
Laura's MIDI Heaven	`laurasmidiheaven.simplenet.com`
MIDI Explorer Search Engine	`musicrobot.hypermart.net`
MIDI Farm	`www.midifarm.com`
MIDI Madness	`www.qin.com/madness/main.htm`
MIDI Town	`krebs.home.texas.net`
Multi Audio	`www.multiaudio.net`

Don't Forget the Newsgroups!

There are several Usenet newsgroups that specialize in posting MIDI files. Look in the `alt.binaries.sounds.midi.*` heirarchy, as well as in the `alt.musc.midi` newsgroup.

The Latest Audio Phenomenon—MP3

Know this: MP3 is revolutionizing the music industry.

MP3 is a new format for compressing music to fit within reasonably sized computer files while maintaining near-CD quality sound. A typical three-minute song in MP3 format only takes up 2Mb of disk space.

Although large record companies despise MP3 (they fear the threat of unauthorized copying), Internet users—particularly college students—love it and have wholeheartedly embraced the format. MP3 has quickly become the standard for music on the Web.

Finding an MP3 Player

Just as you need a CD player to play your compact discs, you need a software-based MP3 player to play your MP3 files. There are a number of popular player programs available, including

➤ MacAMP (www.macamp.com)—for the Macintosh

➤ Microsoft Windows Media Player
   (www.microsoft.com/windows/mediaplayer/download/Win32otherx86.asp)

➤ Sonique (www.sonique.com)

➤ SuperSonic (www.gosupersonic.com)

➤ Unreal Player MAX (www.303tek.com/e/index.html)

➤ Virtual Turntables (carrot.prohosting.com/downloads.html)

➤ Winamp (www.winamp.com)—the most popular player today; *recommended*

➤ X11Amp (www.x11amp.bz.nu)—for Unix users

If you want to play your MP3 files away from your computer, check out the Diamond Rio (www.mp3.com/diamond/); kind of a Walkman for MP3 discs.

Searching for MP3 Files on the Web

MP3 directories and search sites are springing up faster than the dandelions in my back yard, even though many of these sites are illegal sites run by hobbyists—which means that even though they're here today, they may be gone tomorrow. If you try to search for MP3 on a normal search engine, you may stumble across a lot of these fly-by-night sites and miss out on the real treasures.

The best thing to do is to check out the list of more stable MP3 sites in Table 29.3. Most of these sites let you search by artist or song title, and some let you search or browse by genre.

Table 29.3   MP3 Libraries and Search Engines

Site:	URL:
2look4	www.2look4.com
Audiofind	www.audiofind.com
DAILYMP3.COM	www.dailymp3.com
Dimension Music	www.dimensionmusic.com
Lycos FAST MP3 Search	mp3.lycos.com
MP3 2000	www.mp3-2000.com
MP3 Place	www.mp3place.com
MP3.com	www.mp3.com
MP3now.com	www.mp3now.com
MPEG.ORG	www.mpeg.org/MPEG/mp3.html
Multi Audio	www.multiaudio.net
musicseek	www.musicseek.net
Oth.Net	oth.net
Palavista Digital Music Metacrawler	www.palavista.com

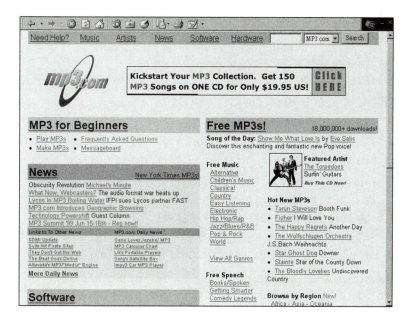

Search for MP3 files, read MP3 news, and learn all about how MP3 works— all at MP3.com.

MP3.com (www.mp3.com) is the big dog of MP3 sites. This hugely popular site—more than 200,000 visitors per day!—features breaking MP3 news, songs you can download, and software links to keep you up-to-date on the latest developments in the world of MP3 music.

Another good source for general MP3 information is the "official" MP3 site at www.mpeg.org/MPEG/mp3.html. Either this site or MP3.com are good sites to start looking because they include a lot of what you'll need to get up and running with this MP3 phenomenon.

As search sites go, it's hard to get any better than the Lycos FAST MP3 Search (mp3.lycos.com), which indexes more than a half million MP3 files—the largest collection of MP3s on the Web!

Searching for MP3 in Usenet Newsgroups

There are a ton of Usenet newsgroups devoted to MP3 information and downloadable files. Here are just a few to check out:

➤ alt.music.mp3
➤ alt.binaries.sounds.mp3
➤ alt.binaries.sounds.mp3.1950s
➤ alt.binaries.sounds.mp3.1960s
➤ alt.binaries.sounds.mp3.1970s
➤ alt.binaries.sounds.mp3.1980s
➤ alt.binaries.sounds.mp3.1990s
➤ alt.binaries.sounds.mp3.bootlegs
➤ alt.binaries.sounds.mp3.ninja.music
➤ alt.binaries.country.mp3
➤ alt.binaries.mp3.bootlegs
➤ alt.binaries.mp3.zappa

Searching for MP3 with Special Software

Even though there are a huge number of Web-based MP3 search sites, you may want to try something a little stronger—software that searches the Internet for MP3 files.

Here are just a few of the MP3 search programs available today—all downloadable from CNET's MP3 Search Tools site (home.cnet.com/category/topic/0,10000, 0-4004-7-274656,00.html):

➤ **Abe's MP3 Finder**   Standard MP3 searching program.
➤ **MP3 Fiend**   Lets you automatically query 11 major MP3 search engines with simple keyword searches; *recommended*.

➤ **Mp3Leech 98**   Search by artist or song and the program returns a list of matching MP3 files for downloading immediately or at a later time.

➤ **MP3-Wolf**   A nice search program that finds MIDI and WAV files, as well MP3 files.

➤ **Planet.MP3Find**   Search program with a Windows Explorer-like interface.

The Least You Need to Know

➤ There are various types of audio files available on the Internet, including WAV, MIDI, and MP3.

➤ Use AltaVista Photo & Media Finder to find WAV and other general audio files on the Web.

➤ Use one of many MIDI search engines or directories to find and download MIDI music files.

➤ Go to MP3.com to find out more about the hot new MP3 music format—and search for MP3 files to download!

Part 8

Getting Particular: How to Find Specialized Information

Okay, so you've read all the preceding chapters and you still have some specific information you need help finding online. If that's the case, this part of the book is for you. Use these chapters to learn how to find the specialized information you just can't find anyplace else, whether that's help with your homework or where to find an ATM machine.

sniff
sniff

Search for College Information

If you're in high school, trying to decide which college to attend, the Internet is your best resource. There are numerous places where you can search for information about specific colleges, as well as search for any available financial aid.

Searching for Which College to Attend

You can find dozens, if not hundreds, of Web sites devoted to helping you learn more about, and choose a college. Table 30.1 lists some of the best college selection sites on the Web.

Table 30.1   Top College Selection Sites

Site:	URL:	Comments:
Admissions Offices	www.yahoo.com/Education/ Higher_Education/College_ Entrance/Admissions_Offices/	Yahoo!'s comprehensive list of links to college admissions offices across the U.S.

continues

Table 30.1   CONTINUED

Site:	URL:	Comments:
All About College	www.allaboutcollege.com	Lists thousands of links to college and university Web sites around the world
American College Entrance Directory	www.aaced.com	Lists and categorizes the most essential college entrance sites on the Internet
Campus Tours	www.campustours.com	Online virtual tours of thousands of college campuses, complete with interactive maps, college Webcams, QuickTime VR tours, campus movies, and pictures
college_base	library.advanced.org/17038	A site (created by two high school students!) that offers help for the SAT/ACT, a collection of college stories written by college students, and an appraisal section that evaluates colleges from the student's perspective
College Board Online	www.collegeboard.org	The official Web site of the non-profit college organization that sponsors the SAT; includes a College Search database of more than 3,200 two- and four-year colleges, a Scholarship Search service, a Career Search service, and online prep for the SAT
College Bound.net	www.cbnet.com	A resource that bills itself as "a student's interactive guide to college life"
College Is Possible	www.collegeispossible.org	From the Coalition of America's Colleges and Universities; a good reference for preparing for, choosing, and paying for college
College Spot	www.collegespot.com	Includes a college search engine, admissions info, scholarship info, and financial aid info
College411	www.college411.org	A collection of links to other college-oriented Web sites

Site:	URL:	Comments:
CollegeDegree.com	www.collegedegree.com	Lists all available distance-learning courses available at major colleges and universities
CollegeEdge	www.collegeedge.com	Contains college planning advice, a scholarship search, and an extensive careers and majors section—as well as one of the most comprehensive college search databases with 5,850 two- and four-year colleges (and vocational/technical schools)
CollegeNET	www.collegenet.com	Offers school searches by major, location, and tuition
Colleges & Careers Center	www.usnews.com/usnews/edu/	From U.S. News Online, a full-service college planning site, and the famous (or infamous) yearly College Rankings
Colleges.com	www.colleges.com	An online "virtual campus" that provides an online community for college students across the country
CollegeView	www.collegeview.com	A complete college portal, with sections on financial aid, careers, résumé writing, and interviewing, as well as a searchable database of all accredited colleges and universities in the U.S. and Canada
CollegeXpress	www.collegexpress.com	Profiles private and independent institutions (no state universities or community colleges)
Critical Comparisons of American Colleges and Universities	www.memex-press.com/cc/	Offers interactive graphs and statistical analyses to help you compare and contrast various schools
Education Resources Information Center	www.accesseric.org	The site of the National Library of Education; includes the ERIC Database, the world's largest source of education information, with more than 950,000 abstracts of documents and journal articles

continues

307

Table 30.1 CONTINUED

Site:	URL:	Comments:
ETS Net	www.ets.org	The official site of the Educational Testing Service; includes information on colleges and universities, careers and jobs, and disabilities and testing
GoCollege	www.gocollege.com	Offers a college search based on desired major, test scores, class rank, location, and tuition; lets you apply to 850 colleges directly online
Kaplan	www.kaplan.com/precoll/	From the giant test prep company, a site packed with free information, including several newsletters, financial aid information, and a college search engine
National Association for College Admission Testing	www.nacac.com	A site created by the NACAC, an association of secondary school counselors, college and university admission officers, and other student counselors; includes a comprehensive listing of college fairs
Student Survival Guide	www.luminet.net/~jackp/survive.html	A wonderful little self-published resource guide for success in college; includes 10 Tips for Survival in the Classroom, 10 Tips for Deciding On or Changing Your Major, 10 Ways to Improve Your Social Life, and numerous other lists of "10s" to help you make your way through your first year at school

308

CollegeEdge is one of the best sites to search for college information—make sure you check out the Pack and Go section, with advice on how to pack for school, what to do your first semester, and how to get along with your roommate!

Check Out College Web Sites

Almost every college has its own Web site. These sites often include a lot of good information about the school, the faculty, the classes, and the campus. In many cases, you'll also be able to access individual student Web pages directly from the main college Web site. One of the best places to search for college Web sites is at Yahoo! College Search (`features.yahoo.com/college/search.html`). You can also guess at a college's URL by entering www.*college*.edu, where *college* is the college's name or initials. For example, enter www.duke.edu to connect to Duke University's Web site, or enter www.ucla.edu to go to UCLA's home page.

Searching for Financial Aid and Scholarships

The Internet also contains a treasure trove of financial aid resources, including applications that you can file electronically, in-depth information about grants and loans, college connections, scholarship searches, and more.

Table 30.2 lists some of the top financial-aid–related Web sites.

Table 30.2   Financial Aid and Scholarship Web Sites

Site:	URL:	Comments:
College Board	www.collegeboard.org	A huge archive with tons of useful information on paying for college
College Guides and Aid	www.collegeguides.com	Links to and reviews of the best financial aid resources—including Web sites, books, software, and more
College Savings Plan Network	www.collegesavings.org/yourstate.htm	A comprehensive list of college savings programs by state
FastWEB	www.fastweb.com	A scholarship search service with a database of 180,000 sources of financial aid
FinAid	www.finaid.org	A full-service financial aid site, including a directory of college aid offices
National Financial Services Network	www.nfsn.com/Educatio.htm	An online directory of lenders for education loans
Office of Postsecondary Education	www.ed.gov/offices/OPE/Students/index.html	A good site to learn all about the different kinds of federal aid; includes a free electronic version of the federal financial application that you can submit directly from the site
Project EASI	easi.ed.gov	Easy Access for Students and Institutions, a Dept. of Education program aimed at streamlining the financial aid process
Sallie Mae	www.salliemae.com	The company that provides much of the money that goes into higher-education loans; their Web site includes an introductory guide to financial aid and a comprehensive database of scholarships and other resources
Think College	www.ed.gov/thinkcollege	The Department of Education's college preparation information resource, providing information about recently enacted government programs

There is probably no better online resource for pre-college students and their parents than the College Board's Web site (www.collegeboard.org). The financial aid section of this immense site archives tons of useful information on paying for college. Some of the more useful sections of this site are the CSS/Financial Aid PROFILE,

CollegeCredit Loans, Expected Family Contribution Calculator, Financial Aid Calculators, and Financial Aid Services.

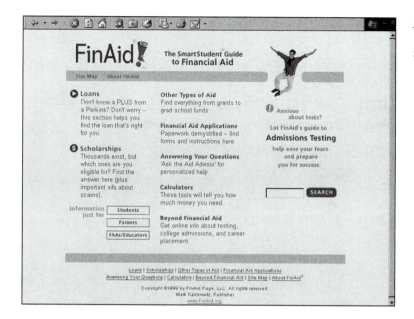

FinAid—one of the best "unofficial" online guides to financial aid resources.

Another good site to examine is FinAid (`www.finaid.org`), a real gold mine of a site. FinAid includes access to scholarship and fellowship databases, information on grants and loans, an extensive bibliography, links to school financial aid offices, and links to most of the other important sources of financial aid information contained on the Web.

Beware of Rip-Offs

Some scholarship search services are excellent resources, but others are scams, according to the FTC. The biggest tip-off is money: If somebody wants a lot of it to conduct a search for you, you're probably dealing with the wrong folks. The bills can quickly outstrip the value of scholarships discovered—and often, they aren't finding anything that you wouldn't come across with some smart online searching of your own.

The Least You Need to Know

➤ There are hundreds of sites you can search that provide information about choosing a college; one of the best is CollegeEdge.

➤ You can also go directly to a college's Web site to obtain information about classes, programs, admissions, and life on campus.

➤ You should also use the Internet to search and apply for financial aid; The College Board and FinAid run two of the best aid-related Web sites.

Chapter 31

Search for Help with Homework

In This Chapter

➤ Discover why homework-helper Web sites can be a lifesaver when your children have homework problems or reports due

➤ Find out which search sites filter out content inappropriate for children

I wish that I had had access to the Internet when I was a kid. Back then when I had a homework assignment or a report to write, I either had to trek down to the library or pull out our family's beat-up set of encyclopedias.

Today, kids just plunk themselves down in front of the computer and let their fingers do the searching for them. In fact, kids don't even have to access the main search engines to look up information—there is a virtual plethora of sites devoted just to helping children do their homework.

Searching for Homework Help on the Web

If you have kids, they have homework. If they're having trouble with their homework, there are numerous Web sites you can access that provide targeted homework help. Most of these sites let you either browse through a list of topics, or search the site for specific types of help.

Table 31.1 lists the top homework-related sites on the Web.

Table 31.1   Top Homework Sites

Site:	URL:	Comments:
About.com Homework Help	homeworkhelp.about.com	Terrific collection of topic-specific links for anyone needing help with homework
Awesome Library	www.awesomelibrary.org	A directory of more than 12,000 sites specifically organized for teachers, students, and parents
Eisenhower National Clearinghouse	www.enc.org	Focusing on math and science education, this site offers online lessons and activities, a database of K-12 curriculum resources, and other services
Grammar Lady	www.grammarlady.com	The Grammar Lady answers your questions about English grammar
Homework Central	www.homeworkcentral.com	Three separate sites for different grade levels (1-6, Middle/High School, and College)
Homework Help	www.startribune.com/stonline/html/special/homework/	Teachers from across the U.S. volunteer and provide answers to questions submitted by stumped students
Homework Helper	www.homeworkhelper.com	From the Electric Library, a good search engine for homework topics
infoplease Homework Center	kids.infoplease.com/homework/	Part of the infoplease Kids' Almanac, specially designed for K-12 home work problems
Kid Info	www.kidinfo.com	Links to curriculum guides, lesson plans, reference sites, and teaching aids—organized by specific curriculum
KidsClick	sunsite.berkeley.edu/KidsClick!/	Created by librarians, an index of more than 5,000 homework-helpful Web sites in various categories for kids ages 1-6

Site:	URL:	Comments:
KidsConnect	`www.ala.org/ICONN/kidsconn.html`	A question-answering, help, and referral service for K–12 students on the Internet; part of the American Library Association's ICONnect site
KY3 for Kids Homework Help	`www.ky3.com/kids/homework`	Links to homework-helpful Web sites
Mad Scientist Network	`www.madsci.org`	Focuses on K-12 science education; scientists answer questions submitted by users, and all the answers are archived at this site
Schoolwork.ugh!	`www.schoolwork.org`	Good collection of resources for students in grade 7 and higher
StudyWEB	`www.studyweb.com`	This directory of educational resources provides links to more than 70,000 sites about topics such as music, language, animals, and politics; includes ratings by grade level and notes whether visual aids are available (helpful if you're writing a report)
WebMath	`www.webmath.com`	Great site for general math and algebra problems; students enter their math problem and receive a step-by-step solution
Word Central	`www.wordcentral.com`	Access Merriam Webster's student dictionary, a kid's Word of the Day, and various word games

I'm a big fan of infoplease's Homework Center. You can search the site from the search box at the top of the home page or click the topic links in the left column. I also like browsing through the **Answers** to questions other students have asked; this helps you get through some sticky problems without having to reinvent the wheel.

The infoplease Homework Center—a good place to search for answers to your homework problems.

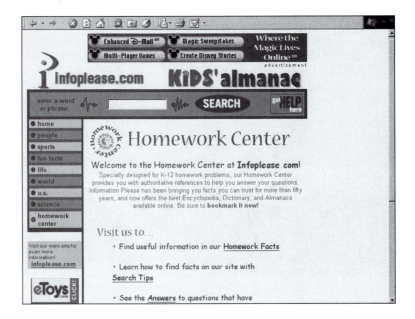

Don't Forget the Libraries!

Other good types of Web sites for homework help and report research are online libraries and encyclopedias. See Chapter 12, "Madame Librarian: Online Libraries and Encyclopedias," for more information.

Look for Your School on the Internet

Many grade schools, middle schools, and high schools have their own Internet sites. If you want to look for your school's Web site, check out the American School Directory (www.asd.com), which lists more than 106,000 K-12 school sites.

Give Your Kids Their Own Safe Search Sites

In addition to the homework-specific sites, there are also several kid-safe search sites on the Web. (These are in addition to the kid-safe filters available at many of the general search sites.) These search sites do a good job of filtering out links to sites with inappropriate content (sex, drugs, dirty language, and so on—the usual suspects). If you want to protect your children from the worst of the Web, make them use any of the sites listed in Table 31.2.

Table 31.2   Top Kid-Safe Search Sites

Site:	URL:	Comments:
Ask Jeeves for Kids!	www.ajkids.com	A unique service where you enter your queries in plain English, and Ask Jeeves! provides the answer via a short list of highly qualified Web sites; the Ask Jeeves for Kids! site filters a sites' appropriateness. (See Chapter 10 for more information on how to use Ask Jeeves!)
Disney Internet Guide (DIG)	www.disney.com/dig/today	Disney's kids' guide to the Internet, listing only those sites considered appropriate
EdView SmartZone	school.edview.com/search/	A collection of more than 7 million teacher-reviewed, kid-safe Web pages, categorized by subject and grade level
Family Web Files	www.familywebfiles.com	Links to family-friendly Web sites in both English and Spanish
infoplease Kids' Almanac	kids.infoplease.com	One of the largest and coolest information-oriented kids' sites on the Web
Searchopolis	www.searchopolis.com	One of the newer and better filtered search engines— *recommended*
Super Snooper	supersnooper.com	A search engine that filters out inappropriate results
Yahooligans!	www.yahooligans.com	Yahoo! for kids, designed for ages 7 to 12, with sites hand-picked for appropriateness; the oldest major directory for children (from 1996)

Yahooligans!—the first, and one of the best, Web directories for kids.

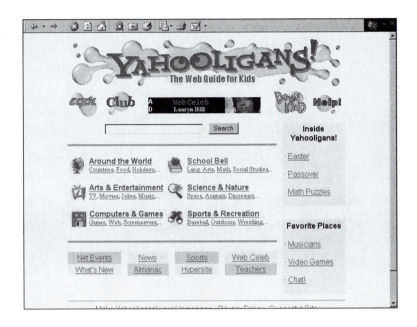

My two favorite sites here are Ask Jeeves for Kids! and Yahooligans! Although Yahooligans! is a good, high-quality directory that is very easy to browse, Ask Jeeves! lets kids search the way they're inclined to search—using plain English questions. As with the main Ask Jeeves! site (discussed in Chapter 10, "The Next Generation: Newer, Better Search Engines"), it's an efficient and effective way to find the Web sites that contain the answers to your questions—and, with the kids' version, the content is filtered for appropriateness.

Sites for and by Teachers

Sites for students are one thing; sites for *teachers* are another. If you're a teacher, check out Education World (www.education-world.com), which lists more than 50,000 sites of interest to educators.

The Least You Need to Know

➤ Homework-helper sites assist children with their homework problems; one of the most popular is infoplease Homework Center.

➤ Kid-safe search engines and directories filter out inappropriate content that otherwise slips into general search sites; two of the best are Ask Jeeves for Kids! and Yahooligans!

PAPER! GET YOUR PAPER HERE!

Chapter 32

Search for Archived News Articles

In This Chapter

➤ Find out where you can find a master list of all the different news sites on the Internet

➤ Discover which sites let you search for articles across multiple news sites and archives

How do you find news on the Net? For current, general news, it's easy enough to go to a dedicated news site, such as CNN Interactive (www.cnn.com) or MSNBC (www.msnbc.com). But what if you want to find news about something more obscure, or about something that happened several months—or years—in the past?

First things first—don't try searching for news items on the general search sites. Most search engines and directories don't index news stories. Or, if they do, they index only major stories from major sources.

What you need are sites that are dedicated to the archiving of news stories. You need to search a news archive.

Search the Sources

Before we get to news archives, I should point out the blatantly obvious—sometimes it's best to go right to the source. By that, I mean that if you know where an article came from, go to that periodical's Web site and search its archive.

For example, if you know that a particular news item came from the *New York Times*, go to the *New York Times'* Web site (www.nytimes.com). Then click the **Archives** link to search through all their old articles.

Because there are a ton of news sources on the Web, there are a ton of sites you can search directly. For a good list of news sites on the Web, go to News and Newspapers Online (library.uncg.edu/news/), a comprehensive directory compiled by the University of North Carolina.

However, not all newspapers and magazines have archives on their Web sites, and even those that do sometimes charge for the privilege of accessing them. Still, if you know where to go, this is a good way to get started with your news searching.

Search the Archives

If you don't know precisely where to go to find a bit of news, go to a site that lets you search or link to other sites. There are a variety of news archives and indexes on the Web; some archive articles in their own databases, and some simply link to the archives of individual news sources. For the best news archives, be prepared to pay for access.

Table 32.1 lists the top news archive and index sites on the Web.

Table 32.1   News Archives and Indexes

Site:	URL:	Comments:
1st Headlines	www.1stheadlines.com	Gathers news from 101 newspaper, broadcast, and online news sources
AJR NewsLink	ajr.newslink.org	From the American Journalism Review, links to and searches of a variety of print and online news sources
Excite News Tracker	nt.excite.com	Excite's news-only search engine; includes an option for a personalized page that tracks news by preselected topic areas
News and Newspapers Online	library.uncg.edu/news/	Probably the most comprehensive directory of news sites on the Web
News Index	www.newsindex.com	Indexes current news stories from hundreds of sources—refreshed hourly; does not archive older stories

Site:	URL:	Comments:
NewsBot	www.newsbot.com	HotBot's search engine for current news
NewsCentral	www.all-links.com/ newscentral/	Links to 3,500 newspapers around the world
NewsHub	www.newshub.com	Searchable current news, updated every 15 minutes
NewsLibrary	www.newslibrary.com	Fee-based archive of articles from more than 50 newspapers
Newspapers Online	www.newspapers.com	Links to newspapers and other periodicals worldwide
NewsTrawler	www.newstrawler.com	A fee-based meta-search engine for news—lets you send queries to hundreds of different news sites simultaneously
Northern Light Current News Search	www.northernlight.com/ news.html	Archives news stories from more than 100 search publications; lots of powerful search options on this site (see Chapter 9 for more information on Northern Light)
Paperboy	www.paperboy.net	Searches more than 300 daily newspapers; more of a global reach than most news archives
TotalNews	www.totalnews.com	Links to and searches most of the major Web-based news sites
WorldWide News	www.worldwidenews.com	Links to newspapers around the world

Of all these sites, I like NewsTrawler and Northern Light the best—even though they both charge reading fees.

NewsTrawler is great because of the huge number of sources indexed and the ease with which you can include and exclude specific sources. You begin by doing a little narrowing down from the home page; you can select to search by various cuts of news sources or by various topics. When the Mega Selection page appears, narrow down your selection a little more, then click the **Select Items** button. Finally, when the next page appears, select which individual periodicals you wish to search, enter your query, then click the **Trawl** button.

Searching for news items at NewsTrawler—you can narrow your search by publication country and category, or by news subject.

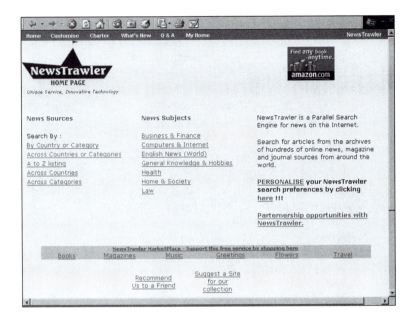

Limit Your Trawling

Because NewsTrawler searches multiple sources simultaneously—the searches aren't done on the NewsTrawler site itself—selecting too many sources can slow your trawl to a crawl. For fastest results, try not to select more than 20 sources for your search. (Note that because all these sources parse their queries differently, NewsTrawler doesn't support either Boolean operators or date-range limits.)

Northern Light is a favorite because of its powerful search features and the way it categorizes results. See Chapter 9, "See the Search Lights with Northern Light," for more information on how to use Northern Light's robust search commands.

When you search a news archive, try to find one that lets you narrow your search by both source and date. Source is important because most of the news you're looking for will fall into specific categories; you don't need to search *Cat Fancy* if you're looking for information on the latest General Motors minivans. Date is important because more often than not, you'll have a date range in mind. For example, if you're looking for stories about the country's current unemployment rate, you don't want your results page to be filled with stories that are five years old—you want to limit your search to more recent stories. For more useful results, make sure you limit your sources and date range.

Search the TV News

What if the news you want isn't in print? Vanderbilt University's Television News Archive (`tvnews.vanderbilt.edu`) is the world's most extensive archive of television news, with more than 30,000 individual network evening-news broadcasts and more than 9,000 hours of special news-related programming from the 1960s to today. You can search the archive online and request copies of those tapes you wish to watch.

The Least You Need to Know

➤ Most online news sites have their own archives that you can search for older news items.

➤ For a master list of all online news sites, go to the News and Newspapers Online site.

➤ To search across multiple sites and publications, use a news archive or an index site. Two of the best are NewsTracker and Northern Light Current News Search.

Chapter 33

Search for Medical and Healthcare Information

In This Chapter

➤ Learn how you can search for important medical information online

➤ Discover MEDLINE, the world's largest medical database

➤ Find out about the latest Internet trend—online drugstores

If you or one of your family members is sick, you want answers *now*. Whether you're dealing with an ear infection or something much more serious, there is no better and faster place to turn than to the numerous health-related sites on the Internet. Online you'll get access to the same medical databases used by most physicians, and your access will be immediate—no waiting for an appointment!

Search for Medical Information Online

Whether you're looking for general health information or in-depth data on a specific medical condition, you can find it on the Web. Although it's hard to recommend that people make their own diagnoses, you can use this information to be better informed before you consult with your doctor.

Table 33.1 lists the top healthcare sites on the Web.

Table 33.1   Medicine and Healthcare Sites

Site:	URL:	Comments:
About.com Family	familymedicine.about.com	Comprehensive Medicine list of links to hundreds of health-related sites, organized by type of medical problem
Achoo	www.achoo.com	Full-service healthcare portal—includes health news and shopping
BeWELL	bewell.com	Free access to MEDLINE, the premiere medical database, one of the best medical resources on the Internet—*recomended*
drkoop.com	www.drkoop.com	A full-service family healthcare portal, led by the former U.S. Surgeon General
E Medicine	www.emedicine.com	Free online medical textbooks for medical professionals and the general public
Health A to Z	www.healthatoz.com	A directory of more than 50,000 Internet health resources
HealthAnswers	www.healthanswers.com	Heath information organized into the following centers: Aging, Alternative Medicine, AIDS/STDs, Men's Health, Nutrition, Pediatrics, Pregnancy, and Women's Health
Health-Net	www.health-net.com	A full-service healthcare portal; part of the Parent Zone Web site
Healthtouch Online	www.healthtouch.com	Includes sections for drug information, pharmacy search, health resource directory, and health information
kidsDoctor	www.kidsdoctor.com	No, not about kids playing doctor, but rather an index of articles pertaining to children's health
Medical World Search	www.mwsearch.com	Full-text search of nearly 100,000 pages from selected medical sites

Site:	URL:	Comments:
MedicineNet	www.medicinenet.com	Full-service site offers medical information, a pharmaceutical reference guide, a medical dictionary, and doctors' answers to user questions
Mediconsult.com	www.mediconsult.com	Articles and information on a variety of medical topics, from acid reflux to women's health
WebMD	www.webmd.com	Site for both patients and doctors

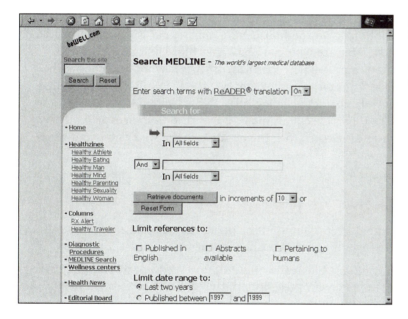

Searching for in-depth medical information in the MEDLINE database, available on the BeWELL site.

Many of these sites are superb resources for all sorts of medical information; they are particularly useful in diagnosing medical conditions and in encouraging preventive healthcare. But when it comes to searching for exact information on medical conditions or procedures, I always turn to BeWELL. Not only does BeWELL have superb wellness centers and a great online handbook of diagnostic procedures, but it also offers free access to MEDLINE, the world's largest medical database.

When you click the **MEDLINE Search** link, you're confronted with a somewhat complex search form. Don't get too overwhelmed, though; this form uses ReADER technology that translates your words into MeSH, the proper medical vocabulary used by the MEDLINE database. For example, if you enter a query for lung cancer, ReADER automatically searches MEDLINE for "lung neoplasms." If you're well-versed in the proper terminology, you can turn ReADER off and enter the terms yourself; for most of us mortal humans, it's better to leave ReADER on and query in somewhat

329

normal English. Note that the other options on the search form allow you to limit your search to certain subsets of patient types, article types, and date ranges.

The MEDLINE database is a terrific resource, and BeWELL's interface to it offers some powerful search options. This is one site that just begs for an in-depth search!

MEDLINE Direct

BeWELL puts a great interface on the MEDLINE database. But if you don't mind a slightly less user-friendly interface, you can also access MEDLINE directly at the National Library of Medicine Web site (www.nlm.nih.gov). When you choose the **Internet Grateful Med** option (yes, that's really what they call it!), you also get access to other medical databases, including AIDSLINE, HealthSTAR, and TOXLINE. While you're there, check out some of the other resources at the NLM site—a lot of it is high-level research, but there's some useful stuff hiding out there, as well.

Searching for Drugstores Online

Hand in hand with online doctors comes online pharmacists. Make no mistake about it—online drugstores are turning into big business.

Most online drugstores work just like real-world drugstores, except with FedEx thrown in for the legwork: They receive your prescription, they fill it, and then they ship it to you. Just like that—no fuss, no muss.

If you're interested in getting your prescriptions filled online, Table 33.2 lists some of the more popular online pharmacies.

Table 33.2   Online Pharmacies

Site:	URL:
Cyber Pharmacy	www.cyberpharmacy.com
Drug Emporium	www.drugemporium.com
Drugstore.com	www.drugstore.com
PlanetRx	www.planetrx.com
Soma.com	www.soma.com

Because of the lower costs of doing business online, many of these online drugstores offer lower prices than some brick-and-mortar pharmacies. The trade-off, of course, is the lack of human interaction. If you need the advice of a pharmacist, use your corner druggist; if you want the convenience and lower prices without the advice, shop online.

Learn About Drugs Online

If you're using an online drugstore and don't have the benefit of a live pharmacist for advice and information, turn to another Web site as a substitute. RxList—The Internet Drug Index (rxlist.com)—is a searchable database of information about prescription drugs, their effects, and possible interaction problems.

The Least You Need to Know

➤ Health-oriented Web sites provide a wealth of medical information for all types of patients.

➤ BeWELL offers user-friendly access to MEDLINE, the world's largest medical database.

➤ In addition to online healthcare sites, online pharmacies enable you to purchase your prescriptions over the Web.

Search for Other Kinds of Information

In the previous 33 chapters of these book, I've covered just about every kind of search engine or directory there is, right?

Wrong! There are still *more* specialized search sites to be found on the Web—and this chapter takes a very fast-paced look at some of the more useful of these.

Search for Someplace to Stay

If you're looking for an apartment to rent, check out SpringStreet (www.springstreet.com). You can search by location, price range, unit type, and desired amenities. If you don't like SpringStreet, try Rent Net (www.rent.net) or Apartments.com (www.apartments.com) as alternatives.

If you're looking to buy a house, try Realtor.com (www.realtor.com). This site lists more than 1.2 million homes from 500 realtors. Other good home-listing sites include Microsoft HomeAdvisor (www.homeadvisor.com), HomeHunter (www.home-hunter.com), and FSBO.COM (www.fsbo.com), where you can find listings of homes for sale by owner. If you're looking to build a new home from scratch, search the NewHomeNetwork site (www.newhomenetwork.com).

On a similar tack, you can search for local realtors by entering the name of your city and the keyword realtor in one of the major search sites. You can also check the locality guides many sites provide for some major cities—often you'll find listings of realtors or a directory of homes and apartments for sale or rent.

Whether you're renting or buying, Virtual Relocation (www.virtualrelocation.com) is a great site to help you plan every aspect of your move. This site includes apartment and real-estate listings, mortgage directories, insurance information, and a good relocation guide.

If you're just passing through and need a good hotel, try the Accommodation Search Engine (ase.net). This site is one of the most comprehensive hotel databases on the Web, with more listings than you can find at most travel sites.

Searching for lodging with the Accommodation Search Engine.

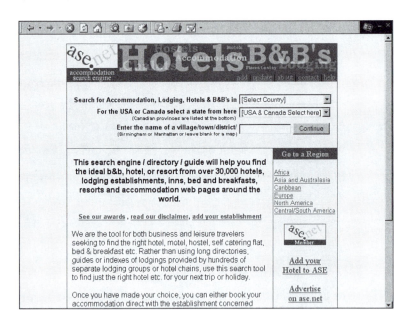

Search for Maps and Directions

Need help getting someplace? Then check out MapQuest (www.mapquest.com) or MapBlast! (www.mapblast.com). Both of these sites let you search for a specific address and then either create an area map or generate door-to-door driving directions. If you want to see something really cool, though, take a look at Microsoft's TerraServer (terraserver.microsoft.com)—it displays detailed satellite photographs corresponding to specific coordinates.

Here's something neat—the Houston Astrodome, as photographed from space, on Microsoft's TerraServer site.

Search for a Money Machine

While you're out and about, you might need some cash. Where do you find the nearest automatic teller machine? The best places to look are at Visa's ATM Locator (www.visa.com/pd/atm/main.html) and the MasterCard/Cirrus ATM Locator (www.mastercard.com/atm/). The Visa site lets you specify a street address or cross street; the MasterCard site lists machines only by city and state.

Search for a Web Site Name

Closer to home, if you're creating a new Web site and would like to reserve your own individual domain name, you need to find a site that lets you search for available domain names—and then register the name that you want. NetNames USA (www.netnamesusa.com) is a good site for this kind of searching, as is the official Network Solutions site (www.networksolutions.com).

Domain Names and Network Solutions

Internet domain names are pretty much available on a first-come, first-served basis. All the administration for assigning domain names is handled by a company called Network Solutions. Many third parties offer domain name registration; however, although they handle all the dirty work for you, they still go to Network Solutions to get the name assigned.

Search for Illegal Software

The Internet is a great way to distribute pirated software, often called *warez*. Anyone with a computer and a modem can access sites filled with illegal software, and download that software directly to their PC, no questions asked.

Where's the Warez?

The type of pirated or cracked software available clandestinely over the Internet is called *warez*. (It's pronounced "where's", *not* "Juarez.") A warez results when computer crackers disable the copy-protection code of a piece of software, and then place the cracked program in a special newsgroup or Web or FTP site. These so-called "warez sitez" are blatantly illegal, yet keep springing up in ever-increasing numbers.

Ignoring the illegal nature of this activity for the moment, how do you find warez on the Web? Some of the top warez sites are 2600: The Hacker Quarterly (www.2600.com); Hack O Matic (www.garden.net/users/zero/newhack/); Invincer's Intraverse Top FTP Sites (www.invincer.com/2600W/FTPsites.html); Search Warez (search.warez.com); and Warez.com (www.warez.com).

Remember, though—not only are warez programs illegal, they're also totally unsupported by the software manufacturer. If you run into any problems using a cracked program, you're totally on your own!

Search the Bible

Looking for a particular passage in the Bible? Then check out one of the many searchable Bibles available on the Internet. Bible Search (www.biblesearch.com) is a good site, as is Bible Gateway (bible.gospelcom.net/bible), which lets you search the Bible in nine languages and multiple Bible versions. There's also Religious Texts (www.hti.umich.edu/relig/), which lets you search four versions of the Bible (Martin Luther translation, King James Version, Revised Standard Version, Rheims 1582 New Testament), the Book of Mormon, and the Koran.

If you're searching for other religious resources, check out Religious Resources on the Net (www.aphids.com/relres/) or Crosswalk.com (search.crosswalk.com/pk/), both of which are searchable databases of religious and Christian Web sites. If you're looking for a particular church, try Net Ministries Church Directories (netministries.org/churches.htm) or NetChurch Search (www.netchurch.com/church_search.asp).

Search for Scientific Information

The best place to search for scientific information is SciCentral (www.scicentral.com), a huge directory with links to more than 50,000 science resources. For serious scientific research, you can go directly to the National Technical Information Service (www.ntis.gov); the huge database at this site includes 370,000 technical publications in all major scientific fields. (You can buy the entire reports offered here or just read the abstracts for free.)

If you're looking for science stuff for kids, try About.com's Science/Nature for Kids site (kidscience.about.com) or General Science Links (www.siec.k12.in.us/~wes/sites/scigen.htm). Both of these sites provide large directories of science sites geared for a younger audience.

Search for Private Information

With a little determination, some time, and the right list of sites, you can find out practically anything about anybody, right from your computer keyboard. (You also may have to pay for some of this information—several of these sites have fee-based access.)

By diligently tracking down someone's public records (marriage licenses, divorce filings, property tax payments, and so on), doing a little basic detective work, and using a smidgen of deductive reasoning, you can find out what someone does for a living, how much money they take home, the names and ages of their spouse and children, the age and make of their car, the location and value of their house, you name it. It's kind of scary.

Where do you start looking for this data? Some of the best sites are FACSNET People Finders/Public Records Databases (www.facsnet.org/report_tools/CAR/carpeopl.htm); Directory of Electronic Public Access Services (www.uscourts.gov/PubAccess.html); WWW Virtual Law Library (www.law.indiana.edu/law/v-lib/states.html); KnowX (www.knowx.com); The American Information Network Inc. (www.ameri.com); and the *Naked in Cyberspace* Directory of Internet Resources (www.technosearch.com/naked/directory.htm).

Search for Legal Information

Looking for a lawyer? Then search through the directories of legal counsel at West Legal Directory (www.wld.com) and Lawyers.com (www.lawyers.com). If it's just general legal advice and information you're looking for, try searching American Law Sources On-Line (www.lawsource.com/also/), 'Lectric Law Library (www.lectlaw.com), or FindLaw (www.findlaw.com).

Search for Government-Related Stuff

Searching for information on a particular politician—excuse me, public servant? Then search through Carroll's U.S. Government Links (www.carrollpub.com). This wonderful site includes thousands of links to officeholders and agencies on the federal, state, and local levels—all the way down to county and city offices. If you can't find what you want there, try About.com's Alphabetical Index of U.S. Government Web Space (usgovinfo.about.com/blindex.htm), with its direct links to just about every conceivable government agency.

To search for U.S. government publications, regulations, and statistics, check out the FedWorld Information Network (www.fedworld.gov). If you want to research congressional legislation and voting, go to the Thomas site (thomas.loc.gov), run by the Library of Congress and named after the library's founder, Thomas Jefferson.

Looking for governments outside the U.S.? Then search through the governments on the WWW site (www.gksoft.com/govt/), with its worldwide listings of parliaments, ministries, offices, law courts, embassies, city councils, public broadcasting corporations, central banks, multinational organizations, political parties, and the like. This massive directory contains more than 11,000 entries from more than 200 countries and territories. If you can't find what you're looking for there, try World World (www.worldworld.com), with its graphical links to foreign governments, international agencies, and the global press.

Search for Entertainment Facts and Trivia

Who was the third actor on the left in that old movie you saw last night? For that matter, what was the name of the movie? If you want to find out just about anything about any movie or movie star, the place to look is the Internet Movie Database (us.imdb.com). This treasure trove of movie trivia lets you search by movie or TV title, cast name, crew name, or character name—and then returns the most detailed movie descriptions (including *complete* cast and crew listings) that you've ever seen, as well as links to online reviews. (Where else can you find out that Michael Zorek played Bubba in the Phoebe Cates clunker *Private School*?)

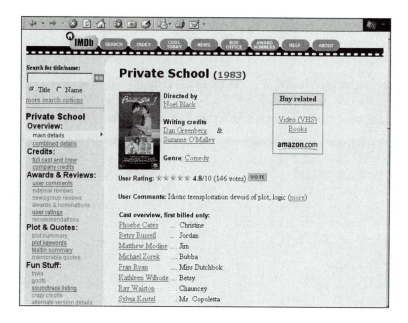

Search for movie information at the Internet Movie Database—you'll find detailed listings for both the best and the worst films ever made, including Private School.

For music, the equivalent of the Internet Movie Database is the All-Music Guide (www.allmusic.com). This site is part of the All-Media Guide network that also includes the All-Classical Guide (www.allclassical.com), the All-Movie Guide (www.allmovie.com), and the All-Game Guide (www.allgame.com). The All-Music Guide lets you search by artist, album, song, style, or record label, and it includes information on 29,659 artists, 354,282 albums, and 1,841,841 individual song titles. The All-Music Guide also lists 179,349 sidemen and 2,659,620 album credits—with 1,369,945 links between people who "worked with" one artist or another. In other words, if its been recorded, it's listed somewhere in the All-Music Guide.

I'd love to point you to a similar repository of book information, but I haven't been able to find one—other than Amazon.com (www.amazon.com), that is. I hate to recommend a retailer site for reference information, but the truth is that Amazon.com contains a wealth of information of interest to any book lover. Not only are Amazon's book descriptions informative, but you also get the benefit of reading reviews written by other readers! And, if you select the Full Search option, you can search for books by author, title, format, subject, ISBN, publisher, or release date. The good thing is that you can browse Amazon.com's site all you want and you don't have to buy anything!

Another good site for bibliophiles is BookFinder.com (www.bookfinder.com), which helps you locate rare and out-of-print books that you likely can't find anywhere else—even on Amazon.com!

The Least You Need to Know

➤ There are numerous search engines and databases that specialize in narrow types of information.

➤ You can find specialized search sites for apartments, realty listings, hotels, ATMs, lawyers, politicians, and movies—all of which provide better results than searching for the same information at a standard search site.

Part 9

Getting Smart: Sanity-Saving Search Secrets

If you've gotten this far, you know where to find just about any type of information on the Internet. Now it's time to learn how to find that information—the best ways to get the best results from your online searches. In this part of the book I share all my search secrets and strategies with you, the things I've learned through years of hard work and hundreds of thousands of extensive search sessions. If you want to be the most effective and efficient searcher on your block or in your office, these are the chapters to read!

Chapter 35

Super-Secret Search Strategies That *Always* Work

In This Chapter

➤ Learn the habits and strategies of effective searchers

➤ Discover 40 sure-fire tips to improve your search sessions

➤ Uncover the 10 most common pitfalls that lead to ineffective searches

What does it take to consistently find what you're looking for on the Internet?

Effective searching requires a combination of innate ability, productive habits, and specific skills. It also helps to have a kind of "sixth sense" about where to look for information and a lot of patience to make it through those long stretches when you can't seem to find anything useful, no matter how hard you try.

In other words, successful searching is a blend of art and science, of intuition and expertise—something some are born to and others have to learn.

Experienced searchers tend to develop routines that help them find specific information with a minimum of fuss and muss. As an experienced searcher myself, I'll share with you my habits and routines, my strategies and secrets, in the hope that you can learn all you need to help you be more productive in your search activities.

How I Search the Web—And Why You Should Care

I'm constantly being asked for my "search secrets"—where I go to find certain types of information, what techniques I use, and so on. (In fact, that's the main reason I decided to write this book.) One of my secrets is that I have a set information-gathering routine I follow daily and some established strategies I use when I have to search for information.

I'm not saying you should duplicate everything I do, because people have to develop their own ways of doing things. I only offer you my routine as an example of how one person effectively finds stuff on the Internet. What works for me may or may not work for you, but—if you don't have any better ideas—it's at least a place to start!

What I Do Every Morning (Besides Shaving and Showering)

One key component of my information gathering is my daily tour of the Web. Every morning as I sip my cup of hot chocolate and check my email messages, I scan about a dozen informational Web sites. It's amazing what you can stumble across by scanning these types of resources on a regular basis.

The sites I scan reflect my immersion in the high-tech industry; you would probably select a different set of sites based on your own particular interests. That said, the sites I visit every morning include

➤ **CNET news.com** (www.news.com)   Great for general computer industry news

➤ **New York Times** (www.nytimes.com)   The online version of the paper—for free! (Registration required.)

➤ **Salon** (www.salonmagazine.com)   An interesting collection of stories about all aspects of today's culture

➤ **SiliconValley.com** (www.mercurycenter.com/svtech/)   Technology news from the *San Jose Mercury News*, in the heart of Silicon Valley

➤ **StarNews.com** (www.starnews.com)   My local newspaper (*The Indianapolis Star*), online

➤ **The Industry Standard** (www.thestandard.net)   Offering technology business news and some good editorial commentary

➤ **Upside Today** (www.upside.com)   Offering news on the business side of the high-tech industry

➤ **Wired News** (www.wired.com/news/)   With trendy reports on high-tech culture

➤ **ZDNet News** (www.zdnet.com/zdnn/)   Offering the technical end of high-tech news reporting

On a less regular basis (weekly, generally), I visit a handful of other Web sites that offer some very focused information. These sites include BookWire (www.bookwire.com), for news about the book publishing industry; Search Engine Watch (www.searchenginewatch.com), for news about searching and search engines; and The Red Herring (www.herring.com), for even more tech business news.

I get most of my "normal" news and financial information from the personal start page I configured at My Excite (my.excite.com). I set up my Web browser so that it launches My Excite every time I connect to the Internet, and I configure My Excite to track specific types of news and information, as well as specific companies in my financial portfolio. My Excite is good about identifying companies featured in recent news articles; when I see a new article about one of my target companies, all I have to do is click and read.

Now, to be fair, I don't read every article I find on every one of these sites. Instead, I scan the headlines, only clicking and reading those articles that are of immediate interest. (This is not unlike reading the newspaper—you can browse the headlines and read only the interesting or important stories.) I probably spend no more than a few minutes at each site; the entire exercise takes less than fifteen minutes.

I also get a lot of daily news delivered to me via email. Numerous email publications are available that deliver customizable information directly to my inbox every morning. Two of the most popular are Netscape's In-Box Direct (home.netscape.com/ibd/index.html) and InfoBeat (www.infobeat.com); both let you subscribe to multiple publications from a single site.

One of my favorite email deliveries comes from CompanySleuth (www.companysleuth.com). I configure this service to track a handful of companies I'm interested in, then every day they send me an email notifying me about any news articles, analyst reports, SEC filings, message board discussions, and insider trades involving those companies. Because I choose to have the emails delivered in HTML format, I can click a link to access any of the items discussed in the message.

What I Do When I Search

When it's time to search for specific information, I have a more-or-less standard procedure I follow, which tends to find what I want more often than it doesn't.

In general, I tend to go broad rather than narrow—it's less efficient, but you can scrounge up all sorts of information that doesn't happen to be filed away neatly and logically. Personally, I'll sacrifice wading through the dreck of too many results against the serendipity of stumbling over something truly useful. I can't tell you how many times my curiosity has led me to information hiding in the strangest places, at sites where I would never have thought to look.

When I construct my queries, I try to think how the people who compile the data or create the Web page think. These masters of data don't necessarily think the way regular people think, but it's their constructs that feed the indexes at the major search sites. So if normal folks think "cell phone" but these technogoobers think "portable communications device," I want to look for `portable communications devices`.

Getting down to the searching itself, I typically start with Yahoo! (`www.yahoo.com`). I tend to ignore Yahoo!'s Category Matches and go straight to its Web Sites and Web Pages results. Then I'll use the links at the bottom of the Yahoo! page to redirect my search to other search engines. That's why I like starting with Yahoo!—you can get anywhere from there!

My second search engine is typically AltaVista (`www.altavista.com`). AltaVista definitely gives quantity over quality—but it does give me a lot of pages that *could* contain the information I'm looking for.

Next, I'll either go to HotBot (`www.hotbot.com`) or to Northern Light (`www.northernlight.com`), both of which provide surprisingly well-targeted results. After that, it's a toss-up between Lycos (`www.lycos.com`), Excite (`www.excite.com`), and Infoseek (`infoseek.go.com`)—although I generally stop before I get to this bottom tier.

If I'm searching on a more narrow topic, I might skip all of the above and go directly to a specialist site. For example, I use CNET's news.com (`www.news.com`) and ZDNet News (`www.zdnet.com/zdnn/`) to look for any computer-related information I need.

If I'm searching for something newsy or want to be informed by opinions and gossip, I'll try a Usenet search at Deja.com (`www.deja.com`). Yes, I know I can search newsgroups from some of the other search sites, but I just like the way DejaNews works!

If I'm looking for phone numbers, addresses, or email addresses, I go right to The Ultimates (`www.theultimates.com`). I like this site because it organizes multiple white and yellow pages searches from a single page—and, unlike more general metasearches, these sites all use pretty much the same syntax for their queries. (I avoid general meta-search sites like the plague, by the way—I don't trust them to return the same results I get from a direct search of individual sites.)

If I'm searching for company financial information (which I do a lot), I generally start with Hoover's Online (`www.hoovers.com`) and The Motley Fool (`www.fool.com`). Hoover's is the most comprehensive site for detailed financial information; The Fool is a great site for ratios and rumors. For more in-depth information, I might visit Multex Systems (`www.multexnet.com`) for analyst reports or the SEC EDGAR Database (`www.sec.gov/edgarhp.htm`) for quarterly and annual financial filings. My daily stock quotes, of course, I get from my personalized My Excite page.

Finally, I try to remind myself that not everything I want is available online. I try to read a variety of newspapers and magazines on a regular basis, such as *The Wall Street Journal*, *Business Week*, and *Newsweek*. And I keep up with industry-specific news by subscribing to a handful of industry newsletters.

The bottom line is that I keep my eyes and ears open all the time for information that might be of some possible use. Even if I don't store the information immediately, I remember where I found it—because that might be a good place to start my search next time.

Should you adopt my routines and procedures? Probably not, because your needs are no doubt different from mine. However, follow in the spirit of my strategies, and I guarantee you successful searching in the future.

40 Tips for Finding What You Want on the Web

Now that you know my general search strategies, let me give you some specific tactics and techniques you can employ in almost all your searches.

Tip #1: Be Curious

Always be on the lookout for information. Think there might be something interesting on a particular Web page? Then check it out! You never know what you might find until you look. If you're not curious, you'll never stumble over anything useful—and there's a lot of stuff on the Net to stumble over! If you're too busy to explore an interesting page, you can always bookmark it and look at it later.

Tip #2: Follow the Links

Find a useful Web page? Then click through a few of the links on that page. Quite often, good information leads to more good information on a related site. Don't stop when you find a good page—use it as a launching pad for further Web excursions!

Tip #3: Make Fast Decisions

Searching can be time consuming. Don't even try to read everything you come across. When you access a page, scan it quickly and decide whether it's useful. Be ruthless in abandoning pages that don't look fruitful. Scan and click, scan and click—the faster you move on, the faster you'll find the right information.

Tip #4: Don't Be Afraid to Try New Things

Don't get stuck in a rut. If you always go to the same search sites and enter the same types of queries, you'll never find anything new or different. Vary your routine on occasion and try some different search engines. Do you always use Yahoo!? Try Ask Jeeves! or Google every now and then. Are you a HotBot fan? Switch to Northern Light for a week. You'll never grow unless you try new things from time to time.

Tip #5: Know What You're Looking For

Know exactly what you're looking for before you go online. It helps to visualize what the ideal answer would look like—then figure out how to target a search for that ideal

Web page. After all, how will you know you've found the right information if you don't know what information you're really looking for?

Tip #6: Do Some Advance Planning

Don't start cold. Planning is necessary before you start your search. Think about what you're looking for, think about the keywords and phrases you want to use, think about which search engines would be best for this particular search. Take the time to thumb through a thesaurus to come up with synonyms for your keywords. Think, then plan, then search.

Tip #7: Use the Right Search Site

Remember—no single search site covers 100 percent of the Internet. Even the biggest search engines index only a fraction of the total Web pages currently available—and they all use different methods to create their indexes.

Do you want some very targeted pages about a popular topic? Then you might want to use a directory, such as Yahoo! Don't have a clue about where to start? Then go to one of the big search engines, such as AltaVista, HotBot, or Northern Light. Looking for industry-specific information? Then hit an industry-specific Web site.

Here's a subtip within a tip: Never use a general search site when a specialty site is available. For example, I never use AltaVista to look for computer information; I go directly to CNET, instead. If you know exactly what you want, you might as well narrow your search from the beginning.

Tip #8: Use Multiple Search Sites

Trust me—you'll seldom find exactly what you want at the first site you visit. If your search of AltaVista isn't panning out, try your query at HotBot or Northern Light. Different sites produce different results; use that variety to your benefit.

Tip #9: Not Sure? Then Guess!

Many times you won't even know exactly what it is you're looking for. In these instances, trust your instincts and take a guess on what keywords to include in your query. You might not hit the jackpot right away, but you can learn from the results generated from your educated guess.

You can also guess at Web site addresses. If you're looking for a specific company's Web site, try entering www.companyname.com, where the center part of the URL is the name of the company. For example, if you're trying to find Microsoft's Web site, it's not a bad guess to enter www.microsoft.com. This trick even works if you're looking for general topics—try www.cars.com if you're looking for cars or www.genealogy.com if you're looking for genealogical information. (Remember to use .edu instead of .com if you're searching for a college—and .gov instead of .com if you're searching for a government agency. For example, try www.irs.gov around tax time.) It's not a perfect technique, but it will generally get you *somewhere*.

Tip #10: Vary Your Vocabulary—And Your Spelling

When you're searching for a particular word, don't assume that everyone spells it the same way—or knows how to spell it properly, period. It wouldn't be out of the question to find Ernest Hemingway's name misspelled on some sites as Hemmingway or even Hamingway—which means that you might want to extend your search to include common misspellings.

Also, don't forget non-American spellings of certain words. Although American English has become the standard language for Internet communications, there are a lot of non-American English speakers on the Net. Remember that British English turns *color* into *colour* and *organize* into *organise*.

Finally, don't forget about synonyms. What you call pink, someone else might call mauve. What's big to you might be large to someone else. Think of all the ways your keyword could be phrased and include them in a Boolean expression using a lot of ORs—as in high OR tall OR big OR giant.

Tip #11: Truncate

If you're not sure whether you're looking for plurals or singulars (or present tense or future tense), truncate your words and use wildcards. For example, search for dog* to return either a single dog or multiple dogs.

Tip #12: If You're Not Sure, Go Wild!

Speaking of wildcards, they're quite useful if you're not sure of a word's spelling. Thinking about Tip #10's British/American issue; if you want to search for both organise and organize, search instead for organi*.

This is also a good strategy if you're not sure of someone's full name. Was your old girlfriend named Sherry or Sheryl or Sherylyn? Searching for sher* will find all three.

Tip #13: Make Your Queries Precise—But Not Too Precise

When you're deciding which keywords to use, try to pick words that are precise but not overly restrictive. If you must use a very general word, try modifying it with a more specific word—or you're apt to generate a huge number of results that have little relevance to the specific information you're searching for. For example, car is a pretty general keyword; ford sports car is a much more precise query.

Tip #14: Nouns Are Good

As you construct your query, remember that nouns make the best keywords. Try to answer the "who, what, when, where, how, and why" through the use of your keywords. Avoid conjunctions, verbs, adverbs, and adjectives unless they modify a more general noun (see Tip #13).

Tip #15: Phrases Are Even Better

Keywords are great; phrases are better. Instead of searching for three keywords (ford sports car, for example), search for a single phrase ("ford sports car") using quotation marks. All major search sites generate more relevant results when you enter multiple-word phrases rather than a string of grammatically unrelated keywords.

Tip #16: Get the Right Order

When constructing your query, put the important stuff up front. Put keywords or phrases that describe your main subject at the start of your query; put less important words and phrases last. Almost all search engines search for the first words first, and then rank results according to how they match these more important keywords.

Tip #17: Use Your Pluses and Minuses

Don't forget to use the + and – modifiers in your queries. If your results must match a word, don't assume the search engine will know this; put a + in front of it just to be sure. And think about how excluding certain words or concepts can clean up your results; use the – command to block pages that contain certain words from your results.

Tip #18: Use Boolean Power—But Use It Carefully

Don't be afraid of Boolean searches. Joining words with an AND or excluding words with a NOT can add a lot of power to your searches. The more you use Boolean operators, the more precise your queries can be.

However, be cautious in your use of Boolean phrases. Remember that different search sites use Boolean operators in slightly different ways. The same Boolean query entered at AltaVista might return wildly different results when used at HotBot. If you want to use Boolean operators, make sure you understand exactly how each search site implements them.

In addition, Boolean logic can sometimes be hard to understand. If you construct a Boolean query just a little bit wrong, you might end up with no results whatsoever. Think of a Boolean phrase as being similar to an algebraic phrase—make sure everything adds up in the end!

350

Tip #19: Use Advanced Options

Almost every search site offers some sort of advanced search page. Find it and use it. These advanced searches typically offer a lot more options that you can use to really fine-tune your search on that site.

Tip #20: Know the Impact

Okay. You know all about + and – and AND and OR—or do you? Do you really know the impact that all these modifiers, operators, and commands have on your searches? Check out Table 35.1 to find out how various techniques and commands impact your search results.

Table 35.1   Likely Results of Various Search Techniques

Action:	Impact on Scope of Query:	Impact on Quality of Results:	Comments:
Focused keywords	Narrows	Higher	As long as they're not *too* focused
General keywords	Broadens	Lower	Generally, they should be modified
Additional keywords	Broadens	Higher	The more keywords, the more the search engine knows about your query
Use of synonyms or alternate spellings	Broadens	Higher	No two people describe things the same way; use OR to connect
Phrases " "	Narrows	Higher	Phrases are better than single keywords
Wildcards *	Broadens	Higher	Necessary to pick up all forms of a word
+	Narrows	Higher	Forcing inclusions creates more precise queries
–	Narrows	Higher	Good for weeding junk out of your results
AND	Narrows	Higher	Linking words improves results

continues

351

Table 35.1 CONTINUED

Action:	Impact on Scope of Query:	Impact on Quality of Results:	Comments:
OR	Broadens	Lower	Great for synonyms
NEAR	Narrows	Higher	A good alternative to precise phrases
NOT	Narrows	Higher	Good for weeding junk out of your results
Parentheses ()	Depends...	Depends...	If you do it right, great; like math, some people have trouble constructing logical formulas
Filters (meta words)	Narrows	Depends...	If used properly, helps to target your search

Tip #21: Don't Overcomplicate Things

The more complex your query, the more likely that you'll make some sort of con-struction mistake and that the search engine will get confused. In general, limit your queries to no more than six to eight keywords and no more than three distinct con-cepts. The reality is that search engine behavior gets a tad unpredictable with longer, more complex queries—so keep it simple!

Tip #22: Don't Get Too Specific

Another problem with complex queries is that they often create such a specific query that few, if any, results are returned. Yes, looking for dog is too general, but looking for small brown elderly cocker spaniel named Sandy is too specific. If you find yourself getting few results, take some of the parameters out of your query to broaden your search.

Tip #23: Search from the Specific to the General...

This tip and the next are contradictory and reflect differing search strategies. The thinking behind this technique is that you can often find exactly what you're looking for quicker with a very specific query; only if you aren't successful do you then broaden your search.

Tip #24: ...Or Search from the General to the Specific

Personally, I prefer the opposite technique from the one in the previous tip. When you start with a general search, you learn a little more about the topic at hand, which can help you better construct a more specific second-stage query. In addition, you're more apt to stumble over information serendipitously with a general search than you are with a specific one. The bottom line—try both methods and see which one works for you.

Tip #25: Mix It Up

Don't get stuck using a particular search technique exclusively. If you always use Boolean searches, try dropping the operators and stringing together a bunch of key-words for a change. If you're big on excluding words with the – modifier, try a more inclusive search next time. If you always do the same thing the same way, you'll never know what you might be missing.

Tip #26: Fine-tune Your Results

Okay. You've executed your search. You've generated your results. Are you done? Of course not!

Look at the results generated from your initial search. Think about the good matches and the bad matches and why they ended up in the results list. Then enter a new query (based on your initial list of results, perhaps) that uses additional or different keywords, operators, and modifiers. (Some search sites even let you add new keywords to an existing query to generate "results from results.")

Your goal—to make the next list of results higher quality than the last.

Tip #27: Dig Around a Little

Find a Web page that contains good information? Then root around other pages on that site to see what else might be there.

If the site has its own internal search engine, use it. Click the site's navigation tools to check out other sections of the site. You can even mess around with the site's URL—by dropping parts off the end of the address—to go to other directories within the site. (For example, if the initial address is `www.mysite.com/directory/subdirectory/thispage.htm`, try entering `www.mysite.com/directory/subdirectory/`, or `www.mysite.com/directory/`, or just `www.mysite.com`.)

Tip #28: Different Day, Different Results

Remember that any search site can generate different results at different times for the same query. This happens because search engines are constantly finding new pages and deleting expired ones, and any page changes impact the relevancy rankings of all remaining pages. So don't expect to duplicate a successful search at a later time and get the same results.

Tip #29: Look for Newer Stuff First

In many cases, the best information is the newest information. On those search engines that let you set a date or age parameter, try looking for information less than a year old. (This advice is especially true if you're looking for technical information.)

If you're looking for recent information, however, remember that the major search engines and directories sometimes take a while to add new pages to their indexes. Depending on the search site, the process of adding a new page may take from a few hours to a few months. For the most recent information, then, you might be better off checking the newsgroup archives at DejaNews or searching directly at a hard news site.

Tip #30: Read the Help Files

You'll never know how to use anything if you don't read the instructions. Take the time to read the Help files and the FAQs at the major search sites—you'll be surprised at what you'll learn.

Tip #31: Ask for Help

There's more than just Web pages online. There are also people online, in newsgroups and on email mailing lists and chat channels. These people can be a great resource in your quest for information—all you have to do is ask them. Find a relevant forum and ask your questions—more often than not, you'll find your fellow users to be quite helpful and very informative.

Of course, you need to ask your questions in the right place in the right way. Don't just barge into an unknown newsgroup and blurt out a stupid question. Take time to learn the standards and "netiquette" of the newsgroup or the mailing list so that you don't annoy the people you want to help you.

The bottom line: if the answer you're looking for isn't readily available online, someone who knows the answer probably is.

Tip #32: Try to Keep Up

As was certainly evidenced as I was writing this book (and making major changes to my manuscript weekly!), the major search sites are constantly changing things and adding new features. Generally, these new features are designed to help you improve your searching. Keep your eyes open for changes at all the search sites you frequent, and learn how to use those new features.

You can also find out about new features and other industry news from Search Engine Watch (www.searchenginewatch.com). This Web site contains all the latest search engine news and even publishes an email newsletter to keep you informed about what's going on. If you're a truly serious searcher, this site is one to bookmark.

Tip #33: Customize Internet Explorer 5 for Faster Searches

If you're using Internet Explorer 5 or later, you can specify which search engines are used when you click the **Search** button or enter a query into the Address box. Just click the **Search** button to open the Search pane, and then click the **Customize** button. Select which search sites you want to use—and you're done. Now you can use your favorite search engines directly from the browser itself.

Unfortunately, Netscape Navigator allows no such customization of its search functions. Sorry.

Tip #34: Be a Pack Rat

Don't dismiss anything you find while engaging in your search activities. You never know when that one little scrap of data will be the key to something more important. It may be a key date here or a link to another page there—whatever you find, no matter how minor, don't throw it away! Print it out, write it down, bookmark it, save the file to disk, whatever—but hold on to anything that may be of value later.

Tip #35: Document Your Travels

Don't rely on your memory to return you to that one perfect page. Use your Web browser's Bookmarks or Favorites feature to keep track of all the pages you've visited and searches you've completed.

Tip #36: Kill Some Trees

Go ahead—print it out! There's nothing wrong with using your printer to make hard copies of the key pages you visit. (Just remember to activate your browser's option to include the page's URL on the printout; that way you'll always have the address if you need to access that Web page in the future.)

Tip #37: Don't Limit Yourself to the Web...

While you're busy searching through umpteen Web sites, don't forget all the other resources available on the Internet. Usenet newsgroups, email mailing lists, chat channels, and even FTP servers often contain truly useful information and files. Don't overlook anything that's available on the Internet!

Tip #38: ...Or to the Internet!

For that matter, don't forget about all the information you can find offline, in the real world. Turn off your computer! Read a newspaper or a magazine! Use an encyclopedia! Visit a library! Talk to people face to face! The Internet is just one resource available to you; don't assume that it's the only resource you should use.

Tip #39: Keep Your Eyes and Ears Open

Always be looking for information. Anywhere. From any source. Don't overlook the opportunity to find something, to learn something, to discover something whenever and wherever you may be. If you're open to finding information only when you're specifically looking, you'll overlook a lot of opportunities that pop up right in front of your face. Quite often, the best information appears when you're least expecting it.

Tip #40: Learn from Your Experience

Try to learn something about searching from every search you made. Did using this modifier effectively weed out irrelevant results? Did searching for a phrase rather than separate keywords produce higher-quality hits? If it worked once, it'll work again. The more you search, the better the searcher you can be—if you truly learn from what you do.

10 Common Mistakes You Don't Have to Be an Idiot to Make

Even the best searchers screw up, sometimes. As we all learn from our mistakes, I'll let you learn from *someone else's* mistakes and present the 10 most common foul-ups made when searching the Web—so you can avoid making them yourself!

Mistake #1: Not Knowing What You're Looking For

How can you find something if you don't know what you're looking for? You can waste a lot of time searching if you aren't sure what exactly it is you expect to find.

Mistake #2: Surfing Instead of Searching

Admit it, it's happened to you. You're in the middle of a long and boring search when you start randomly clicking a few links. Then, before you know it, you're pages and pages away from anything relevant, surfing your way across the vastness of the World Wide Web, your search all but forgotten.

Get disciplined! You can search when you're surfing; keep your mind on the task at hand. If you find yourself wandering, you're probably trying to do too much for too long. Try scheduling shorter (but more frequent) search sessions, just like you would schedule formal meetings. And while you're at it, schedule some break time so you don't burn out!

Mistake #3: Relying Exclusively on Your Own Assumptions

Don't assume you know everything. Don't assume that you have the right spelling for a keyword or the right URL for a Web site. Don't assume you have the right date for an event or the right name of a publication. Don't assume that anything you think you know is 100 percent accurate. And, most of all, don't assume you know exactly where to find the right information—or that the information actually exists. You could be wrong.

Mistake #4: Searching Too Broadly

Broad searches equal huge lists of results. Huge lists of results equal many irrelevant matches. So if you really want to look for Ford minivans, don't search for cars— search for ford minivans! You'll get more relevant results that way.

Mistake #5: Being Too Specific

This is the flip side of the previous pitfall. If you use too many modifiers and operators and narrow your parameters too much, you won't find anything—literally. When your search returns zero results, go back and rethink your query, taking away some of the limiting parameters.

Mistake #6: Using the Wrong Search Site

If you're looking for specialized information, don't use a general search site. If you're looking for a large number of matches, don't use a small directory. If you're looking for high-quality results, don't use a large search engine. Pick the right search site for your specific search. Refer to the tear-out card at the front of this book—and don't assume the same site will be good for all your different searches.

Mistake #7: Using the Wrong Boolean—Or Using the Right Boolean, Wrongly

Remember that different search sites use different variations of Boolean logic. Some sites use NOT to exclude words; others use AND NOT. Read the Help files at a specific site before you start doing Boolean searches at any given site.

Also, know that it's difficult to construct a Boolean phrase. Anybody—and I mean *anybody*—can make a mistake and goof up the whole logical equation. Run through your Boolean logic before you click the **Search** button or you might be disappointed in the results.

There's one more Boolean thing to mention: If your queries are too complex (especially if you nest too many phrases within other phrases), some search engines will just go nuts. Complex Boolean searches are not always handled well by all search engines. That's just the way it is. If you find your complex queries producing strange—or nonexistent—results, go back and simplify things.

Mistake #8: Getting Unbalanced

One very common mistake people make when they're constructing complex queries is getting their parentheses unbalanced. If you have a left parenthesis, you need a right parenthesis; they have to match. (This is Algebra 101, folks—check your math!)

Mistake #9: Misspelling a Word

The reason the search engine couldn't match your keyword could be because you didn't spell it right. I know of only one search engine that includes a spell checker (Ask Jeeves!); you have to check your own spelling everywhere else. Remember, search engines are pretty dumb—they'll search for whatever you enter, no matter how it's spelled.

Mistake #10: Stopping Too Soon

Please, *please* don't settle for the first page of results at the first search engine you query. There is always something more relevant on the next page, on the next search site, or resulting from the next query. Unless you're positive you've found the perfect match, keep looking!

The Least You Need to Know

➤ Effective searchers employ a combination of curiosity, intuition, and specific skills when searching for information.

➤ You can learn how to improve your searching by following the tips and techniques used by experienced Web searchers.

➤ Even the most experienced Web searchers make mistakes; always be on your guard against the most common pitfalls.

WHOA...

Chapter 36

How Not to Find Sex Sites When You Search

In This Chapter

➤ Learn about the options offered by several of the Big Seven search sites that let you filter out objectionable content

➤ Uncover specialized search engines that filter out all undesirable sites from their search results

➤ Find out about software programs you can install on your PC to monitor all your Internet activities

➤ Discover the secret keywords that can filter out adult-oriented sites from search queries at any Web site

---

How many times have you searched for something rather innocuous, only to find that multiple sex sites pop up in your results list? Why is it that search engines return these seemingly unrelated adult sites in response to a simple non–adult-oriented query?

The problem is that search engines and spiders are relatively dumb, and the administrators of adult Web sites are relatively smart. These purveyors of porn know how to manipulate search engine results so that their sites appear to match just about any type of query, no matter how unrelated. (If you want to learn these same techniques, see Chapter 39, "How You Can Manipulate Search Engine Results.")

How can you outsmart these "spamdexers" and remove adult sites from your search results? It's possible, even though it does take a bit of work.

Let Someone Else Do It: Using Search Filters

Many of the Big Seven search sites offer special filters that you can use to weed out offensive content from your search results. Using these filters helps to ensure that when your children search on these sites, they won't see a lot of pages with adult or other inappropriate content.

These filters all work pretty much the same. Someone, somewhere, compiles a list of offensive words and topics. Then software at the site (or, in some cases, people at the site) searches through the site's index for pages that contain those words or topics and excludes them from the newly filtered site index. That way, when you do a search at that site using that filter, you never see any offensive Web pages that might otherwise have been included in your results.

The following are the filtering options available at the Big Seven sites:

➤ **AltaVista—AV Family Filter**   The AV Family Filter uses both its own editors and SurfWatch software editors to automatically categorize potentially offensive pages and separate them from the rest of the search results. Lists are updated weekly to block content in the following categories: drugs/alcohol/tobacco, gambling, hate speech, sexually explicit subject matter, and violence.

➤ **Infoseek—GOguardian**   GOguardian filters out adult content from all Infoseek searches. Automatically activated within Infoseek's Kids and Family Centers.

➤ **Lycos—Search Guard**   Search Guard blocks out pornographic or offensive words and denies access to Lycos's chat, email, and message board functions.

➤ **Yahoo!—Yahooligans!**   Although the main Yahoo! directory doesn't offer any filtering options, Yahoo! does offer the separate Yahooligans! directory, with specially selected sites just for children.

Of these, Lycos Search Guard probably does the best job of filtering out offensive content, although AV Family Filter is giving Search Guard a run for its money. At the present time, Excite, HotBot, and Northern Light don't offer any filtering options.

In addition, there are other sites that specialize in offering filtered searches specifically for children. These sites include

➤ Ask Jeeves for Kids! (www.ajkids.com)

➤ OneKey (www.onekey.com)

➤ Searchopolis (www.searchopolis.com)

➤ Super Snooper (www.supersnooper.com)

These sites, created specifically for children to use, typically are even "cleaner" than the filters at the major search sites.

The Safe-Surfing Software Solution

In addition to the filters built into certain Web sites, you can also install software on your computer that performs filtering functions for all your online sessions. This software all works pretty much the same (and some of the software drives some of the search-site filters)—the software guards against either a preselected list of sites or a preselected list of topics, and it blocks access to sites that meet the selected criteria.

More Kid-Safe Sites

For more sites specifically designed with children in mind, check out Chapter 31, "Search for Help with Homework."

The following are five of the most popular filtering programs:

➤ **Cyber Patrol** (www.cyberpatrol.com; $29.95)   Blocks access to a preselected list of Web sites; also detects sites with objectionable words or images.

➤ **Cyber Snoop** (www.pearlsw.com; $29.95)   Tracks where your child has visited and saves the list as an activity log for parents to review; it can also block access to specified Web sites and Usenet newsgroups.

➤ **Cybersitter** (www.solidoak.com/cysitter.htm; $39.95)   Blocks access to a preselected list of Web sites, FTP sites, and Usenet newsgroups; also detects offensive words and phrases. One of the most popular filter programs, with more than 1.7 million users; *recommended*.

➤ **Net Nanny** (www.netnanny.com; $39.95)   Blocks access to a preselected list of Web sites, Usenet newsgroups, and chat rooms.

➤ **SurfWatch** (www.surfwatch.com; $49.95)   Blocks access to a preselected list of Web sites, Usenet newsgroups, and chat rooms; large initial list of banned sites (25,000 URLs); *recommended*.

Of these, I tend to like Cybersitter and SurfWatch the best—Cybersitter for its ease of use and SurfWatch for its massive list of suspect URLs.

Some Guidelines for Children on the Web

Before you let your kids on the Internet, you might want to consider some of these guidelines to make their surfing and searching a little safer:

➤ Make sure your children know never to give out any identifying information (home address, school name, telephone number, and so on) nor to send their photos to other users online.

➤ Never allow a child to arrange a face-to-face meeting with another computer user without parental permission and supervision. If a meeting is arranged, make the first one in a public place and be sure to accompany your child.

➤ Consider making Internet surfing an activity you do together—or make it a family activity by putting your PC in a public room, rather than in a private bedroom.

➤ Set reasonable rules and guidelines for computer use by your children; consider limiting the number of minutes/hours they can spend online each day.

➤ Monitor your children's Internet activities. Ask them to keep a log of all Web sites they visit; oversee any chat sessions they participate in; check out any files they download; even consider sharing an email account (especially with younger children) so that you can oversee their messages.

➤ Consider giving each of your children an online pseudonym so they don't have to use their real names online.

➤ Tell your children never to respond to messages that are suggestive, obscene, belligerent, threatening, or that make them feel uncomfortable—and encourage your children to tell you if they receive any such messages.

➤ Let your children know that people online may not be who they seem; just because someone says she's a 10-year-old girl doesn't necessarily mean that she really is 10 years old, or a girl.

The bottom line is that you have to take responsibility for your children's online activities. Provide the guidance they need to make the Internet a fun and educational place to visit.

No Sex, Please—Filtering Your Queries at Any Search Site

Although search filters are the best way to avoid objectionable content, they can also filter out sites that you actually want to visit. Instead, you might try using your own search filters by adding parameters to your queries that exclude certain words and phrases from your search results. This approach has the added benefit of filtering the queries you make at any search site, whether the site offers built-in filtering or not.

Which words should you exclude from your queries? Some of the more common words used in the titles and META tags of adult Web sites are "sex" and "hardcore." If you tell a search engine to exclude these words from your search (by using either the "–" command or the NOT Boolean operator), any pages containing these two words won't be returned.

Let's see how this works. Pick a search engine and enter a search for `breasts`. Chances are that you'll get a few adult sites mixed in with a results list that also includes sites about breast cancer and breast feeding. Now enter this search: `breasts –sex –hardcore` (or, in a Boolean search, `breasts NOT sex NOT hardcore`) and see what you get. It should be a slightly cleaner search.

Note that this isn't a perfect tactic, because not all adult sites include the words "sex" and "hardcore" in their META tags; in addition, some adult sites use splash pages that tend to foil filtering schemes of all types. Still, it helps a little, so you might want to give it a try.

The Least You Need to Know

➤ AltaVista, Infoseek, and Lycos offer options that let you filter out objectionable content from your search results.

➤ There are several specialized search engines—such as Searchopolis and Super Snooper—that offer filtered searches.

➤ Numerous software programs—such as Cybersitter and SurfWatch—let you filter all your Internet surfing.

➤ Excluding the words "sex" and "hardcore" from your queries will manually filter out a lot of adult-oriented Web sites.

Chapter 37

Let Your Software Do the Searching with Specialized Search Programs

In This Chapter

➤ Discover how you can initiate Web meta-searches from your desktop with search software programs

➤ Learn how to search-enable your own personal Web site

Searching the Web doesn't have to be done from the Web. There is now an entire category of software programs that provides search functions from your own personal computer—and, in some cases, *of* your personal computer. Most of this software is available freely over the Web as shareware, although commercial versions are also offered. (Of course, you're supposed to pay for shareware if you like it…it isn't supposed to be free forever!)

Micromanaging the Search Engines with Search Software

If you like meta-search sites (as discussed in Chapter 13, "Kill Two Birds with One Stone at Meta-Search Sites"), why not install a meta-search engine on your own personal computer? There are several companies that offer software programs that you can use to send queries to multiple search engines and to compile and sort your results in various ways. Many of these programs let you download results in the background—or even when you're away from your computer, doing other tasks. Some even let you download the actual pages corresponding to the search results so that you can view the results of your search even if you're offline.

The following are some of the more popular search programs currently available. Most let you download a trial version so you can test them out before you plunk down your hard-earned cash. (These are all Windows 95/98/NT programs; if you're a Mac user, the pickings are slimmer.)

➤ **BullsEye** (www.intelliseek.com)   Offers a wide range of predefined searches, such as news, business, and software; it attempts to group downloaded results in similar categories. The commercial version sells for $49.

➤ **Copernic** (www.copernic.com)   Offers a variety of specialty searches, including music, movies, jobs, and sports; searches 10 Web search engines, as well as Usenet newsgroups and email mailing lists. The commercial version sells for $29.95.

➤ **CyberSearch** (www.frontiertech.com)   Queries five Web search engines and returns results in separate folders. The commercial version sells for $99.

➤ **Cybot** (www.theartmachine.com/cybot.htm)   Queries five Web search engines and returns results in Microsoft Access database format. The commercial version sells for $49.95.

➤ **Mata Hari** (www.thewebtools.com)   The commercial version sells for $34.95.

➤ **NetAttache Pro** (www.tympani.com/products/NAPro/NAPro.html)   The commercial version sells for $39.95.

➤ **Search4** (www.intermania.com/search4/)   Free utility that runs in the Windows taskbar and queries eight search sites.

➤ **SSSpider** (www.pkware.com/catalog/ssspider.html)   From the makers of PKZIP, this software queries multiple search engines using 27 languages, then combines and ranks results by relevancy. The commercial version sells for $29.95.

➤ **Teleport Pro** (www.tenmax.com/pro.html)   In addition to querying search engines, this program can download and mirror complete Web sites. The commercial version sells for $39.95. *Recommended.*

➤ **WebFerret** (www.ferretsoft.com/netferret/)   One of the easiest-to-use search programs, limited to Web searching only (queries 18 sites). Standard version is free; WebFerretPro sells for $26.95. *Recommended.*

➤ **WebSeeker** (www.bluesquirrel.com)   Searches more than 100 sites with an easy-to-use interface; also lets you highlight text to search from within desktop applications. The commercial version sells for $49.95. *Recommended.*

A Whole Family of Ferrets

If you like WebFerret, check out its siblings InfoFerret (which queries Web databases and archives), EmailFerret (which searches for email addresses), FileFerret (which searches for files to download), IRCFerret (which searches for IRC chat channels), PhoneFerret (which searches for phone numbers and addresses), and NewsFerret (which searches Usenet newsgroups)—all available from FerretSoft (www.ferretsoft.com).

Which—if any—of these search programs should you use? I'll be honest—I've tried several of these programs, but I don't use any of them on a daily basis.

Why? These programs all suffer from the same problems you find with meta-search sites—because every search engine uses a slightly different query format, you don't get optimal results from the "vanilla" queries submitted by the meta-search tools. I prefer to go directly to the sites I want to use, individually, and submit the "perfect" query for that site. Meta-search tools—whether Web sites or software—simply aren't that accurate, even if they are somewhat time saving.

If you do want to try some of these programs, however, I recommend that you check out Inforia Quest (which searches the most number of sites), Teleport Pro (which lets you mirror complete sites on your hard disk), WebFerret (which is the easiest to use), or WebSeeker (which lets you initiate Web searches from within your regular desktop applications). You might find they're beneficial to your searching style, even if they aren't to mine.

Ferreting for information with WebFerret software.

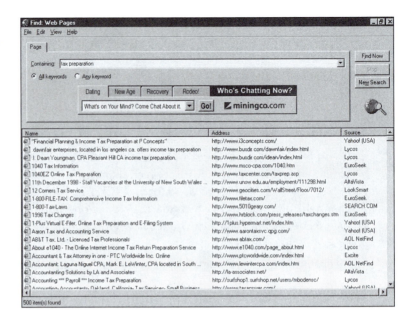

Make Your Own Search Engine: How to Search-Enable Your Web Site

Searching the entire Web is one thing; searching your own Web site is another. If you run a large Web or intranet site, you may want to incorporate your own private search engine so users can search for information within your site. There are lots of companies—including many of the major Web search engine companies—that offer site-search software both for individual and commercial use.

These packages vary wildly in what they offer and require of you. Some of these solutions require some programming skill on your part; some don't. Some are free; some aren't. Some allow you to customize the look-and-feel of your search results; some provide a canned interface.

Table 37.1 presents a rundown on some of the more popular site-search packages currently available.

Table 37.1   Search Software for Web Sites

Software/Company:	Located At:	Comments:
ALISE	www.alise.com	For Windows NT, with versions for HTML, Visual Basic, and Visual C developers
Alkaline Search	www.vestris.com/alkaline	For Windows NT, Linux, and Solaris SunOS; free for noncommercial sites or $350 for commercial use
AltaVista	altavista.software.digital.com	The popular Web search engine offers a variety of programs for indexing desktops, Web sites, and intranets
Cha Cha	cha-cha.berkeley.edu	Experimental sites-search software, available for individual or commercial use
DataWare	www.dataware.com	Offers the Knowledge Query Server site-search software
Excalibur	www.xrs.com	Multimedia and text-based site-search software
Excite for Web Servers (EWS)	www.excite.com/navigate/	Easy-to-use site-search software, suporting both keyword and concept searching
Extense	www.extense.com	For Linux, Sun Solaris, and AIX; free if indexing 200 or fewer pages
FreeFind	www.freefind.com	Site-search software for individual or commercial use
ht://DIG	http://htdig.sdsu.edu/	For UNIX; free software that features both Boolean searching and fuzzy searching
Hyperseek	www.hyperseek.com	Commercial software; $399 for a single domain
IndexFinger	www.indexfinger.com	Site-search software for individual or commercial use
IndexSite	www.indexsite.com	For Windows 95/98/NT; pricing from $69 to $195
Infoseek	software.infoseek.com	Ultraseek Server software, same as that used on the Infoseek site
Inmagic	www.inmagic.com	Offering a variety of site-search software, including Lycos's DB/Text Intranet Spider

continues

369

Table 37.1 CONTINUED

Software/ Company:	Located At:	Comments:
InQuizit	www.itpinc.com	Site-search software featuring natural language processing
Intelligenx	www.intelligenx.com	Site-search software featuring a full-text search system
InText	intext.com	For Windows 95 and other platforms
Isearch	www.cnidr.org/ir/isearch.html	Site-search software for individual or commercial use
Limit Point	www.limit-point.com	For Macintosh servers, featuring Boolean search
Links	www.gossamer-threads.com/ scripts/links/	Price is $150 for commercial use and free for noncommercial sites
LookSmart SmartLinks	www.looksmart.com/ smartlinks/	Free HTML code to incorporate the LookSmart SmartLinks panel on your own Web page
Lycos Site Spider	www.lycos.com/software/ software-intranet.html	For Windows NT; search soft ware from Lycos and Inmagic
Magnifi	www.magnifi.com	Commercial site-search software for both text and multimedia files
Muscat	www.muscat.com	Commercial site-search soft-ware
News Index New Ticker	www.newsindex.com/ tickercust.html	A Java-based search engine that crawls selected news sites and displays a news ticker on your Web page
Open Text	www.opentext.com	For Windows NT and UNIX; Livelink site-search software
Oracle	www.oracle.com	Oracle's ConText software allows searches of information contained within its database packages
PC Docs/ Fulcrum	www.pcdocs.com	Site-search software for commercial and individual sites
Phantom	www.maxum.com/Phantom/	For Windows95/NT and Macintosh
PLS	www.pls.com	Free site-search software, from a subsidiary of America Online
Quadralay	www.quadralay.com	For Windows NT, Solaris, SunOS, IRIX, HP/UX, AIX, and Linux; WebWorks Search is priced under $500

370

Software/ Company:	Located At:	Comments:
SiteSurfer	`www.devtech.com/SiteSurfer/`	Java-based site-search engine
SWISH-E (SWISHEnhanced)	`sunsite.berkeley.edu/SWISH-E/`	Site-search software that supports Boolean operators and wildcard searches
Thunderstone Webinator	`www.thunderstone.com/webinator/`	For Windows NT and UNIX; available both in free and commercial versions
Tippecanoe Systems	`www.tippecanoe.com`	For Windows NT; Tecumseh site-search software
Verity	`www.verity.com`	Commercial site-search software
Virage	`www.virage.com`	Multimedia search software; used by AltaVista Image Finder
WebGlimpse	`glimpse.cs.arizona.edu/webglimpse/`	Site-search software for commercial and individual use
Whatuseek IntraSearch	`www.whatuseek.com/intraSearch/`	Site-search software for commercial and individual use
Wisebot	`www.tetranetsoftware.com`	For Windows 95/98/NT; Wisebot site-search software
ZyLab	`www.zylab.com`	For Windows NT users; ZyIndex site-search software

Want More Info?

If you want to learn more about adding search functionality to your own Web site, check out Search Tools (`www.searchtools.com`). This site offers listings of various search software, as well as useful articles and news about site-search software.

The Least You Need to Know

➤ There are many software programs that provide meta-search capabilities from your personal computer desktop.

➤ The best search programs are Inforia Quest, Teleport Pro, WebFerret, and WebSeeker.

➤ If you run your own Web site, there are many programs available that let you add search functionality within your site.

Chapter 38

Search the Lazy Way: Use Your Web Browser for Quick Searches

In This Chapter

➤ Learn how to initiate a Web search from within Microsoft's Internet Explorer

➤ Find out how to search the Web from within Netscape Navigator

➤ Discover how Sherlock lets you search the Web—or your hard disk—in Mac OS 8.5

Did you know that you don't actually have to go to a search site to search the Web? Both Microsoft's Internet Explorer and Netscape Navigator let you start your searching right from your Web browser—you don't even have to enter the URL for AltaVista, Yahoo!, or any other search site!

Two Cool Ways to Launch a Search from Internet Explorer

The latest version of Internet Explorer, version 5, has a number of features that let you start a search without actually hitting the search site first. When you use these search methods, Internet Explorer 5 does all the site accessing automatically.

Method One: Search with the Search Button

When you click the **Search** button on Internet Explorer 5's toolbar, the browser displays a separate Search pane. Within the Search pane is the Search Assistant, which allows you to search for Web pages, email addresses, businesses, and maps.

Address box

Search directly from Internet Explorer 5's Address box, or click the **Search** *button to display the Search pane.*

Search pane

Search button

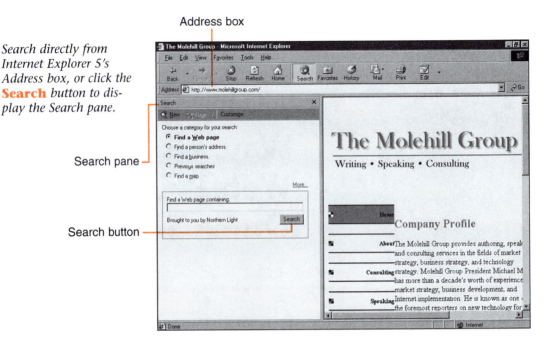

When the Search Assistant first appears, you select what kind of search you want to perform. Just check which you want to do: Find a Web Page, Find a Person's Address, Find a Business, view your Previous Searches, or Find a Map.

If you choose to Find a Web Page, Search Assistant uses one of Microsoft's chosen search providers—AltaVista, Euroseek, Excite, GoTo, Infoseek, Lycos, MSN Web Search, Northern Light, or Yahoo! The very first time you use Internet Explorer 5, one of the services is selected at random; this search service remains your default choice from that point on unless you customize your settings.

To use the Search Assistant, enter your query into the Search box, and then click the **Search** button. The Search Assistant then disappears from the Search pane and is replaced by the search results from the chosen search service. When you click a specific listing in the results, the selected page loads into Internet Explorer's main pane (on the right). This way you can view your search results and the actual Web pages simultaneously.

After you've done a search, you can easily transfer your query to another search engine. Just click the **Next** button in the Search pane and your query will be sent to the next search service on your list. You can also pull down the **Next** button (click the arrow next to the button itself) to select a specific search engine to redirect your query to.

When you want to initiate a new search, click the **New** button in the Search pane and start it again. If you ever want to look at the results from past searches, check the **Previous Searches** option in the Search pane, and then click the query you wish to re-examine.

374

Customize the Search Assistant

You can customize the search services used by Internet Explorer 5's Search Assistant by clicking the **Customize** button in the Search pane. When the Customize Search Settings window appears, select which search service you want to use by default and move it to the top of the services list. You can also move any service up or down in the list; when you click the **Next** button in the Search pane, you toggle through this list of search services in order. You can also choose not to use certain search services by unchecking the box next to a specific service. Click the **OK** button to finalize your choices.

Method Two: Search from the Address Box

You can also search from the Address box in Internet Explorer 5, using something that Microsoft calls *Autosearch*.

If you enter one or more words into the Address box (without a www. at the beginning or a .com at the end), Autosearch assumes you're entering a query, and it displays a page of results (from the MSN Search service) that matches your query. You can also force Autosearch to search when you enter a single keyword by entering a question mark (?) before the keyword in the Address box—such as ? microsoft.

If you want to use the Address box to search a service other than MSN Search (and you may want to—MSN Search isn't that great), click the **Customize** button in the Search pane, click the **Autosearch** button, and then select which search service you want to use.

Find Related Sites

After you've accessed a specific Web site, pull down the Tools menu and select **Show Related Links**. This displays a Related List pane that contains a list of Web sites that are somehow related to the displayed page. This feature—and a similar feature employed in Netscape Navigator—is powered by technology supplied by Alexa. (Go to www.alexa.com to learn more about Alexa's full menu of navigation services.)

The Several Ways to Start a Search with Netscape Navigator

Similar to the way Internet Explorer 5 integrates search functions into its Web browser, Netscape Navigator (version 4.5 or later) also lets you initiate searches without actually accessing a search site first. The features and functions are similar to those in Internet Explorer 5, but with Netscape's own particular twist.

You can either Smart Browse or search from Navigator's Location box—or click the **Search** *button to go to Netcenter's Net Search page.*

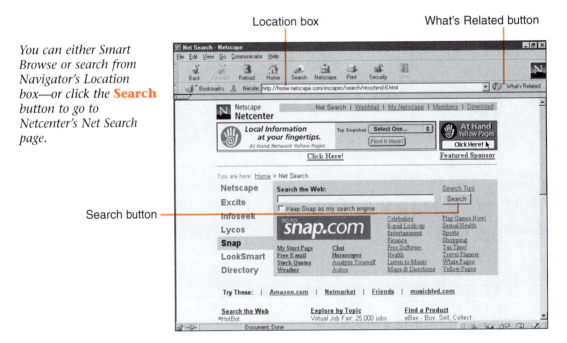

Method One: Smart Browsing from the Location Box

Just as Internet Explorer 5 includes Autosearch from its Address box, Netscape Navigator includes a feature called Smart Browsing from its Location box. Just enter a keyword into the Location box, and Smart Browsing will take you to the most likely Web site that matches the keyword. (Again, entering `microsoft` takes you to `www.microsoft.com`.) However, Navigator is a little different because if you enter a more generic word (such as `cars`), it doesn't take you directly to `www.cars.com`; instead, it displays a list of pages that possibly match your keyword.

Note, however, that the list displayed by Smart Browsing isn't really a list of search results. Instead, it's a shorter list prepared by Netscape showing those domain names that are close matches to your keyword.

Method Two: Traditional Searching from the Location Box

You can also perform traditional (that is, non-Smart Browsing) searches using Navigator's Location box. Just enter a question mark (?) in front of your keyword(s) in the Location box, and Navigator accesses Netscape Search (powered by Excite) to perform a normal Web search.

To summarize, if you enter microsoft into the Location box, Navigator activates Smart Browsing and takes you to www.microsoft.com. If you enter ? microsoft, Navigator accesses Netscape Search to display a list of sites that match your keyword query.

Find More Sites with What's Related

After you've accessed a specific Web site using Smart Browsing, click the **What's Related** button to display a list of Web sites related to the displayed page. Click any site listed in the What's Related menu to access that specific site. (The technology behind this is supplied by Alexa—who supplies similar technology for Internet Explorer.)

Method Three: Search with the Search Button

Finally, when you click Navigator's **Search** button (located on the Navigation toolbar), you're taken directly to Netscape Netcenter's Net Search page (described in Chapter 10, "The Next Generation: Newer, Better Search Engines"). From here you can initiate any type of search you want.

Make Searching Elementary with Apple's Sherlock

If you're a Macintosh user—and you've either purchased a new iMac or upgraded your old Macintosh to Mac OS 8.5—you actually have Web browsing built into your operating system in the form of a technology called *Sherlock*.

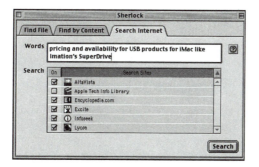

Search the Web from your Macintosh desktop with Sherlock.

Sherlock lets you query multiple Web search engines simultaneously (click the **Search Internet** tab), search your hard disk for specific files by name (the **Find File** tab), or search your hard drive for specific information (the **Find by Content** tab). Sherlock uses relevance ranking to sort your search results, provides a three-line summary for each Web site listed, and enables you to save your search queries for later use.

For more information on Sherlock, read your Apple owner's manual, or go to `www.apple.com/sherlock/`.

The Least You Need to Know

➤ Internet Explorer enables you to initiate Web searches by clicking the **Search** button or by entering a query into the Address box.

➤ Netscape Navigator enables you to initiate Web searches by clicking the **Search** button or entering a query into the Location box.

➤ Mac OS 8.5 includes a built-in search function called Sherlock, which enables you to search either your hard disk or the World Wide Web.

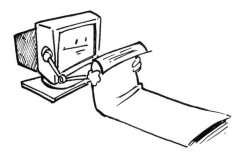

Chapter 39

How You Can Manipulate Search Engine Results

In This Chapter

➤ Discover how different search sites rank their results

➤ Learn how and where to place keywords on your page to improve your page's relevancy

➤ Uncover the dirty tricks you can use to fool the search engines and give your site a higher relevancy ranking

You perform a search on AltaVista, and site X is at the top of the results. You perform the same search on HotBot, and site Y is the number-one listing. Then you go to Northern Light and find that site Z sits atop all the other listings.

How do different search engines rank their search results? Are there ways for Webmasters to tweak their sites to impact their rankings with specific search engines? Just how much can you trust the relevancy rankings generated by the various search sites?

Relevancy of results is a big issue in the search engine world. Read on to discover just how good the results really are at your favorite search sites.

The Relevant Issue: How Search Engines Rank Their Results

So here's the $10,000 question: How *do* search engines go about determining relevancy?

The answer isn't simple because each site ranks its results using slightly different methods—which is one reason why the same search on different search engines produces different results.

Location, Location, Location

Probably the most important factor in relevancy ranking is the location of the keyword on a Web page. It's kind of a "first come, first served" rule.

For example, pages with keywords appearing in the title are assumed to be more relevant than pages without the keywords in the title. Search engines also check to see whether the keywords appear near the top of the page's text, such as in the headline or in the first few paragraphs. The assumption is that any page relevant to the topic will mention those words right from the beginning.

What's the Frequency, Kenneth?

Frequency is the other major factor in how search engines determine relevancy. Practically all search engines analyze how often keywords appear in relation to other words in a Web page. Those with a higher frequency are often deemed more relevant than other pages.

Sometimes Life Really Is a Popularity Contest

Some engines may also give "popular" Web pages a boost. For example, some search engines can tell which of the pages in its index have a lot of links pointing at them. A much-linked-to page is ranked higher in the search results because there's probably a good reason that page is popular.

Sites that use link popularity to rank their results include AltaVista, Excite, and Infoseek.

Familiarity Helps

Some search sites that also have their own Web directories may give a relevancy boost to sites they've reviewed in their directories. The logic is that if the site was good enough to earn a review, it's probably more relevant than an unreviewed site.

Sites that use familiarity to rank their results include Excite and Infoseek.

Crawling from the Wreckage

All search engines use spiders to "crawl" the Web and report back what they find. But there are different ways to crawl, believe it or not.

Some spiders use what is called a *deep crawl*, which finds the many individual pages from a Web site, even if the pages are not explicitly submitted to them. A shallow crawl lists far fewer pages from a site—in many cases, just the home page and any manually submitted pages.

Search engines using a deep crawl include AltaVista, HotBot, and MSN Search.

Tag—You're It!

META tags are the code placed in the HTML header of a Web page, providing information that is visible to Web browsers but not to Web users. Many search engines use META tags to help index the content of a Web page; some engines assign a higher relevancy ranking if keywords appear in the META tags.

Sites that use META tags to rank their results include Infoseek, HotBot, and MSN Search.

Which Words?

Just what information gets indexed when a spider crawls a site? It differs from spider to spider:

➤ **Full body text**   This indexes all the text found on a Web page. All spiders perform a full body text index, although some will not index *stop words*.

➤ **Stop words**   These are words (such as "and" and "the") that are too frequently used to have much relevancy to most queries. Some search engines either leave out stop words when they index a page (to save space) or may not search for these words during a query (to speed up the search). Infoseek is one of the sites that doesn't index stop words.

➤ **ALT text**   This is the "alternate" text associated with images on a Web page; if the picture doesn't load, the ALT text is displayed. Only a few of the search engines (specifically AltaVista, Infoseek, and Lycos) index ALT text.

➤ **Comments**   Some Web pages contain "hidden" text as comments to the Web page designers. These comments are indexed by HotBot and MSN Search but are pretty much ignored by the other search engines.

Pay the Penalty

Believe it or not, there are some things you can do to your site that will cause some search engines to give you a *lower* relevancy ranking—or to totally exclude your pages from their index!

Here are some of the spanners you can throw in the spider works:

➤ **Frames**   This common design technique can actually throw off some spiders, which might only index the main frame on a multiframe page. In particular, AltaVista has some trouble dealing with framed pages.

➤ **Image maps**   Image maps are graphics with hyperlinks, and some search engines can't follow the links embedded in the pictures. In particular, AltaVista and Infoseek have trouble spidering image maps.

➤ **Password protection**   Spiders can't enter protected sites if they don't have the right password. If you limit access to your site, you limit your indexing potential, as well.

In general, the simpler your site, the more easily it can be indexed.

Size and Freshness

In addition to the way they crawl or index, some search engines simply index *more* Web pages than others, which adds a degree of complexity to their rankings. In addition, some search engines index Web pages more often than others, and this freshness factor will also impact rankings. The result of the size and freshness factors is that no two search engines have the same collection of Web pages to search through—no matter how similar their ranking methods may be.

Force Your Way to the Top: How to Optimize Your Site's Ranking

If you're running a Web site, you want to be at the top of the list when someone is searching for sites such as yours. There's nothing worse than being site number 957 out of a thousand results.

So, what can you do to improve your chances of hitting the top of the lists?

There are a variety of techniques you can use to improve your relevancy ranking with the major search engines. Although most of these techniques are tried and true and acceptable to all, know that some of the more controversial techniques (those known as *spamdexing*) are frowned upon by the Internet community and could actually result in your pages being excluded from some search indexes.

Spamdexing—Should You Do It?

Any optimization of a Web page with intent to deceive a search engine's spider and result in a higher or misleading ranking is called *spamdexing* or *spoofing*. Should you try to spamdex the major search engines or just go the honest route and take the ranking you deserve?

Here's what you need to know:

First, different spamdexing techniques don't always work with all search engines. In fact, some search engines may detect your spamdexing and actually delete your page from their index.

Second, spamdexing usually focuses on specific and very popular keywords. Guess what? If you're focusing on these keywords, so are your competitors. If you attempt to wrest control of these keywords from other sites, be prepared for an ongoing and time-consuming battle—because your competitors will be doing the same thing! Your time and effort might be better spent on improving and promoting your site using more traditional methods.

Finally, deceiving a search engine is one thing, but do you really want to deceive your site visitors? Your site's content should stand on its own, without artificially pumping up content that may or may not justify the attention.

The bottom line: There's nothing wrong with making sure that search engines notice your site and all that it contains. But trying to fool the spiders into seeing something that isn't there probably isn't the best strategy in the online world.

Pick Your Keywords Carefully

How do you think people will search for your Web page? Think like the user and make sure you actually use those keywords somewhere on your page. In fact, try to put those words near the top of your page and include them in the page's title and META tags.

While you're doing this, also make sure you pick *multiple* keywords—because not all users search the same way. For example, if your page is about Golden Age comic book collecting, you may want to choose `comics`, `comic books`, `golden age`, and `collecting` as your keywords.

Use META Tags

A META tag is one of the codes placed in the HTML header of a Web page. The most important META tags (noticed most by spiders) are KEYWORDS and DESCRIPTION. The KEYWORDS tag lets you emphasize the importance of certain words and phrases on your page; the DESCRIPTION tag lets you control the text of the summary displayed in some search engine results listings. Putting your keywords in your META tags increases your chances of getting indexed by most search engines.

Make Your Text Count

Just cramming your page with keywords doesn't mean a thing if the keywords don't have anything to do with what your page is actually about. Your keywords need to be reflected in the page's content. And as far as most spiders are concerned, your content is your page's HTML text—*not* any pictures on your page!

What does this mean? If your page contains images of Marilyn Monroe but no text, you won't show up in the results when someone searches for Marilyn. But if you add some text to the page that talks about Ms. Monroe, you'll get indexed.

Text equals content equals indexing. Remember that.

Submit Your Pages

This sounds like a no-brainer, but it's worth pointing out anyway. Most search engines (and almost all directories) accept submissions for inclusion in their indexes. You should submit your key pages to all the major search sites so that they can either be added manually or so that the site's spider can be directed to your URLs for indexing. (For a list of links directly to the submission pages of the major search engines, go to www.tiac.net/users/seeker/searchenginesub.html.)

Check Your Registrations—and Fine-tune Your Site

Don't just assume that because you submitted your site to a search engine, it will automatically be spidered or indexed. For any given search engine, it may take anywhere from a few days to a few months for registrations to actually become effective. In some cases, you may have to submit your site several times before it gets registered.

After your site starts showing up in a search engine's results lists, take note of where your site ranks. If you're not as high as you'd like (and you probably won't be), go back and fine-tune your site, focusing on frequency and placement of keywords. Examine other sites that rank higher than yours; what are they doing that you're not?

If you want the highest possible ranking, you have to work at it!

Pay Somebody Else to Do It

You can submit your page manually to every single search site (which could total several hundred submissions!), or you can avail yourself of one of many different multiple-site submission services. Some of these services are free, but most will cost you something. While the pros typically continue to submit one site at a time because they can better fine-tune their submissions to specific sites, using a submission service can be a real time-saver for the mere mortals among us. Some of the more popular services include AutoSubmit (`autosubmit.com`), BigSubmit (`bigsubmit.com`), Cyber Submit (`www.cybersubmit.com`), Linkosaurus (`sffa.com/linkosaurus.html`), Submit Away (`www.submit-away.com`), Submit Pro (`www.submit-pro.com`), Web Site Garage (`www.register-it.com`), and Webpage-Register.com (`www.webpage-register.com`).

Spoof at Your Own Risk

There are other techniques you can use to try to trick search engines into improving your relevancy. These techniques often work against you because many search engines specifically look for these spoofs and automatically exclude these spamdexed pages from their indexes.

What are some of the most common spamdexing techniques? Here are a few to consider, at your own risk:

➤ **Keyword stuffing**   This technique involves the repeating of keywords and keyword phrases many times in a row, either in the page's text or in the META tags. (For example, if your site is about feet, you would insert the text `feet feet feet feet feet` somewhere on your page or in the META tags.)

➤ **Unrelated keywords**   Let's say your site is about something boring, such as pound cake. You could increase your hits by telling everyone it was about something more interesting, such as sex. You add the unrelated keyword `sex` to your title and META tags and whatnot, so your site will pop up whenever someone searches for `sex`. This is also called lying about your site content, but a lot of sites do it.

➤ **Invisible text**   This technique involves making your text "invisible" by choosing the same color for the text and for the page's background. An example of this is white text on a white background—invisible to the user, but capable of being seen by spider software. Some sites use invisible text to stuff keywords on a page in a way that users won't notice.

➤ **Tiny text**   This technique involves placing very small text on your page, usually at the bottom, where most users won't notice it. Again, this is a way to keyword stuff a page without interfering with the user experience.

I can't recommend any of these techniques because they've all been widely used and abused—and they can actually work against you with some vigilant search engines. But they do work, sometimes, and lots of sites employ them. Use them or not—it's your call!

When All Else Fails—Buy Your Way to the Top!

Up until quite recently, search engines prided themselves on the fact that their search results were pristine and totally separate from their site advertising. Most sites have allowed *keyword purchasing* for some time, where specific banner advertisements pop up to correspond with specific "purchased" search queries. But the results themselves were true.

Not anymore.

AltaVista has taken a lot of heat recently for its auctioning of key search results. The way it works is that a site pays AltaVista a sum of money for a certain keyword; whenever that keyword is entered in a query, the site that paid the cash gets the top listing. Not an ad, but a real listing in its own little box (titled "AV Relevant Paid Links").

But AltaVista wasn't the first site to sell its results. GoTo (www.goto.com) takes pride in the fact that it sells all its listings to the highest bidders. Where AltaVista at least segregates its paid listings, GoTo just puts the paid ones at the top of the list. To me, that obviates the integrity of the site, and forces me to not recommend GoTo as a reliable search engine.

To date, AltaVista and GoTo are the only sites selling their search results—but will they be the last? Stay tuned for future developments...

The Least You Need to Know

➤ Different search engines use different criteria to index and rank Web pages.

➤ Frequency and position are the two most important factors in determining Web page relevancy.

➤ Spamdexing techniques can fool some search engines into improving your relevancy rankings—or get you kicked from some search engine indexes.

The Complete Idiot's Search Site Directory

Site:	URL:	Type of Search:
1st Headlines	www.1stheadlines.com	News
2600 Irregulars' Warez Ring Index	www.webring.org/cgi-bin/ webring?index;ring=2600warez	Warez
2600: The Hacker Quarterly	www.2600.com	Warez
2look4	www.2look4.com	MP3
411Locate	www.411locate.com	White pages, email, yellow pages
4work	www.4work.com	Jobs
About.com	www.about.com	General
About.com Alphabetical Index of U.S. Government Web Space	usgovinfo.about.com/ blindex.htm	Government
About.com Family Medicine	familymedicine.about.com	Health
About.com Homework Help	homeworkhelp.about.com	Homework
About.com Science/ Nature for Kids	kidscience.about.com	Science
About.com Web Clip Art Links	webclipart.about.com	Clip art
Accommodation Search Engine	ase.net	Hotels
Achoo	www.achoo.com	Health

continues

CONTINUED

Site:	URL:	Type of Search:
Acses	www.acses.com	Shopping
ActiveX.com	www.activex.com	Computers
AdAmerica	www.adamerica.com	Classifieds
Adult411	www.adult411.com	Adult
AJR NewsLink	ajr.newslink.org	News
All About College	www.allaboutcollege.com	College
All-Classical Guide	allclassical.com	Music
All-Game Guide	www.allgame.com	Games
All-Movie Guide	www.allmovie.com	Movies
All-Music Guide	www.allmusic.com	Music
AltaVista	www.altavista.com	General
AltaVista Photo & Media Finder	image.altavista.com	Pictures and sounds
Amazing Picture Machine	www.ncrtec.org/picture.htm	Pictures
Amazon.com	www.amazon.com	Books
Amazon.com Auctions	auctions.amazon.com	Auctions
American College Entrance Directory	www.aaced.com	College
American Information Network, Inc.	www.ameri.com	People and DMV records
American Law Sources On-Line	www.lawsource.com/also/	Legal
American School Directory	www.asd.com	K-12 schools
Ameritech Yellow Pages	yp.ameritech.net	Yellow pages
Anarchist Cookbook	www.anarchist.free-online.co.uk	Anarchy
Anarchy Rules.com	www.anarchyrules.com	Anarchy
Ancestry.com	www.ancestry.com	Genealogy
AngelFire	www.angelfire.com	Personal Web pages
Annoyances.org	www.annoyances.org	Computers
Annual Reports Library	www.zpub.com/sf/arl/	Financial
AnyWho	www.anywho.com	White pages, yellow pages
AOL NetFind	www.aol.com/netfind/	General
Apartments.com	www.apartments.com	Apartments
Argus Clearinghouse	www.clearinghouse.net	Library
Armchair Millionaire	www.armchairmillionaire.com	Financial

390

Site:	URL:	Type of Search:
Art Today	www.arttoday.com	Clip art and pictures
Arthur	www.ahip.getty.edu/arthur/	Pictures
Ask Jeeves!	www.askjeeves.com	General
Ask Jeeves for Kids!	www.ajkids.com	Children
At Hand Network Yellow Pages	www.athand.com	Yellow pages
Auction Universe	www.auctionuniverse.com	Auctions
Auction Universe Network	www.aun.com	Auctions
Auction Watchers	www.auctionwatchers.com	Auctions
AuctionGuide.com	www.auctionguide.com	Auctions
AuctionInsider	www.auctioninsider.com	Auctions
AuctionPage	www.auctionpage.com	Auctions
Auctions Online Supersite	guestservices.hypermart.net	Auctions
Audiofind	www.audiofind.com	MP3
Awesome Library	www.awesomelibrary.org	Homework
Bank Rate Monitor	www.bankrate.com	Financial
Barry's Clip Art Server	www.barrysclipart.com	Clip art
Beaucoup	www.beaucoup.com	Search engine list
BellSouth Real Yellow Pages	yp.bellsouth.com	Yellow pages
Berkeley Digital Library SunSITE	sunsite.berkeley.edu	Library
BeWELL	bewell.com	Health
Bible Gateway	bible.gospelcom.net/bible/	Religious
Bible Search	www.biblesearch.com	Religious
Bidder's Edge	www.biddersedge.com	Auctions
BidFind	www.bidfind.com	Auctions
Bigbook	www.bigbook.com	Yellow pages
BigCharts	www.bigcharts.com	Financial
Bigfoot	www.bigfoot.com	White pages, email, yellow pages
BigYellow	www.bigyellow.com	Yellow pages
BizProLink	www.bizprolink.com	Business
BizRate	www.bizrate.com	Shopping
BookBlvd.com	www.bookblvd.com	Shopping
BookFinder.com	www.bookfinder.com	Books

continues

391

CONTINUED

Site:	URL:	Type of Search:
Bottom Dollar	www.bottomdollar.com	Shopping
Builder.com	www.builder.com	Computers
BullsEye	www.intelliseek.com	Search software
Business and Technology Research Library	www.brint.com/interest.html	Business
Buyer's Index	www.buyersindex.com	Shopping
Campus Tours	www.campustours.com	College
CareerBuilder Network	www.careerbuilder.com	Jobs
CareerMosaic	www.careermosaic.com	Jobs
CareerPath	www.careerpath.com	Jobs
CareerSite	www.careersite.com	Jobs
Carroll's U.S. Government Links	www.carrollpub.com	Government
Catalog City	www.catalogcity.com	Shopping
Celebrity Email	www.celebrityemail.com	Celebrities
Chip's Celebrity Home and Email Addresses	www.addresses.site2go.com	Celebrities
CityAuction	www.cityauction.com	Auctions
Classical MIDI Archives	www.prs.net/midi.html	MIDI
Classifieds 2000	www.classifieds2000.com	Classifieds
Classmates Online	www.classmates.com	Alumni
ClickTheButton	www.clickthebutton.com	Shopping
Clip Art Review	www.webplaces.com/html/clipart.htm	Clip art
Clipart Directory	www.clipart.com	Clip art
ClipArtConnection	www.clipartconnection.com	Clip art
ClipArtNow	www.clipartnow.com	Clip art
CMPnet	www.cmpnet.com	Computers
CNET	www.cnet.com	Computers
CNN Interactive	www.cnn.com	News
CNNfn	cnnfn.com	Financial
College Board Online	www.collegeboard.org	College
College Bound.net	www.cbnet.com	College
College Guide	www.pathfinder.com/money/colleges/	College
College Guides and Aid	www.collegeguides.com	College
College Is Possible	www.collegeispossible.org	College

392

Site:	URL:	Type of Search:
College Savings Plan Network	www.collegesavings.org/yourstate.htm	College
College Spot	www.collegespot.com	College
college_base	library.advanced.org/17038/	College
College411	www.college411.org	College
CollegeDegree.com	www.collegdegree.com	College
CollegeEdge	www.collegeedge.com	College
CollegeNET	www.collegenet.com	College
Colleges & Careers Center	www.usnews.com/usnews/edu/	College
Colleges.com	www.colleges.com	College
CollegeView	www.collegeview.com	College
CollegeXpress	www.collegexpress.com	College
Common Threads	www.gensource.com/common/	Genealogy
CompaniesOnline	www.companiesonline.com	Business
Company Sleuth	www.companysleuth.com	Financial
Compare.Net	www.compare.net	Shopping
ComparisonShopping.net	www.comparisonshopping.net	Shopping
Computer Academic Underground World Headquarters	www.caughq.org	Warez
Computer Industry Almanac	www.c-i-a.com	Computers
Computer Intelligence Infobeads	www.ci.infobeads.com/INFOBEADS/Pages/Main/MAIN.ASP	Computers
Computer News Daily	computernewsdaily.com	Computers
Computers.com	www.computers.com	Computers
ConsumerInfo.com	www.consumerinfo.com	Financial
Copernic	www.copernic.com	Search software
Corbis	www.corbis.com	Pictures
Corporate Information	www.corporateinformation.com	Financial
Critical Comparisons of American Colleges and Universities	www.memex-press.com/cc/	College
Crosswalk.com	search.crosswalk.com/pk/	Religious
CyberMatch Worldwide	www.cmww.com	Personals
CyberSearch	www.frontiertech.com	Search software

continues

CONTINUED

Site:	URL:	Type of Search:
CyberStacks	www.public.iastate.edu/~CYBERSTACKS/	Library
Cybot	www.theartmachine.com/cybot.htm	Search software
Cyndi's List of Genealogy Sites on the Internet	www.cyndislist.com	Genealogy
DAILYMP3.COM	www.dailymp3.com	MP3
Dataquest	www.dataquest.com	Computers
Deja.com	www.deja.com	Usenet newsgroups
Dialog	www.dialog.com	Professional
DialogWeb	www.dialogweb.com	Professional
Digital Library Net	www.digitallibrary.net	Library
Dimension Music	www.dimensionmusic.com	MP3
Direct Hit	www.directhit.com	Search engine technology
Directory Guide	www.directoryguide.com	Search engine list
Directory of Electronic Public Access Services	www.uscourts.gov/PubAccess.html	Federal court records
Directory of Free Classified Ad Sites	www.windsorbooks.com/adsites/	Classifieds
Disney Internet Guide (DIG)	www.disney.com/dig/today	Children
Dogpile	www.dogpile.com	Meta-search
Download.com	www.download.com	Files
drkoop.com	www.drkoop.com	Health
Dun & Bradstreet	www.dnb.com	Financial
E Medicine	www.emedicine.com	Health
EarthWeb	www.earthweb.com	Computers
eBay	www.ebay.com	Auctions
Education Network	www.ccounsel.org	College
Education Resources Information Center	www.accesseric.org	College
Education World	www.education-world.com	Education
EdView SmartZone	school.edview.com/search/	Children
Eisenhower National Clearinghouse	www.enc.org	Homework
Electric Library	www.elibrary.com	Library

Site:	URL:	Type of Search:
Email Address Book	www.emailbook.com	Email
EmailChange.com	www.emailchange.com	Email
EmailFinder	www.emailfinder.com	Email
Encarta Online	www.encarta.msn.com	Encyclopedia
Encyclopaedia Britannica Online	www.eb.com	Encyclopedia
Encyclopedia.com	www.encyclopedia.com	Encyclopedia
ePages Classifieds	www.ep.com	Classifieds
ETS Net	www.ets.org	College
Excite	www.excite.com	General
Excite News Tracker	nt.excite.com	News
Excite Shopping	www.excite.com/shopping/	Shopping
FACSNET People Finders/Public Records Databases	www.facsnet.org/report_tools/CAR/carpeopl.htm	People
Family History Research Register	symbiosis.uk.com/fhistory/	Genealogy
Family Web Files	www.familywebfiles.com	Children
FamilySearch	www.familysearch.org	Genealogy
FAST Search	alltheweb.com	General
FastWEB	www.fastweb.org	College
FedWorld Information Network	www.fedworld.gov	Government
FileMine	www.filemine.com	Files
FilePile	filepile.com	Files
FinAid	www.finaid.org	College
Find mE-Mail	www.findmemail.com	Email
FindLaw	www.findlaw.com	Legal
FindLinks	www.findlinks.com	Business
FirstAuction	www.firstauction.com	Auctions
Flirt	www.flirt.com	Personals
FoneFinder	www.primeris.com/fonefind/	Area codes
Forbes Digital Tool	www.forbes.com	News
Forrester Research	www.forrester.com	Computers
Free Classified Ads	www.freeclassifiedlinks.com	Classifieds
Free-Help	www.free-help.com	Computers

continues

CONTINUED

Site:	URL:	Type of Search:
Friendfinder	www.friendfinder.com	Personals
FSBO.COM	www.fsbo.com	Houses/mortgages
Funk & Wagnalls Knowledge Center	www.fwkc.com	Encyclopedia
Gamecenter.com	www.gamecenter.com	Games
Genealogical Research at the National Archives	www.nara.gov/genealogy/ genindex.html	Genealogy
Genealogy Home Page	www.genhomepage.com	Genealogy
Genealogy Online	www.genealogy.org	Genealogy
Genealogy Resources on the Internet	members.aol.com/ johnf14246/internet.html	Genealogy
Genealogy.com	www.genealogy.com	Genealogy
General Science Links	www.siec.k12.in.us/ ~west/sites/scigen.htm	Science
GeoCities	www.geocities.com	Personal Web pages
Globe, The	www.theglobe.com	Personal Web pages
GoCollege	www.gocollege.com	College
GOD: Global Online Directory	www.god.co.uk	General
Google!	www.google.com	General
GoTo.com	www.goto.com	General
Governments on the WWW	www.gksoft.com/govt/	Global government
Grammar Lady	www.grammarlady.com	Homework
GTE SuperPages	yp.gte.net	Yellow pages
GVU Center's WWW User Survey	www.cc.gatech.edu/gvu/ user_surveys/	Computers
Hack O Matic	www.garden.net/users/ zero/newhack/	Warez
HeadHunter.NET	www.headhunter.net	Jobs
Health A to Z	www.healthatoz.com	Health
HealthAnswers	www.healthanswers.com	Health
Health-Net	www.health-net.com	Health
Healthtouch Online	www.healthtouch.com	Health
HEART Career.com	www.career.com	Jobs
Home Shark	www.homeshark.com	Houses/mortgages
Homebuyer's Fair	www.homefair.com	Houses/mortgages
HomeHunter	www.homehunter.com	Houses/mortgages

396

Site:	URL:	Type of Search:
Hometown AOL	`hometown.aol.com`	Personal Web pages
Homework Central	`www.homeworkcentral.com`	Homework
Homework Help	`www.startribune.com/stonline/html/special/homework/`	Homework
Homework Helper	`www.homeworkhelper.com`	Homework
Hoover's Online	`www.hoovers.com`	Financial
Hot Jobs	`www.hotjobs.com`	Jobs
HotBot	`www.hotbot.com`	General
HotBot Shopping Directory	`shop.hotbot.com`	Shopping
Hytelnet	`www.lights.com/hytelnet/`	Hytelnet information
Icon Bank	`www.iconbank.com`	Clip art
ICQ Power Search	`www.icq.com/search/`	Instant messages
IDG.net	`www.idg.net`	Computers
In-Box Direct	`home.netscape.com/ibd/index.html`	Email publications
Industry Standard, The	`www.thestandard.net`	News
InferenceFind	`www.infind.com`	Meta-search
InfoBeat	`www.infobeat.com`	Email publications
infoplease Homework Center	`kids.infoplease.com/homework/`	Homework
infoplease Kids' Almanac	`kids.infoplease.com`	Children
Inforia Quest	`www.inforia.com`	Search software
informIT	`www.informit.com`	Computers
Infoseek	`infoseek.go.com`	General
InfoSpace	`www.infospace.com`	White pages, email, yellow pages
Inktomi	`www.inktomi.com`	Search engine technology
Inter-Linked Communications	`www.inter-linked.com`	Business
International White and Yellow Pages	`www.wajens.no`	White pages, yellow pages
Internet Address Finder	`www.iaf.net`	Email
Internet Movie Database	`us.imdb.com`	Movies
Internet Personals	`www.montagar.com/personals/`	Personals
Internet Public Library	`www.ipl.org`	Library

continues

CONTINUED

Site:	URL:	Type of Search:
Internet Sex Guide	www.sexguide.net	Adult
Internet Sleuth	www.isleuth.com	Meta-search
Internet.com	www.internet.com	Computers
invest-o-rama	www.investorama.com	Financial
InvestorLinks	www.investorlinks.com	Financial
Invincer's Intraverse Top FTP Sites	www.invincer.com/2600W/ FTPsites.html	Warez
IRC Networks and Server Lists	www.irchelp.org/irchelp/ network.html	IRC chat channels
ITKnowledge	www.itknowledge.com	Computers
iVillage Personal Home Pages	pages.ivillage.com	Personal Web pages
Job Options	www.joboptions.com	Jobs
jobfind.com	www.jobfind.com	Jobs
JobWeb	www.jobweb.com	Jobs
Jumbo	www.jumbo.com	Files
Kaplan	www.kaplan.com/precoll/	College
Kid Info	www.kidinfo.com	Homework
KidsClick	sunsite.berkeley.edu/ KidsClick!/	Homework
KidsConnect	www.ala.org/ICONN/ kidscomm.html	Homework
kidsDoctor	www.kidsdoctor.com	Health
Kim Komando's Komputer Klinic	www.komando.com	Computers
KnowX	www.knowx.com	Public records
KY3 for Kids Homework Help	www.ky3.com/kids/ homework/	Homework
Laura's MIDI Heaven	laurasmidiheaven. simplenet.com	MIDI
Lawyers.com	www.laywers.com	Legal
'Lectric Law Library	www.lectlaw.com	Legal
Letsfindout Kids' Encyclopedia	www.letsfindout.com	Encyclopedia
LEXIS-NEXIS	www.lexis-nexis.com	Professional
Library of Congress	lcweb.loc.gov	Library
LibrarySpot	www.libraryspot.com	Library

Site:	URL:	Type of Search:
List of Lists, The	`www.catalog.com/vivian/` `interest-group-search.html`	Mailing lists
Liszt	`www.liszt.com`	Mailing lists
Liszt's IRC Chat Directory	`www.liszt.com/chat/`	IRC chat channels
Liszt's Usenet Newsgroup Directory	`www.liszt.com/news/`	Usenet newsgroups
LoanGuide	`www.loadguide.com`	Houses/mortgages
LookSmart	`www.looksmart.com`	General
Lovecity	`www.lovecity.com`	Personals
Lycos	`www.lycos.com`	General
Lycos Auctions Search	`www.lycos.com/auctions/`	Auctions
Lycos FAST MP3 Search	`mp3.lycos.com`	MP3
Lycos FTP Search	`ftpsearch.lycos.com`	Files
Lycos Image Gallery	`www.lycos.com/picturethis/`	Pictures and sounds
Lycos Top 5%	`point.lycos.com/categories/`	General
Mad Scientist Network	`www.madsci.org`	Homework
Mailtown	`www.mailtown.com`	Email
Mamma	`www.mamma.com`	Meta-search
MapBlast!	`www.mapblast.com`	Maps
MapQuest	`www.mapquest.com`	Maps
MasterCard/Cirrus ATM Locator	`www.mastercard.com/atm/`	ATM
Mata Hari	`www.thewebtools.com`	Search software
Match.com	`www.match.com`	Personals
Matchmaker	`www.matchmaker.com`	Personals
Media Metrix	`www.mediametrix.com`	Computers
Mediabuilder	`www.mediabuilder.com`	Clip art
Medical World Search	`www.mwsearch.com`	Health
MedicineNet	`www.medicinenet.com`	Health
Mediconsult.com	`www.mediconsult.com`	Health
Meeting Place, The	`www.nis.net/meet/`	Student Web pages
MeetMeOnline	`www.meetmeonline.com`	Personals
MESA MetaEmail SearchAgent	`mesa.rrzn.uni-hannover.de`	Email
MetaCrawler	`www.go2net.com/search.html`	Meta-search
Michigan Electronic Library	`mel.lib.mi.us`	Library

continues

CONTINUED

Site:	URL:	Type of Search:
Microsoft HomeAdvisor	homeadvisor.msn.com	Houses/mortgages
Microsoft Investor	investor.msn.com	Financial
Microsoft Knowledge Base	support.microsoft.com/ servicedesks/directaccess/	Computers
MIDI Explorer Search Engine	musicrobot.hypermart.net	MIDI
MIDI Farm	www.midifarm.com	MIDI
MIDI Heaven	mysp.com/p/midiheaven/ midi.html	MIDI
MIDI Madness	www.qin.com/madness/main.htm	MIDI
MIDI Town	krebs.home.texas.net	MIDI
Mining Co.; see About.com	www.about.com	General
Monster.com	www.monster.com	Jobs
Morningstar	www.morningstar.com	Financial
Motley Fool	www.fool.com	Financial
MP3 2000	www.mp3-2000.com	MP3
MP3 Place	www.mp3place.com	MP3
MP3.com	www.mp3.com	MP3
MP3now.com	www.mp3now.com	MP3
MPEG.ORG	www.mpeg.org/MPEG/ mp2.html	MP3
MSN Search	home.microsoft.com	General
MSNBC	www.msnbc.com	News
Multex	www.multexnet.com	Financial
Multi Audio	www.multiaudio.net	MP3, MIDI
musicseek	www.musicseek.net	MP3
My Virtual Encyclopedia	www.refdesk.com/ myency.html	Encyclopedia
My Virtual Reference Desk	www.refdesk.com	Library
My WebMD	www.mywebmd.com	Health
my.email.address.is	my.email.address.is	Email
National Association for College Admission Testing	www.nacac.com	College
National Financial Services Network	www.nfsn.com/Educatio.htm	College
National Libraries of the World	www.ifla.org/II/natlibs.htm	Library

400

Site:	URL:	Type of Search:
National Library of Medicine	www.nlm.nih.gov	Health
National Technical Information Service	www.ntis.gov	Science
NationJob	www.nationjob.com	Jobs
Ncrtec Good Photograph and Image Sites	www.ncrtec.org/tools/ picture/goodsite.htm	Pictures
Net Ministries Church Directories	netministries.org/ churches.htm	Religious
NetAttache Pro	www.tympani.com/products/ NAPro/NAPro.html	Search software
NetChurch Search	www.netchurch.com/ church_search.asp	Religious
NetNames USA	www.netnamesusa.com	Domain names
Netscape Netcenter Personals	digitalcity.netscape.com/ personals/	Personals
Netscape Open Directory	directory.netscape.com	General
Netscape Search	home.netscape.com	General
Network Solutions	www.networksolutions.com	Domain names
New York Public Library Digital Library Collections	digital.nypl.org	Library
New York Times	www.nytimes.com	News
New York Times Technology	www.nytimes.com/ yr/mo/day/tech/	Computers
NewHomeNetwork	www.newhomenetwork.com	Houses/mortgages
News and Newspapers Online	library.uncq.edu/news/	News
News Index	www.newsindex.com	News
News.com	www.news.com	Computers
NewsBot	www.newsbot.com	News
NewsCentral	www.all-links.com/ newscentral/	News
NewsHub	www.newshub.com	News
NewsLibrary	www.newslibrary.com	News
Newspapers Online	www.newspapers.com	News
NewsTrawler	www.newstrawler.com	News
Nitemare	www.garden.net/users/zero/ index.html	Warez
Northern Light	www.northernlight.com	General

continues

CONTINUED

Site:	URL:	Type of Search:
Northern Light Current News Search	`www.northernlight.com/news.html`	News
NUA Internet Survey	`www.nua.ie/surveys/`	Computers
Office of Postsecondary Education	`www.ed.gov/offices/OPE/Students/index.html`	College
One & Only Internet Personals	`www.one-and-only.com`	Personals
One Nation Worldwide	`www.onww.com`	Personal Web pages
OneKey	`www.onekey.com`	Children
OneSeek	`www.oneseek.com`	Meta-search
Online Career Center	`www.occ.com`	Jobs
Onsale atAuction	`www.onsale.com`	Auctions
Oth.Net	`oth.net`	MP3
Palavista Digital Music Metacrawler	`www.palavista.com`	MP3
Paperboy	`www.paperboy.net`	News
PC Data	`www.pcdata.com`	Computers
PC Quote	`www.pcquote.com`	Financial
PcPips.com	`www.pctips.com`	Computers
People Finder	`www.peoplesite.com`	People
PeopleSearch	`www.peoplesearch.net`	White pages
Personal Home Page Directories	`www.bltg.com/people/`	Personal Web pages
Personal Pages Worldwide	`www.utexas.edu/world/personal/index.html`	Personal Web pages
PI Mall	`www.pimall.com`	Private investigators
Portal Hub.com	`www.portalhub.com`	Search engine information and reviews
PR Newswire	`www.prnewswire.com`	News
Project EASI	`easi.ed.gov`	College
Pronet	`pronet.ca`	Business
ProQuest Direct	`www.umi.com/proquest/`	Professional
Public Eye	`www.thepubliceye.com`	Shopping
Public Libraries with WWW Services	`sjcpl.lib.in.us/homepage/PublicLibraries/PubLibSrvsGpherWWW.html`	Library
Publicly Accessible Mailing Lists	`www.neosoft.com/internet/paml/`	Mailing lists

Site:	URL:	Type of Search:
Quicken.com	www.quicken.com	Financial
QuickenMortgage	www.quickenmortage.com	Houses/mortgages
QuoteCom	www.quote.com	Financial
Realtor.com	www.realtor.com	Houses/mortgages
Recruiters Online Network	ipa.com	Jobs
Recycler.com	www.recycler.com	Classifieds
Red Herring	www.herring.com	News
Register.com	www.register.com	Domain names
Religious Resources	www.aphids.com/relres/ on the Net	Religious
Religious Texts	www.hti.umich.edu/relig/	Religious
Rent.Net	www.rent.net	Apartments
ReunionNet	www.reunited.com	Alumni
Reverse Phone Directory	www.reversephonedirectory.com	White pages
Romance Makers	www.romancemakers.com	Personals
Rootsweb	www.rootsweb.com	Genealogy
RxList	rxlist.com	Health
Saint's List of IRC Networks and Servers	www.geocities.com/ ~saintslist/	IRC chat channels
Sallie Mae	www.salliemae.com	College
SavvySearch	www.savvysearch.com	Meta-search
School Libraries on the Web	www.voicenet.com/~bertland/ libs.html	Library
Schoolwork.ugh!	www.schoowork.org	Homework
SciCentral	www.scicentral.com	Science
Search Engine Watch	www.searchenginewatch.com	Search engine information and reviews
Search Engines in Review	www.blueangels.net	Search engine information and reviews
Search Spaniel	www.searchspaniel.com	Meta-search
Search Warez	search.warez.com	Warez
Search.com	www.search.com	General
Search4	www.intermania.com/search4/	Search software
Searchopolis	www.searchopolis.com	Children
SEC EDGAR Database	www.sec.gov/edgarhp.htm	Financial
Shareware Place	www.sharewareplace.com	Files
Shareware.com	www.shareware.com	Files

continues

403

CONTINUED

Site:	URL:	Type of Search:
ShopFind	www.shopfind.com	Shopping
Shopper.com	www.shopper.com	Shopping
SiliconValley.com	www.mercurycenter.com/svtech/	Computers
SMARTpages	www.smartpages.com	Yellow pages
Smithsonian Institution Libraries	www.sil.si.edu	Library
Smithsonian Photo Archive	photo2.si.edu	Pictures
Snap	www.snap.com	General
Spider's Apprentice	www.monash.com/spidap.html	Search engine information and reviews
SpringStreet	www.springstreet.com	Apartments
SSSpider	www.pkware.com/catalog/ssspider.html	Search software
Student Homepages	www.westegg.com/students/	Student Web pages
Student Survival Guide	www.luminent.net/~jackp/survive.html	College
Student.com Personal Page Direct	www.student.com/feature/ppd/	Student Web pages
StudyWEB	www.studyweb.com	Homework
Super Snooper	supersnooper.com	Children
SuperSeek	www.super-seek.com	Meta-search
Switchboard	www.switchboard.com	White pages, email, yellow pages
Swoon	www.swoon.com	Personals
Techni-Help	www.freepchelp.com	Computers
TechSupportSites	www.techsupportsites.com	Computers
TechWeb	www.techweb.com	Computers
Teleport Pro	www.tenmax.com/pro.html	Search software
Television News Archive	tvnews.vanderbilt.edu	News
TerraServer	terraserver.microsoft.com	Maps
Terrorist's Handbook	www.meaning.com/library.boom/thb/	Anarchy
Think College	www.ed.gov/thinkcollege/	College
Thomas	thomas.loc.gov	Government
Thunderstone	www.thunderstone.com	Search engine technology

Site:	URL:	Type of Search:
Time Life Photo Sight	www.pathfinder.com/photo/index.html	Pictures
Today's Mortgage Information	www.hsh.com	Houses/mortgages
Tom's Hardware Guide	www.tomshardware.com	Computers
Topica	www.topica.com	Mailing lists
TotalNews	www.totalnews.com	News
Tripod	www.tripod.com	Personal Web pages
Tucows	www.tucows.com	Files
uBid	www.ubid.com	Auctions
Ultimates, The	www.theultimates.com	White pages, email
United States Postal Service ZIP Code Lookup and Address Information	www.usps.gov/ncsc/	ZIP codes
University of Minnesota Gopher	gopher://gopher.micro.umn.edu	University gopher
Up4Sale	www.up4sale.com	Auctions
Upside Today	www.upside.com	News
U.S. Business Advisor	www.business.gov	Business
U.S. West Dex	yp.uswest.com	Yellow pages
Virtual Relocation	www.virtualrelocation.com	Moving
Virtual World of Intelligence	www.dreamscape.com/frankvad/covert.html	Anarchy
Visa's ATM Locator	www.visa.com/pd/atm/main.html	ATM
Vital Records Information	www.vitalrec.com	Genealogy
Warez.com	www.warez.com	Warez
Web100	www.metamoney.com/w100/	Business
WebAuction	www.webauction.com	Auctions
webCATS	www.lights.com/webcats/	Library
WebCrawler	www.webcrawler.com	General
WebFerret	www.ferretsoft.com/netferret/	Search software
WebMath	www.webmath.com	Homework
Webpersonals	www.webpersonals.com	Personals
WebSEEk	www.ctr.columbia.edu/webseek/	Pictures
WebSeeker	www.bluesquirrel.com	Search software
WebTaxi	www.webtaxi.com	Meta-search

continues

CONTINUED

Site:	URL:	Type of Search:
West Legal Directory	www.wld.com	Legal
whatUseek	www.whatuseek.com	General
WhoWhere	www.whowhere.lycos.com	White pages, email, yellow pages
WhoWhere Homepages	homepages.whowhere.com	Personal Web pages
WinSite	www.winsite.com	Files
Wired News	www.wired.com/news/	News
Word Central	www.wordcentral	Homework
World Alumni Net	www.infophil.com/World/ Alumni/	Alumni
World Email Directory	www.worldemail.com	Email
World Trade Search	world-trade-search.com	Business
World Wide Web Virtual Library	www.vlib.org	Library
World World	www.worldworld.com	Global government
WorldPages	www.worldpages.com	White pages, email, yellow pages
WorldWide News	www.worldwidenews.com	News
WWW Virtual Law Library	www.law.indiana.edu/ law/v-lib/states.html	State government agencies
XFinder Adult Search Engine	www.xfinder.com	Adult
Yahoo!	www.yahoo.com	General
Yahoo! Auctions	auctions.yahoo.com	Auctions
Yahoo! Classifieds	classifieds.yahoo.com	Classifieds
Yahoo! College Admissions Offices	www.yahoo.com/Education/ Higher_Education/college_ Entrance/Admissions_Offices/	College
Yahoo! College Search	features.yahoo.com/college. search.html	College
Yahoo! Finance	quote.yahoo.com	Financial
Yahoo! Image Surfer	ipix.yahoo.com	Pictures
Yahoo! People Search	people.yahoo.com	White pages, email, yellow pages
Yahoo! Personals	personals.yahoo.com	Personals
Yahoo! Shopping	shopping.yahoo.com	Shopping
Yahoo! Yellow Pages	yp.yahoo.com	Yellow pages

Site:	URL:	Type of Search:
Yahooligans!	www.yahooligans.com	Children
ZDNet	www.zdnet.com	Computers
ZDNet Help	www.zdnet.com/zdhelp/	Computers
ZDNet News	www.zdnet.com/zdnn/	Computers
ZDNet Software Library	www.zdnet.com/swlib/	Files
Zip2	www.zip2.com	Yellow pages
ZurfRider	www.zurf.com	Search software

Index

N

O